BEAUTY, TRUTH AND LOVE

Edited by Patrick Hannon and Eugene Duffy

Beauty, Truth and Love
ESSAYS IN HONOUR OF ENDA MCDONAGH

the columba press

First published in 2009 by
the columba press
55A Spruce Avenue, Stillorgan Industrial Park,
Blackrock, Co Dublin

Cover by Bill Bolger
Cover picture by Tony O'Malley, 'From Sixteenth Century Sculpture of Rury O'Tunney – St Mary's, Callan'. The painting was presented by Jane O'Malley to Enda McDonagh on the occasion of the Conference organised by the Galway Mayo Institute of Technology and the Western Theological Institute
on 13 October 2007.
Origination by The Columba Press
Printed in Ireland by ColourBooks Ltd, Dublin

ISBN 978-1-85607-662-3

Copyright © 2009, The Contributors

Table of Contents

Foreword   7

Preface
  Archbishop Michael Neary   9

1   Mayo Theology for Enda McDonagh
  John F. Deane   11

2   Enda McDonagh's Bekan – his native parish
  Nollaig Ó Muraíle   14

3   Enda McDonagh: A Friend Amongst Us
  Nuala Bourke   20

4   Enda McDonagh, the Scholar
  Seán Freyne   24

5   Facing the Truth
  Brendan Hoban   30

6   What would a Christian University look like?
  Stanley Hauerwas   36

7   A Response to Stanley Hauerwas
  Patrick Hannon   58

8   Enda McDonagh's dialogue with Vatican II
  Charles Curran   62

9   A Response to Charles Curran
  Vincent MacNamara   87

10   Respect for life and the problem of scriptural violence
  Joseph O'Leary   93

11   A Response to Joseph O'Leary
  Linda Hogan   121

12	HIV/AIDS: The Expanding Ethical Challenge *James F. Keenan SJ*	126
13	A Response to James F. Keenan SJ *Raphael Gallagher CSsR*	149
14	Just Love: Reordering the debate about sexual morality *Linda Hogan*	157
15	Conflicts and Human Rights: A Global Perspective *Noel Dorr*	165
16	Listening to the Voices from the Margins *Stanislaus Kennedy*	184
17	Theology and Poetry: 'Loose-leafed through the Cosmos' *Patrick O'Brien*	199
18	Art: A Gateway to the Transcendent *Anne Harkin-Petersen*	207
19	Reclaiming Beauty *Mary Gordon*	219

List of Contributors   235

Foreword

Enda McDonagh is a moral theologian of international standing, a man of the university, and one of Ireland's public intellectuals. Since his retirement as Professor of Moral Theology at Maynooth in 196, his distinction in these contexts has been regularly acknowledged, not least in that he continues to be called on to contribute to public life and to the university, as well as to moral theology abroad and at home. But he is also a priest of the Archdiocese of Tuam, a native of Bekan in County Mayo, and those who know him know how deeply significant these connections have been both for his life and for his work.

It is therefore fitting that when the faculty of Theology at Maynooth decided to honour him it chose the golden jubilee of his ordination as a priest as the occasion of a conference to which former coleagues and students and distinguished international visitors contributed. It was also fitting that his west of Ireland roots have been honoured, in a conference organised by the Galway-Mayo Institute of Technology in association with the Western Theological Institute.

The papers and other contributions of both conferences are here collected, arranged according as they concern local and personal, *polis* and *ekklesia* in Ireland, and questions and challenges that confront church and society worldwide. The title was suggested by Patrick Kavanagh's poem, 'Stoney grey soil', and its aptness will be obvious to anyone already familiar with Enda McDonagh's work, but obvious also, it can be hoped, to a reader whose introduction to the work or the man is by way of *Beauty, Love and Truth*.

The task of the editors was made easier by the ready and

BEAUTY, TRUTH AND LOVE

warm co-operation of each of the contributors, itself a measure of the regard in which the subject of their tributes is held.

Eugene Duffy
Patrick Hannon
June 2009

Preface

Archbishop Michael Neary

On a November morning in 1963, priests in St Jarlath's College, recognising the long tradition and close links between the college and the Columbans, were bringing members of our Leaving Certificate class to visit Dalgan Park in Navan. I was travelling with my fellow townsman, the late Mgr Tommy Waldron. He decided to go via Maynooth. It was my first time in the college and my first meeting with Enda McDonagh. As we made our way to Dalgan, Tommy spoke about Enda, one of Jarlath's best and brightest. What Tommy said then was borne out for me within a few short years. I recall the way theology students who were a few years senior to me spoke of the freshness and excitement which Enda brought to the subject. His significant contribution to theology has been highlighted by the various speakers at the Conference here in Claremorris.

Enda ranges with ease through the three great traditions of the Hebrew scriptures: law, wisdom and prophecy. Recognising the contribution of each area, he hews his theology sometimes from one tradition, at other times combining all three in a synthesis, enabling us to become acutely aware of the mystery that is God and our feeble attempts to understand and enter into a relationship with God.

My becoming Archbishop of Tuam coincided with Enda's retirement in Maynooth. The first parish which I offered to a priest of the diocese was to Enda. I emphasised that he was entirely free with regard to my offer and I fully understood and appreciated his decision, given his commitments in the Dublin area.

In his professional work he has close contacts with the politicians, the presence today of former Taoiseach, Dr Garret FitzGerald, underlines this fact.

In a world and a society in which the influence of the media is of such importance, Enda understood the media, used a language which the media understood, and in turn was understood by them.

Black and white would never be the favourite colours of a theologian. As the quintessential Mayo man however, Enda preferred to see things in terms of Green and Red. And like all Mayo followers in recent years he too has travelled what has become our *via dolorosa* to Croke Park.

His generosity in donating his vast library to the Galway-Mayo Institute of Technology is in keeping with his love for the West and his concern to promote theology in the place where he derives so much of his inspiration.

I join with you all in expressing our deep appreciation of this fact. Considering his contributions and significant achievements, Enda has very much of which he can be proud.

There is one area however which may be something of an embarrassment to him – the fact that he has taught so many of the Irish bishops! But come to think of it, and perish the thought, what might we be like if we hadn't come under his influence!

Mayo Theology

John F. Deane

There were high brown candles about the coffin,
the vague gesturing of their light
imaged in the sheen on the wood; I listened, hurt,
to the ongoing jeremiads and could believe
a ganglion of devils cavorted in the air;
I had to stand outside during the services, the valley –
with its dark church rising out of its copse of alders –
being an alien place, inhabited by dark invaders;
we had to stand among the gravestones that leaned,
greening, over against one another, and suffer
the ministry of midges, their almost invisible insistence
not letting us settle, as they bit and bothered
scalp and wrist and nostril.
                                      Nanna
on her best days, stood comfortable in her body,
murmuring as she worked, her hands soothed
by flour to the elbows, relishing her skills
with potato-cake, potato-farl, and mash;
when Mrs Harriet Graham-Black, widow, called
to sell black roses made of crepe paper and green
pipe cleaners, Nanna was gracious; sure, she said,
the Protestants now are down on their luck.
Later she sang, as the butter melted on the hot
potato delicacies:
> *Slievemore, Slievemore you are standing there,*
> *your head so high and your sides so bare*
> *some day please God you will surely fall*
> *and bury the Colony Jumpers all.*

In the spring a young man's fancy turns
to spiritual heights; Nangle, foreigner,
boasting the weight of his white beard, white hair,
came angling for souls on the western coast;
potatoes failed: but there were sea-foods,
dillisc, carrageen, periwinkle, crab; the Irish

grew lean and tough as sticks of kelp; Nangle
offered soup, a hospital, a school, and built
an ordered village, set-square-shape, buying
half the side of a hill; the old men twisted caps
in their red hands, the women smiled and tried
the Gaelic tongue; it was God, dragging them
by the arms, now left, now right, they abandoned
their crooked village, straggling away uphill
over stones and bog-pool and the wet turf,
carrying the ever-heavier burden of their faith
down, with faint hope, into the next valley.
                        A man can not,
by his own efforts, draw down God; but you become
obsessed with justice, of God and men, obsessed, too,
with the difficult notion of mercy. A terrible thing it is
to fall into the hands of the living God.
                        Lucas
Cranach the Younger painted him,
a sombre plump-faced man, with internal troubles,
watching a little upwards, with troubled eyes;
our dear Eleutherius, shocked at our abject failure
to achieve the perfection of the Christ; Luther –
this is the leper and the loathsome fellow
with the brain of brass and the nose of iron;
truculent, the bible pages open to show
the history of God. Blank walls before him. Anxieties
skittered like marbles across his brain, the Christ
accusing, Hell's maw gaping.
                        Nanna
Sat on the steps of the stairs, her head
hidden in her hands, her index fingers
in her ears; she hummed loudly, to drown
the rattling of thunder; the devils, she said,
are playing loose among the skillets and pans.
November, All Souls, like a fall of rain, upwards,
the creatures released from pain when we, she said,
go in and out the chapel doors, and say the prayers;

CHAPTER ONE

I heard the small-growth-rustling of her rosaries,
the beads clicked softly against the polished
wood of the pew.
       Braving Satan
I hammered on the door of their grey church,
listened to the hollow sound, like the anxious pounding
of the human heart. What, then is faith? a black
body, the inside structured grey, with plaques
to the titled dead and the lost of many wars;
an everywhichway Church, loose cannons? or a rag-
and-bone and regimented tagglebunch, marshalled
into the corral of Rome? Wittenberg, the theses;
Dugort, the darkened graves waiting
under the drawling western mist. The fall of earth
down on the polished wood was like fingernails
fibulating in my gut; I watched
a ruly goldcrest on the old high yew, its acrobatic
busyness and mastery and remembered:
where two or three are gathered together
honouring the name of Christ he steps out of shadows
to interrupt.
      Their Christmas cards, Nanna said, are robins
hopping in the snow, or horse-drawn carriages
drawing up to lamp-lit houses; they carol
Good King Wenceslas and talk mulled wine
and boxing day. The hymns they sing, said Nanna,
are square like chests of tea and go on and on
interminably; and the words they use are square,
abide, vouchsafe, and gladsome. We have cribs,
an adult baby Jesus, shepherds stunned by baroque
organs in the sky; we sing Adeste, have Stephen's Day
and three wise men come offering their gifts.

Cujus regio, eius religio, a mighty fortress is our God; faith
of our fathers – we settle down to polite antagonisms.

CHAPTER TWO

Enda McDonagh's Bekan – his native parish

Nollaig Ó Muraíle

Bekan, the parish in which Enda McDonagh was born in 1930 is now an entirely rural parish in south-east Mayo. I say 'now' because I am referring here to the present Catholic parish, which is not quite identical to the historic parish of which we have record for more than seven centuries. The latter – the civil or medieval parish – encompassed half of the town of Ballyhaunis and stretched north-east of the town as far as the border with Co Roscommon. In 1894 the boundaries of the Catholic parish were revised; 27 townlands in that north-eastern wing were transferred to the parish of Annagh while, in compensation, 30 others to the south-east were taken from Annagh and given to Bekan. For convenience, references to the parish (as in the book *Béacán/Bekan: Portrait of an East Mayo Parish*, ed. M. Comer & N. Ó Muraíle, with foreword by Enda McDonagh, 1986) will generally include all of those 57 townlands plus a core of 37 others which were in the medieval parish and have remained in the Catholic parish – giving a total of 94 (with a total area of just over 23,000 acres – or 94 square kilometres – which is about one-sixtieth of the area of Co Mayo). The parish is bounded on the north by the parish of Aghamore, on the west by Knock and Kilcolman, on the south by a small portion of Kilvine and by Annagh, which also bounds it on the east. The portion which formerly stretched north-eastwards to the Roscommon border touched the parishes of Kilkeevin and Tibohine in the latter county. As a final clue to its location, we may mention that Bekan lies between Kilkelly – about five miles to the north – Knock – a mile and a half to the west – Claremorris – four miles to the south-west – and Ballinlough – three miles to the east,

CHAPTER TWO

with Ballyhaunis lying partly within the old civil parish, but a little over a mile to the east of the Catholic parish's boundary.

Like the parishes round about, Bekan made no great impact on Irish history, being mentioned on no more than a handful of occasions prior to the nineteenth century. Nevertheless, the area possesses some intriguing remnants of a respectable antiquity. Among the most notable of these are a couple of pillar-stones – out of a total of no more than thirteen in the whole of Connacht – which bear inscriptions in the enigmatic ancient script called ogam. One of the inscriptions, in Kilmannin, commemorates a man called Lugaddon son of Lugadeks, while the other, in Island, bears the name of one Cunalegos son of Qunacanos. Both of these named individuals were no doubt men of some importance in the neighbourhood of Bekan as much as a millennium and a half ago – perhaps around the time of St Patrick. But there is evidence of human habitation going back a further two or three thousand years in the megalithic tombs and burial mounds in Greenwood, Feamore, Belesker and Larganboy. Other reminders of a distant past include bronze implements retrieved from Carrickmacantire and Bracklagh bogs and a celebrated musical instrument found in a local bog in 1791 and known as the Bekan Horn.

Bekan was located in the territory of an ancient people known as the Ciarraighe of Connacht – the local branch were called the Ciarraighe of Nairne, from the old name of Mannin Lake, Loch Nairne. The area features marginally in the cult of the national apostle, St Patrick. Local centres of the cult may have included Cúil Phádraig in Feamore and the townlands of Lispatrick and, especially, Holywell (in Irish Tobar Phádraig), while a holy well in Kildarra testified to the cult of St Brigid. Another holy well in Ballinvilla, Tobar Mhic Dhuach, may arguably reflect the Fons Mucno mentioned by Bishop Tírechán in his late-seventh-century account of St Patrick.

With the arrival of the Anglo-Normans in early-thirteenth-century Connacht, families such as Costello, Waldron, Jordan, Burke, Fitzmaurice, Hopkins, Prendergast and others put down deep roots in the area. Throughout the later middle ages almost the only names we have from Bekan are those of the parish clergy, both of Gaelic and Norman ancestry, recorded in the *Calendar of Papal Letters*: O Conor, Ó Gamhnáin, Prendergast, Ó Cuileannáin, Fleming, O Healy, O Ruane, Joyce, Burke, and so on. It is not entirely certain that all of these were based in Bekan because there is uncertainty about the equation of now-obsolete names such as Cill Ó nAodhagáin and Ráth Churnáin with Díseart Béacáin. This last form seems to lie behind the name by which the parish has been known for the past four and a half centuries at least – Béacán or, in anglicised form, Bekan. (Various aspects of the parish's correct original name are mired in a degree of confusion and uncertainty and cannot be satisfactorily untangled in the space available here.)

The wars and confiscations of the traumatic seventeenth century did not leave Bekan altogether unscathed. In the middle of that century the dreadful Cromwellian era produced in the Bekan-Ballyhaunis area a local martyr, Fr Fulgentius Jordan, a member of the Augustinian community which had been based in Ballyhaunis for more than two centuries before that. Fr Jordan, who was known from his eloquence as 'Béalórga' (goldenmouthed), was brutally done to death by parliamentary soldiers – either at the abbey in Ballyhaunis while exhorting his people to stand firm or while saying Mass at Redpark in Cloontumper. Local traditions about the terrible incident have some variation in detail.

When political disputation and war disturbed the country once more towards the close of the century, a native of the parish who came to prominence was Gerald Dillon of Feamore. A distinguished lawyer, he was an MP in the Jacobite Parliament of 1689. Two years later he was one of the seven signatories of the Treaty of Limerick, after which he followed Patrick Sarsfield into exile in France.

In the dark era of the Penal Laws, Bekan became for a time the hub of the Catholic Archdiocese of Tuam. For a period of 25 years – 1723-48 – two men with Bekan associations ruled the archdiocese: Bernard O Gara, 1723-40, and, following him, his brother Michael, 1740-8. Bernard had been parish priest of Knock in 1715 and later, at the time of his appointment as archbishop, parish priest of Bekan and Annagh. It appears that, during most of his time in charge of the archdiocese, he resided in Carrickmacantire and used Tulrahan old church as his pro-cathedral. It was Bernard, too, who in 1739 erected an inscribed altar-tomb in Ballyhaunis abbey in memory of his father, Charles, and family. (That Charles was a son of Fergal O Gara, prince of Coolavin and MP for Sligo, who had provided much-needed patronage for the team of Irish scholars known as the Four Masters when, in the 1630s and under the guidance of the Franciscan lay-brother Mícheál Ó Cléirigh, they produced their monumental work, *Annála Ríoghachta Éireann*, The Annals of the Kingdom of Ireland.)

Among the principal landowners in the Bekan area in the eighteenth century were the Burkes of Spotfield (Bracklagh), and one of that family, Frank Burke, was the subject of the only Irish poem, or song, known to have been composed about Bekan in that century. Known as 'Plaincstí Bhéacáin' and preserved in a single manuscript in the Royal Irish Academy, Dublin, it is a simple ballad of just two verses singing the praises of this young gentleman of the locality. (When I put the piece into print for the first time a quarter of a century ago, accompanied by a modicum of annotation, little did I dream that it would one day furnish a vital clue to a man named Robert Burke of Dún Laoghaire who was searching for details of his ancestors – the exciting story of how he was thus enabled to bring his quest to a successful conclusion is recounted in his fascinating book *Annie's Letter* (2003).)

Although the storms of conflict associated with the terrible 'Year of the French', 1798, buffetted the borders of Bekan, the parish escaped the worst horrors of the period. Likewise, the even greater horrors of the Great Famine of the 1840s led to hardship and some deaths in the locality, but the parish – largely due to the benevolence of the principal local landlord, Lord

Dillon – was spared the worst excesses of hunger and disease experienced by so many thousands of others in other parts of Mayo, and indeed throughout much of Ireland. Indeed little more than a decade after that great disaster came a development which would link Bekan with the outside world as never before when the Midland and Great Western Railway was extended into Co Mayo in the later 1850s, passing through the very heart of the parish. In addition, towards the end of 1861 not one but two railway stations were opened within the bounds of Bekan civil parish – Ballyhaunis Station in Cherryfield and Bekan Station in Cuilbeg. The latter served to make Bekan's name known far away from East Mayo, being listed on train timetables, railway maps, etc. It was to continue in existence for just over a century until – in the 1960s – a perverse view of 'progress' dictated that it be closed.

Towards the close of the nineteenth century and in the early twentieth the parish was not entirely immune to the dramatic social and political developments associated with the Land War and with the later struggle for independence, not forgetting a degree of local involvement in the awful conflict that convulsed Europe and much of the world and was remembered as the Great War. Great landed families such as the Nolans of Logboy, the Creans of Ballinvilla, the Trestons of Feamore, the Ronans or Ronaynes of Bunduff, Lurgan and Bekan, the Burkes of Spotfield, and others, declined or disappeared entirely while Lord Dillon's estate was bought out and divided among his tenants. A branch of the United Irish League was established in Bekan in 1904 and remained in existence down to the eve of the First World War. Willie Kelly – who for an incredible 66 years served as sacristan in Bekan – was probably the best-known local veteran of the Great War. Among the local men who took part in the War of Independence were Mícheál Ó Cléirigh, later a TD, Maurice Mullins, P. and Aughty Kenny and Tommie Flatley. One of the best-remembered episodes of the period was the abortive Holywell Ambush of August 1920.

Following Independence, Bekan made its contribution to the

CHAPTER TWO

new democracy, remarkably producing three TDs – one for each of the principal political parties! Thomas J. O Connell of Falmore (1882-1969) was a TD for the Irish Labour Party from 1922 to 1932 – for the first five years for Galway and for the second five for South Mayo; moreover, from 1927 to 1932 he was leader of the Labour Party. He served several terms, in the 1940s and 1950s, as a member of the Seanad. In addition, he was secretary of the Irish National Teachers' Organisation from 1916 to 1948 and was co-founder of the Educational Building Society. Micheál Ó Cléirigh of Cossallagh (1897-1988) – already mentioned as a veteran of the War of Independence – served as Fianna Fáil TD for one or other of the two Mayo constituencies from 1927 until 1944, when he became County Registrar for Dublin. Finally, the inimitable Michael 'Dalgan' Lyons of Turlough/Greenwood (1910-91) served as Fine Gael TD for South Mayo from 1965 to 1969 and later served in Seanad Éireann from 1969 to 1977. (Another TD who came from outside the parish but was a former pupil of Bekan National School – and contemporary there of Enda McDonagh's – was P. J. Morley of Cloonfaughna, in Knock parish, who was Fianna Fáil TD for East Mayo from 1977 to 1997.)

This, then, is the parish into which Enda McDonagh was born. As he remarks himself in a warmly affectionate article, 'Between Heaven and Bekan Cross', which he penned nearly thirty years ago for the *Mayo Yearbook*, it was once noted as a parish without three Ps – no pub, policeman or Protestant. (For some decades now, it has at least had a pub!) The title of the article just referred to echoes a line from the poem by Francis Thompson, 'O World Invisible We View Thee' – '… between Heaven and Charing Cross' – while the author closes it with a parody of Yeats's line, 'My country is Kiltartan Cross', declaring proudly 'My country is still Bekan Cross'.

CHAPTER THREE

Enda McDonagh: A Friend Amongst Us

Nuala Bourke

It is a great pleasure to speak today about Enda McDonagh as a friend and I hope that I can in some way do him justice without sounding as if he were no longer with us. Happily Enda is alive and well and very much with us.

Tá seanfhocal ann a deireann 'Má's maith leat moladh, faigh bás.' Buíochas le Dia níl Enda caillte. Tá sé fós linn agus ba mhaith liomsa an moladh atá tuillte aige a thabhairt dó inniu.

I think I met Enda before any of the contributors to this volume did.. We are both from Mayo and Enda was practically the boy next door. His parish priest, Fr Moane, used to engage Enda to drive him on regular visits to my father, and his parents were great friends of our cousins across the road. In our house, as in many others, great store was put on intellectual ability and as children we heard a lot about Mr McDonagh's son who was brilliantly clever. We were in awe of this rather shy young cleric from Maynooth and when we heard he was going to study in Rome his reputation soared. However, when on one occasion he managed to accidentally spray us all with lemonade at the dinner table his embarrassment did wonders for his image.

Enda disappeared from our lives for a while. He was in his own words 'en route to theology'. While we pursued more mundane lives, falling in love, getting married and having children, he made friends with the great and the good and the giants of learning in Rome and Germany, Oxford and Cambridge, all places spoken of in reverent terms in those quiet times in Ireland. Fortunately for the Irish church, and most especially for his friends, he returned to teach theology in Maynooth in the 1960s.

The next time I met Enda was through a very dear mutual

CHAPTER THREE

friend, Tommy Waldron, who was involved in setting up what is now Accord in the diocese of Tuam. By this time the shy cleric had vanished but he was charming as ever, carried his learning lightly, and everyone received kind and courteous attention. When speaking to us then he presented a theology of marriage which emphasised the goodness of this very human relationship, an understanding which was new and somewhat surprising to those who were reared on St Augustine.

Enda has always rejoiced in his roots and so our paths have crossed regularly over the last so many years. The Mayo books of theology provided such a wonderful forum for many who would perhaps have previously regarded theology as the preserve of the few, not a discipline we could aspire to. But an ever gracious Enda welcomed all our contributions and encouraged us to be involved in the relationship between ourselves and God and the world we live in. Mol an óige agus an tsean aois agus tiocfaidh siad!

His recent gift of all his books and papers to the third level college of his native county will ensure that any one wishing to under take study or further research will have fabulous resource material to draw on, not only in theology but in the humanities, the sciences and beyond. The name of Enda McDonagh will be for ever blessed!

When Eugene Duffy, Enda Lyons and Eamonn Conway made a brave decision to transfer some theological education to the West of Ireland, Enda was again interested and available to contribute to the West of Ireland Pastoral Theology Association with characteristic generosity. More recently the launching of the magazine *Céide* was a point of contact with the West. It was yet another effort on Enda's part to bring the margins to centre stage, to gather us in and to provide a forum for an alternative view. It was of course a privilege to be involved in this venture and to have the opportunity to experience again Enda's wit and wisdom, his ability to enthuse others and to observe how he could relieve them of a 'few bob' for his current project. Good wine was a good lubricant!

Enda's friends span the globe from Bekan to Burma, from the Áras to Africa, they are drawn from every walk of life and every religious faith. His recent elevation to canon of the Church of Ireland is testimony to his ecumenism and a sign of hope to all. He is always at ease and has the facility to make each friend feel special. To his friends Enda has been a marrying priest and a burying priest. He has celebrated in great joy with them at weddings and baptisms, and has brought great consolation and comfort to those who needed him in moments of grief and anguish. He has invested much in friendship and has in turn been sustained by his multitude of friends. And if his friends have sometimes felt that his great scholarship, often cleverly concealed by cardigan and slippers, has not so much been unrecognised as unrewarded, we are aware that had high clerical office been thrust upon him we might not have had such easy access to his time and his company.

Professor of Moral Theology seems such a stern and forbidding title and maybe a rather surprising one for a science graduate. In spite of this lofty title Enda as professor was always gracious to everyone and greeted even what were then regarded as lowly students with courteous charm. He was always fair and when, on a bad day, he failed a certain now rather famous candidate in the faculties examinations he apologised to him when his normal good humour returned and ensured his success at the next interview. There are countless students who tell endless stories of the enormous help and encouragement which Enda gave them, and the wonderful worldwide contacts he had when anyone needed an 'introduction' in a foreign land or even in a not so foreign land.

He always eschews condemnation and has therefore been able to accompany many on difficult moral journeys. He has been able to find good in every committed and loving relationship and his work with the marginalised in any context is well known. Nonetheless, he has often been able to say very challenging things by using his unique language which is so non threatening that even the most difficult message can be acceptable.

CHAPTER THREE

Enda's many talents are being celebrated here to day, but in truth there is none more important than his extraordinary ability to reach out in genuine friendship to people of every race and every faith, to engage with them and to grace their lives.

Ba mhaith liom buíochas ó chroí a gabháil le hEnda as ucht a chuid oibre agus a thacaíocht do gach aon duine a chuir suim sa diagacht.

I would like to thank Enda for all he has contributed to broadening theology, helping us to get involved in a subject that is at the heart of our faith, but most especially let me say thank you on behalf of all his friends for his love of life and his gift of friendship.

CHAPTER FOUR

Enda Mc Donagh, the Scholar

Seán Freyne

The usual perception of 'the scholar' is that of somebody who is closeted away from real life, living in his or her ivory tower, immersed in books and uninterested in the daily affairs of the world around them. Perhaps this stereotype is a left-over from the medieval world of the monks, where some of these aspects did indeed apply. On the other hand, in today's world one often hears the label 'academic', or 'theologian', being used pejoratively, to denote varying degrees of irrelevance and pedantry from the perspective of our modern secularised society. I am happy to report that in the case of Enda Mc Donagh, we are dealing with neither a recluse nor an irrelevant voice in terms of the world we live in.

Rather, Enda is somebody who throughout his whole life has been at the forefront of Irish intellectual and political discussion, an activist for peace and justice from Ireland to Africa, from Europe to America, from Bekan to Maynooth. He is also a writer whose work continues to explore the deepest yearnings of the human heart with profundity and originality. In his case, certainly, the label 'scholar' cannot be used in isolation from his life and person, since his theology is not based on books only, but on a reflective and sensitive personality who feels deeply about the joys and sorrows of the human condition and who has never lost contact with his Mayo and West of Ireland roots. The two books of Mayo theology which he conceived and edited, as well as the promotion of the now sadly defunct *Céide*, are testimony to his genuine love of his native hills.

Enda's star had begun to rise very early. I had heard of him before I entered St Jarlath's College, Tuam in 1948. The word that reached Tooreen from the farthest reaches of Bekan was

CHAPTER FOUR

that we had a genius in our midst, but that you would never know it when meeting this shy and unassuming young man. In our Jarlath's days Enda was repeatedly held up to us by teachers such as Joe Cunnane, Doc Mooney and Páraic O'Brien as an example of the heights we could reach if we applied ourselves properly. By then he was already blazing a trail in Maynooth, studying science no less, a most unlikely subject for anybody who had graduated from the science teaching of those far off days in St Jarlath's! Yet it was typical of Enda's inquiring mind and pioneering approach to learning not to take one of the relatively easy options, such as Celtic Studies or Classics, for his first degree, but to choose instead a subject area where he would be challenged, despite the fact that he would not have had the usual background preparation from his previous schooling.

I mention this remote and, at this distance, inconsequential anecdote because in many ways it set a pattern for his life of scholarship. At a slightly later point in his career, when he had been appointed to the Chair of Moral Theology in Maynooth in 1958, he soon realised that he should not take the familiar and well worn path of doing a second Doctorate (his first one was on an ecumenical topic to do with the Anglican Church, as I recall) in Canon Law in Rome – a pre-requisite for any self-respecting Catholic moralist in those days. Enda opted instead to cross the Alps to Munich, where he quickly became acquainted with some of the leading Catholic theologians of the day, including the great Karl Rahner. He returned to Maynooth to take up his Chair two years later, having completed a German doctorate on church-state relations with specific reference to the special status of the Catholic Church according to Article 44 of the Irish Constitution, an article that was later removed by referendum of the Irish people.

In retrospect these choices – for science and for a topic with political as well as religious significance – were indicative of the subsequent direction of Enda's academic career. He never allowed himself to be restrained by the tyranny of the disciplines, as these were and are defined in academia, but rather saw the whole of knowledge, like the whole of life, as a web of interconnected patterns to be contemplated, explored and explained insofar as this was humanly possible. With such an understanding of the way things are, science and theology were not as distant from each other as some have claimed. It is this capacity to range far and wide and to reconcile what might appear to be opposites that makes Enda's writing so attractive and so insightful. A visit to his Maynooth rooms could easily become a distraction, as one felt immediately tempted to spend the time browsing amid the collection he had amassed over the years. You could be always certain that it would be representative of the best and latest in literature, philosophy, history, politics, biblical studies, poetry and of course theology in all its branches. This magnificent collection, so impressive in its range and depth, has now been generously donated to his native Mayo, a gesture of generosity and selflessness that is so typical of the man, as anybody who has ever visited him will readily attest.

Among this wide ranging collection are of course a number of books which Enda himself has authored, 15 in all as well as 15 others edited or co-authored – a highly impressive output, given his many other engagements and commitments. Reviewing one of his recent works, *Vulnerable to the Holy*, I wrote that he was never one to write the theological block-buster, but had rather opted for the essay as his favoured mode of exploration of various topics and issues. This, I am sure, was a very deliberate decision, since Enda never believed that he, or anybody else for that matter, could say the last word on any topic. To give the impression of having done so would be to engage in deception and self-delusion. I well remember an enthralling evening listening to him and David Tracy, an eminent theologian from the University of Chicago, as they animatedly discussed the perennial issue of the relationship of faith and reason. Significantly, both of them chose the notion of 'fragments' as a metaphor for the brokenness of our knowledge of God, echoing for me St Paul's remark: 'We see now darkly as in a mirror.' But Enda went on to explain that for him the fragment was not a broken shard of a lost mosaic,

CHAPTER FOUR

but rather a metaphor for the whole that is disclosed to us in fleeting insights of illumination that are given as viaticum for the journey. The title of his latest collection, *Immersed in Mystery*, expresses the same idea, but in a less jagged image: the script may be torn but it is still legible for those who want to read the signs and are open to the mystery.

The more one examines the later writings, the more one sees how the range of his interests have somehow begun to coalesce, articulating his deep sense of the divine who has revealed itself as love in the life and death of Jesus of Nazareth. Any occasion or topic can become the launching pad for a deep meditation on the God who is Other, and yet very near. More and more, art and poetry speak to him of the mystery in which we are all immersed. But there are people also. Enda has always been a lover of people and a nurturer of human friendships. His theology is marked by a deep awareness of the relatedness of the human condition. To be human is, for him, to be related with others, and it is in exploring the significance of this reality that he has, perhaps, made his most lasting contribution to his own particular specialism of moral theology.

To grasp the significance of his contribution in this regard, we have only to remind ourselves of the state of the discipline when Enda began his teaching career all of 50 years ago. For those of you whose memory does not go back that far, we were still in the days of the pre-Vatican II Catholicism, when law was more important than love, and morality was about obeying the rules rather than responding to the call of the gospel. I well remember one Maynooth professor telling us that the Council would have several difficult issues to decide on, the most important of which would be what precisely constituted 'servile work' on the Sabbath, as described by the Maynooth catechism! Enda arrived back from Munich, ready to launch those of us who were fortunate enough to have him as a lecturer into the new thinking about Christian morality, where the primacy of charity or love was to be affirmed above law. Of course this thinking was not new, but a retrieval of the old and original gospel message of Jesus and Paul, something that had been lost sight of in the post-Reformation period when Roman Catholicism became more Roman than it was Catholic in the true sense of that word, namely, universal in terms of its proclamation of God's love and concern for all peoples and the whole of the creation, as this was revealed in the ministry of Jesus Christ.

For some, this new vision was, and sadly still is, seen as the opening of the floodgates that has led to the moral and spiritual chaos that we find ourselves in today. Being a moral theologian in the post-Vatican II church has not been an easy career and Enda, like others, has had to pay a high price on occasions because of his courageous espousal of these values, while at the same time retaining a remarkable loyalty to the community of the church. Yet the insights that he brought back to us in Maynooth in the early 60s were the ones that would become enshrined in Vatican II. Applying those insights to the ever more complex situations we are faced with in our global village calls for sensitivity, compassion, good judgement and insight, and Enda has those qualities to an outstanding degree. We are today faced with issues that Vatican II never dreamed of – the ecological crisis, new developments in human procreation, the AIDS pandemic, the power of the multi-nationals to control the world's resources, genetic engineering of crops and humans, our capacity to destroy the planet in nuclear war – the list is endless, and then there are the hardy perennials of personal morality – the use of contraceptives and the issue of abortion. Negotiating the balance between moral ideals and human weakness and tragedy is an art as well as a science, and there are no easy or clear-cut answers. It calls for wisdom, experience and courage, especially when loyalty to one's own tradition is called into question, simply because one is prepared to take the risk of relying on God's love rather than on human self-righteousness.

Risk is a word that is increasingly part of Enda's vocabulary – the risk of theology, the risk of God, even. One must indeed reckon that one could be wrong. Yet the risk-taking that Enda speaks of is not some reckless, head-in-the-sand approach, but a considered, reflective judgement on the meaning of life as gift and response to the call of the Other, that is God, incarnated in the daily others we encounter on the way. Increasingly, his risk-taking is nourished by an emphasis on the importance of prayer so that the active life is properly focused, and alive to the possibilities and challenges that come our way each day. Prayer, poetry and politics are part of the epitaph that he would choose for himself, I suspect. An alternative might be that of the Roman philosopher and statesman, Terence: *Homo sum et nihil humanum a me alienum puto* – 'I am human and I consider nothing human foreign to me'. It would sum up Enda McDonagh the scholar, but more importantly, Enda McDonagh, the person. Go mairigh sé i bfhad!

CHAPTER FIVE

Facing the Truth

Brendan Hoban

In 1904, when Sir Horace Plunkett wrote his book, *Ireland in the New Century*, he concluded that the Irish character displayed a striking absence of self-reliance and moral courage and that the Irish Catholic clergy could not be exonerated from some responsibility for this. He excluded from that criticism a number of priests including Fr Jeremiah O'Donovan, a Clonfert priest who was involved (with Plunkett) in the movement for national regeneration. O'Donovan shared Plunkett's assessment of the Irish clergy, to such a degree indeed that it eventually impinged on his decision to leave the priesthood. O'Donovan, a cultured and literate man, travelled the world extolling the potential of the co-operative movement and became, in his day, a prominent and sometimes controversial figure, noted for his liberal and secular views. His bishop, Thomas O'Dea, put a halt to his gallop when he told him that, instead of gallivanting around the world, he should be in Loughrea hearing confessions on Saturday evening. First things first. The Irish church, in the early years of the last century, was a cold place for a liberal or even independent voice. O'Donovan dealt with his experience in fictional form in his novel, *Fr Ralph*, published some years later. Louise Fuller has written of how Catholicism, by the end of the 19th century, had become 'the badge of the Irish nation' and by Catholicism was meant not a rich, cultural and religious heritage but a hybrid of Tridentinism, folk-religion and Victorian Puritanism. 'The Catholic ethos,' Fuller has written, 'that developed in Ireland in the nineteenth century placed a heavy emphasis on discipline and could be characterised as authoritarian, legalistic and prescriptive.'

I don't have to spell out how that version of Irish Catholicism

CHAPTER FIVE

has served our church so badly and yet survived so long. The poet Paul Durcan, in an RTÉ Radio broadcast, *The Giant on my Shoulder*, described 1950s Ireland as 'a sort of medieval iron-curtain country, a Celtic cross theocracy, a cocktail of Israel and Iran, an island of Ayatollahs, mullahs, Pharisees, zealots ... a closed tyrannical society controlled by the Catholic Church and male politicians in much the same way as the Soviet Union was controlled by the Communist Party.' An exaggeration, perhaps, but substantially true.

The divinely inspired antidote to all that darkness and tyranny was the light and promise offered by the Second Vatican Council. Few would deny that the Irish church missed that tide, as it would in subsequent decades miss so many more tides. In Durcan's phrase, all the Irish bishops who attended the session in Rome could offer were 'a few teaspoonfuls of negativity'. They had the experience but they missed the meaning, and their translation of that vision to their people was summed up in the historic phrase, 'No change.' Even before they arrived home from Rome, the thrust of the Vatican II enterprise was being strangled by stealth, well before it was more centrally and officially strangled. The Irish bishops knew better than to trust the odd instincts of a peasant Pope.

At the close of the Vatican Council the Irish church – with a resilient people, a talented priesthood and an intellectually-rigorous episcopate – was in pole position to digest the new wisdom of accountability and collegiality, to put flesh on the great insights of the Council and to build a new church that would engage with a changing world. But it was not to be. There was a failure of imagination on a grand scale; there was a failure to trust the divinely-inspired wisdom of the Council; and there was a failure to facilitate the development of other voices which would bring an openness, a breadth and a richness to a new church.

The old failures came back to haunt us. Even though our church was full of energy and talent we were actively encouraged to believe that no matter how important or refined or even providential the wisdom of the Council, it was less important than the insights of our leaders. Father knew best. The influence of the authoritarian, legalistic and prescriptive ethos of nineteenth century Irish Catholicism continued into the second half of the twentieth century. And that absence of a spirit of self-reliance and moral courage in the Irish clergy, that Sir Horace Plunkett and Gerard O'Donovan decried decades earlier, reasserted itself again. Priests were encouraged to toe the party line, to keep their own thoughts to themselves, to perpetuate the old clerical system that promoted that absurd species of clerical life that Neil Kevin called 'the Safe Man' and that doled out comfortable parishes and empty titles if you played by the rules. Say no more. Rule One was that priests never confronted bishops because the bishop always knows best, even when the dogs in the street knew that his judgement was skewed. And because the Association of Irish Priests wasn't obeying the rules, the bishops decided that the National Conference of Priests would come into being. In Cardinal William Conway's celebrated phrase, 'We left a gap.' And just as priests never confronted bishops, so bishops never confronted or opposed what emanated from Rome, even when what emanated from Rome was patently absurd. I am reminded of Bishop Michael Harty's famous comment, made shortly before his death, that the Irish bishops had forgotten that it was possible to say 'No' to Rome.

We've paid a huge price for the failures of bishops and priests to own their own authority and to trust the spirit and the impetus of the Second Vatican Council. We were too careful, too afraid, too amenable to the wisdom of a narrow clerical world, too reluctant to own our own truth, to use our own minds ... and, if the truth be told, too many of us were too ambitious at a personal level to upset the clerical consensus. Say nothing. Keep your head down.

It might have been very different. If instead of control, we had placed a premium on freedom of speech. If instead of shuffling people like Enda McDonagh to the sidelines of church life, we had trusted in his faith in a Christian God. If we had noted

CHAPTER FIVE

his ability to articulate the possibilities of a changing world, if we had appreciated his insight and intelligence and his facility for engaging with those outside the narrow focus of confessional Catholicism, if we had made him a bishop instead of waiting for St Patrick's Cathedral to make him a Prebendary of Clondalkin, if instead of an ageing and diminishing coterie of Vatican II *aficionados* gathering together as if to keep ourselves warm or looking for shelter on occasions like this, if instead of our marginal and ineffective position on the edge of a disappearing church, if instead of all that if the spirit of Vatican II had been at the heart of the church for the last 40 years, how different things might have been. How we might have learned to name so many uncomfortable truths! And how our church might have been better served if we had spoken the truth and faced the demons of the past.

There were, I think, two significant failures. One was the refusal to hear different voices in the church. The concept of a loyal opposition in the church quickly became anathema to a church given to centralised control and the oppression that often followed. If all you have is a hammer, someone said, sooner or later everything looks like a nail.

Shortly after *Humanae Vitae* was promulgated in 1968 and was repudiated by nineteen priests in Washington DC, the theologian Charles Curran wrote *Dissent In and For the Church*, arguing for space for dissent and individual conscience and for elbow room for theologians in a church that found it difficult to deal with a loyal opposition. But even though a few years later, in 1971, through the influence of Pope Paul VI, the Congregation of the Clergy issued a document minimising the nature of the Washington dissent, ominously the wagons began to circle. And the concept of a loyal opposition was reserved for those who played safe games and made quiet noises in the secluded interior. Within a few years a cold wind from the north, by way of Poland, ushered in a more bitter winter for dissent.

The second significant failure was the subservience of the clergy to the wisdom of those who told them they knew better.

People who know more about psychology than I do tell me that a high percentage of priests are of a psychological personality type that places a premium on loyalty. That's the benign interpretation. A less benign interpretation is that, more than a hundred years after Sir Horace Plunkett adverted to the striking absence of a spirit of self-reliance and moral courage in Irish society and among Irish priests, could it be that more than a hundred years later little has changed? Why is it that Irish priests give little indication of owning their wisdom and intelligence and experience, and often seem happy to deny that wisdom and intelligence and experience or to stand their own truth in their own ground when the very dogs in the street know what needs to be said? Is it that we're too nice? Or too careful? Or too cute? Or too afraid to speak the truth as we see it? Or could it be that we're too ambitious? Like Master Rich in *A Man for All Seasons*, are we selling our souls for some equivalent of some Wales? One of a priest's first services to the world, someone said, is to tell the truth.

In his book *Sacred Silence: Denial and Crisis in the Church*, Donald Cozzens asks the question: What are we afraid of? It's a question that I admit to being obsessed about all my life. Isn't there something extraordinary about a priest who has worked in a parish for 10 or 20 or 30 or 40 years and who in private can name important truths, but who loses his voice when the chips are down or the bishop arrives for Confirmation? The question: what are we afraid of? hides a hundred other questions that we need to ask and to answer if we want to serve the gospel and the church, honourably and authentically even if it means exclusion from the clerical club, the unwanted attention of our superiors, the confusion of our parishioners, even sometimes the hurt of our families. When the history of the last 40 years is written, and when a question is posed about what loyalty to gospel and church actually meant during the last few decades, the verdict of history will place it all in due perspective. Many of us won't be here to hear that verdict but I suspect that what often passes for loyalty in today's church will be held up to the light and found wanting.

CHAPTER FIVE

Unquestioning loyalty is, in effect, a contradiction in terms. How best is the gospel and the church served: by invariably agreeing with the official word or standing on the ground of one's own judgement? One honest voice calling out an unpalatable truth may serve the church a thousand times better than the silent many who accept the status quo in a spirit of unquestioning loyalty. In that climate, we appreciate and we value those who questioned the consensus, especially those who had the learning and the intelligence and the courage to name their own truth and who weren't side-tracked by episcopal disapproval, the pressure of their clerical peers or the lure of place, position or power.

In the desert of the last 40 years, there were exceptional voices, like that of Enda McDonagh, prophets in their own land who were prepared to name the truth, individuals who had the personal freedom not to be dissuaded from speaking the truth even when ecclesiastical carrots were held out before them.

There was a price to be paid for what for many was a kind of self-imposed exile from the centre of their own church but there has been a long and honourable tradition of voices prepared to pay that price.

One of Enda McDonagh's many valuable contributions to the Irish Roman Catholic Church was that by standing against the political consensus in his church he helped others to find a voice too. For those who have given their lives to work for the church they love, outside the camp was often a cold and lonely place to be but when people of the stature and humanity of Enda McDonagh were prepared to stand outside in the cold, it made facing the truth about ourselves and our church a bit easier to do. For that and for much more so many are so grateful for the prophetic voice of Enda McDonagh.

CHAPTER SIX

What Would a Christian University Look Like?
Some Tentative Answers Inspired by Wendell Berry

Stanley Hauerwas

The most fundamental kind of thinking is invariably provincial, in one form or another.
— Robert Pogue Harrison[1]

1. *The Challenge Before Us*

'There are also violent and nonviolent ways to milk cows,' I observed in a sermon on the occasion of the Installation of Dr Gerald Gerbrandt as President of the Canadian Mennonite University on 28 September 2003.[2] I made the comment to commend the parochial character of the Canadian Mennonite University. The Canadian Mennonite University, as its name suggests, is Mennonite and Canadian and you cannot get more parochial than that. My comment about milk, therefore, was meant to raise why such a university would have no reason to distinguish between theoretical and practical forms of knowledge.

My sermon, and I think it important to observe that this is a university that assumes it is appropriate to have a sermon as part of their inaugural event for the first president of this institution, expressed my hope that the Canadian Mennonite University would not be just another 'Christian liberal arts college.' I think it is now clear that Christian liberal arts colleges have turned out to be more liberal than Christian. It is not my particular interest in this essay to try to understand why the

---
1. Robert Pogue Harrison, *Forests: The Shadow of Civilization* (Chicago: University of Chicago Press, 1992), p 246.
2. The sermon entitled, 'On Milk and Jesus' can be found in my book, *Disrupting Time: Sermons, Prayers, and Sundries* (Eugene, Or: Cascade Books, 2004), pp 142-148.

Christian liberal arts college has failed to sustain itself as Christian, but rather to begin to explore what a university responsive to the church might look like.[3]

'To begin to explore what a Christian university might look like' is, of course, a far too grand project. What I am really interested in is to try to spell out what difference there may be between violent and nonviolent ways to milk cows. The focus on milking cows might suggest I assume that university curriculums should not be determined by presumptions about the necessity to sustain 'high culture.' I think it important, however, that universities teach Plato, Aquinas, Dante, and Darwin because I think one of the tasks of the university is to be a memory of a people. But too often Christian justifications of the university focused on the need to preserve the 'classics' of western civilisation have created universities that serve class interests more than Christian purpose. Why and how Plato is read at the Canadian Mennonite University may be quite different from why and how Plato is read at Duke University.

I think, moreover, that Wendell Berry's criticism of the university is very important to help us understand the difference between violent and nonviolent ways to milk cows. Berry is an unrelenting critic of the contemporary university. I am deeply sympathetic to his criticisms of the university as we know it, but his criticisms are so radical that it is not unreasonable to conclude that Berry has no hope that the university can be reclaimed for humane – much less Christian – purposes. I hope to show that Berry's work also suggests how we need to begin to live and, thus, think if we are to begin to imagine what a university shaped by Christian practices might look like.

I have, like Berry, often been a critic of the contemporary university. Of course to be a critic of the university is to mark oneself as a university person. After all, universities are often associated with people who think thinking – if it is to be thinking –

---

3. This way of putting the matter often raises the questions, 'Which church?' and 'Does such a church exist?' The answer is, 'The Church of the Holy Family (Chapel Hill, North Carolina) is church and it exists.'

must be 'critical'. So critics of the university often discover that their criticisms of the university are criticisms that only people trained at universities could produce. Therefore our very critiques reproduce the practices that we critique. The truth of the matter is that in America it is very hard to sustain a life of study without being parasitic on the university. I am more than willing, therefore, to acknowledge that my criticisms of the university, I hope, reveal my profound love of the university.

I hope I am a Christian, but the university has been more my home than the church. I went to Southwestern University in Georgetown, Texas in September 1962. As they say, 'the rest is history,' because from that time to the present I have always lived in a university. The only way I know to make a living is to be at a university. I did not necessarily set out to be a university person. My life just worked out that way. I was brought up to be a bricklayer – honest work. I have tried not to forget what it means to be 'in the trades,' but for better or worse I am an academic.

After Southwestern I spent six years at Yale Divinity School and Yale Graduate School where I received the Bachelor of Divinity degree and my Ph.D. I taught two years at Augustana College in Rock Island, Illinois, fourteen years at the University of Notre Dame, and I am now in my twenty-third year of teaching in the Divinity School at Duke. My life has been made possible by people who care about sustaining the university. I no doubt owe the university more than I know.

Yet the history recounted in the last paragraphs is not one characteristic of those who have sought to have an academic career. I have always served the university, I have always used as well as been used by the university, because I am a Christian. I am a theologian. Theology is not generally considered a legitimate field in the university. Of course that was not the official position at Augustana or Notre Dame. Lutherans and Catholics still thought and think that theology should matter, though how it matters is in dispute. Theology is tolerated at Duke because we are a Divinity School, but the Divinity School is regarded by many at Duke as a 'cultural lag'. Theologians in the modern university bear the burden of proof, which turns out to be very good for theology because if you are a theologian you need to know what your colleagues in other disciplines know, but they do not have to know what you know.

Yet my identity as a theologian means I have always been in the university but not of it. Berry has been more 'out' of the university than 'in' the university. Berry, of course, would not be Berry without the university. He is a graduate of a university. He has a graduate degree. He has taught at the University of Kentucky and other universities from time to time. But Berry has clearly chosen to 'think' and write outside the university. I may, therefore, have more of a stake in making the university 'work' than Berry may have. Nonetheless I hope to show how Berry can help us begin to rethink what a university might look like in order to be of service to the church. Having said this, I should warn the reader that I may also be using Berry's work to sustain a project that Berry thinks hopeless.

2. Berry on the University
'Abstraction is the enemy wherever it is found.'[4] If any sentence could sum up Berry's work and, in particular, his criticism of the modern university it is this one. In order to appropriately appreciate Berry's criticism of abstraction, however, I think it wise to attend to his early, but very important essay, 'Standing by

---

4. Wendell Berry, *Sex, Economy, Freedom, and Community* (New York: Pantheon Books, 1992), p 23. Not to be missed are the implications about power involved by presumptions concerning the necessity of abstractions. No one has seen this more clearly than Sheldon Wolin who observes that modern power is reflected materially in the structure and attributes of theoretical knowledge as understood by the knowledges represented by the development of the mathematical sciences. Wolin notes this conception of power was unlimited because 'the knowledge that made power reproducible had selected nature as its object and conceived it to be a field of inexhaustible forces... abstraction and dehistorization conjoined to clear the way for a form of knowledge that could freely construct its objects and their relationships.' *Tocqueville between Two Worlds: The Making of a Political and Theoretical Life* (Princeton: Princeton University Press, 2001), pp 20-21.

Words.'⁵ Berry is very careful not to reproduce dualisms that only create the problem he is trying to help us avoid. He is not, for example, advocating subjectivity as an alternative to objectivity, nor is he recommending the particular over the universal. Rather he is trying to help us resist our tendency to speak nonsense.

Berry seldom betrays any knowledge of philosophy or philosophers. I suspect, like many poets, he is suspicious of philosophers. But his understanding of language, the criticism of the abstractions that we are taught to speak at universities, cannot help but remind some of us of lessons we have learned from Wittgenstein. In *Standing by Words* Berry argues that the disintegration of communities and persons in our time is a correlative of our loss of accountability in our use of language.

According to Berry, for any statement to be complete or comprehensible three conditions are required:
1. It must designate its object precisely.
2. Its speaker must stand by it: must believe it, be accountable for it, be willing to act on it.
3. This relation of speaker, word, and object must be conventional; the community must know what it is.⁶

Berry suggests that these common assumptions are becoming uncommon through the development of specialisation. As a result language is increasingly seen as a weapon to gain power over others or as a medium of play. Or some, even poets such as Shelley, think the subjectivity of language must be emphasised in order to resist objectification. Yet, according to Berry, when that unhappy choice is accepted only pathos can result making language nothing more than a medium of self-pity.

It is extremely important to note that Berry is not denying the need for generalisation. There is truth in the claim that 'the particular has no language' – but there are nonetheless two forms of precision that allows the particular to be communicated. The

---

5. Wendell Berry, *Standing by Words* (Washington, DC: Shoemaker and Hoard, 1983), pp 24-63.
6. Berry, *Standing by Words*, p 25.

first form of precision is the speech of people who share the same knowledge of place and history. 'The old hollow beech blew down last night.' Berry calls this community speech which he praises because it is precise and open to ongoing testing against its objects. Such speech is the 'very root and foundation of language.'[7]

The second form of precision is that which 'comes of tension either between a statement and a prepared context or, within a single statement, between more or less conflicting feelings, or ideas.'[8] To illustrate this form of precision Berry contrasts Shelley's complaint against our mortality, 'I could lie down like a tired child,' with Robert Herrick's, 'Out of the world he must, who once comes in ...' observing that the latter satisfies our need for complexity and thus does justice to our actual experience.[9] Such precision is hard won, requiring us to battle against our proclivities to engage in fantasies.

One form such fantasies take is to produce sentences that try to be 'objective' by avoiding all personal biases and considerations. Berry thinks such language is often found used by scientists. He gives the example of transcribed conversations of members of the Nuclear Regulatory Commission during the crisis of Three Mile Island, who worked to 'engineer a press release' to avoid frightening the public that a meltdown might happen. Thus one commissioner suggested they say, 'In the unlikely event that this occurred (i.e. the meltdown) temperatures would result and possible further fuel damage.' Berry observes what is remarkable and frightening about such language is the inability of those who speak in such a way to acknowledge what it is they are talking about.[10]

---

7. Berry, *Standing by Words*, p 33. Note Berry does not say the 'particular' defies all language.
8. Berry, *Standing by Words*, p 34.
9 Berry, *Standing by Words*, p 35.
10. Berry, *Standing by Words*, p 38. James Scott provides ample documentation to show how this kind of language is a correlative of state power designed to destroy the concrete. Scott identifies 'the old hollow beech blew down last night' with *methis*, that is, speech that requires

The perversion of speech illustrated by attempts to be 'objective' serves the political purpose of securing the power of those who use it without their being held accountable. They say such speech aims to bring people together for some common project. Accordingly they try to create the illusion that we all speak the same language –

> meaning either that they will agree with the government or be quiet, as in communist and fascist states, or that they will politely ignore their disagreements or disagree 'provisionally,' as in American universities. But the result – though power may survive for a while in spite of it – is confusion and dispersal. Real language, real discourse are destroyed. People lose understanding of each other, are divided and scattered. Speech of whatever kind begins to resemble the speech of drunkenness or madness.[11]

Berry offers another example of this passion for objectivity that interestingly enough has to do with cows. In an article entitled, 'The Evolution and Future of American Animal Agriculture,' G. W. Salisbury and R. G. Hart argue for the importance of the transformation of American agriculture from an art to a science. Art, they suggest, is only concerned with the 'hows', but science with the 'whys'. Accordingly they recommend that a cow be described as 'appropriate manufacturing unit of the twentieth century.' Berry notes that such language relieves those who use it of any accountability indicated by a farmer's statement, 'Be good to the cow, for she is our companion.'[12]

The latter sentence, Berry observes, requires a world that is organised in a hierarchical sequence of nature, agriculture, community, family, person. Such a hierarchy is based on the assumption that these systems are interrelated and whatever affects

---

exemplification in concrete situations. *Methis*, in other words, is close to what Aristotle meant by practical reason. See Scott, *Seeing Like a State: How Certain Schemes to Improve the Human Condition Fail* (New Haven: Yale University Press, 1998), pp 319, 335.
11. Berry, *Standing by Words*, p 40.
12. Berry, *Standing by Words*, pp 43-44.

one will affect the other. The former sentence, that is, the cow as 'an appropriate manufacturing unit,' reverses this hierarchy with one that runs from industrial economy, agriculture, dairy, dairyman. This latter hierarchy is meant to disintegrate the connecting disciplines by turning farming into a profession and a profession into a career.

Berry's subsequent criticism of the university can now be seen as the development of his concern that in the university we are taught to speak in a manner in which we are unable to 'stand by our words'. Thus my claim that the two questions you cannot ask in the modern university are: 'What is the university for?' and 'Who does it serve?' That the university has no 'learned public' to serve – and a learned public might be one that knows how to milk cows – is at the heart of our problem.

Berry thinks the modern university is at least one of the institutions that should be held responsible for the corruption of our language. The university at once legitimates as well as reproduces the disintegration of the life of the mind and of communities through increasing specialisation. According to Berry,

> The various specialties are moving ever outward from any centre of interest or common ground, becoming ever farther apart, and ever more unintelligible to one another. Among the causes, I think, none is more prominent than the by now ubiquitous and nearly exclusive emphasis upon originality and innovation. The emphasis, operating within the 'channels' of administration, affects in the most direct and practical ways all the lives within the university. It imposes the choice of work over life, exacting not only the personal costs spoken of in Yeats poem ('The Choice'), but very substantial costs to the community as well.[13]

---

13. Wendell Berry, *Life is a Miracle: An Essay Against Modern Superstition* (Washington DC: Counterpoint, 2000), p 61. Yeat's poem reads:
　The intellect of man is forced to choose
　Perfection of the life, or of the work,
　And if it take the second must refuse
　A heavenly mansion, raging in the dark.

Specialisation of the disciplines, however, Berry argues is thought to be crucial if the university is to receive the support it needs from a capitalist society. If universities are to grow, and the assumption is that they must always grow, they will need money. But, equally important, universities must accept the fundamental economic principle of the opposition of money to goods. Berry, who otherwise betrays no Marxist sympathies, seems to know in his bones that there is no 'abstraction' more abstract than money. Labour is not only appropriated from the worker in the name of money, but the worker is expected to use that money to buy goods that cannot be represented by money.

The incoherence of university curriculums reflects the university's commitment to legitimate the abstraction effected by money. For example, it is crucial that the university insure that learning be organised not to be a conversation between disciplines, but rather that disciplines be representatives of competing opposites. As a result accountability is lost. The sciences are sectioned off from one another so they might serve their respective corporations. 'The so-called humanities, which might have supplied at least a corrective or chastening remembrance of the good that humans have sometimes accomplished, have been dismembered into utter fecklessness, turning out "communicators" who have nothing to say and "educators" who have nothing to teach.'[14] Indeed universities no longer are sources of literacy. Accordingly the English department itself has become a 'specialty', and even in those departments writing has become a sub-specialty of the freshman writing programme. The result is the clear message that to write well is not necessary.[15]

Berry confesses he has no idea how the disciplines might be reorganised, but he is doubtful that anyone knows how to do

---

    When all that story's finished, what's the news?
    In luck or out the toil has left is mark:
    The old perplexity an empty purse,
    Or the day's vanity, the night's remorse.

14. Berry, *Life Is a Miracle*, p 123.
15. Berry, *Life Is a Miracle*, p 68.

that. However he is convinced that the standards and goals of the disciplines needs to be changed. He observes:

> It used to be that we thought of the disciplines as ways of being useful to ourselves, for we needed to earn a living, but also and more importantly we thought of them as ways of being useful to one another. As long as the idea of vocation was still viable among us, I don't believe it was ever understood that a person was 'called' to be rich or powerful or even successful. People were taught the disciplines at home or in school for two reasons: to enable them to live and work both as self-sustaining individuals and as useful members of their communities, and to see that the disciplines themselves survived the passing of the generations.[16]

The incoherence of university curriculums reflects the acceptance of the assumption that there is nothing odd about unlimited economic growth or consumption in a limited world. Education is now job preparation for a career in a profession.[17] But work, whether it is done in the academy, a profession, or industry, is now designed so that the worker is separated from the effects of their work. The worker is permitted 'to think that they are working nowhere or anywhere – in their careers or specialties, perhaps, or in "cyberspace".'[18] The university, therefore, becomes the home for the homeless, or in Wallace Stegner's wonderful description, the 'boomers.'[19]

The dominance of science in the modern university reflects the captivity of universities to industrial societies. For the ab-

---

16. Berry, *Life is a Miracle*, p 130.
17. Wendell Berry, *Another Turn of the Crank* (Washington DC: Counterpoint, 1995), pp 13-14.
18. Wendell Berry, *Citizenship Papers* (Washington DC: Shoemaker and Hoard, 2003), p 33.
19. Berry, *Another Turn of the Crank*, p 82. Berry reports that boomers are people 'who expect or demand that the world conform to their desires. They either succeed and thus damage the world, or they fail and thus damage their family and themselves.'

stractions of science are readily assimilated to the abstractions of industry in which:

> everything is interchangeable with or replaceable by something else ... One place is as good as another, one use is as good as another, one life is as good as another – if the price is right. This is the industrial doctrine of the interchangeability of parts, and we apply it to places, to creatures, and to our fellow humans as if it were the law of the world, using all the while a sort of middling language, imitated from the sciences, that cannot speak of heaven or earth, but only of concepts. This is the rhetoric of nowhere, which forbids a passionate interest in, let alone a love of, anything in particular.[20]

For Berry the assumption that education is the solution to all our problems is a correlate to the increasing violence of what is taught. Berry thinks the violence of education is, as we should suspect from his analysis in *Standing by Words*, to be found in the destruction of language and community. Berry observes that 'education has become increasingly useless as it has become increasingly public. Real education is determined by community needs, not by public tests.'[21]

Berry's distinction between community and public may seem odd, given the assumption that the public names the goods of the community, but Berry understands the term 'public' to mean simply people abstracted from any personal responsibility or belonging. Thus a public building is one that belongs to everyone, but no one in particular. A community, in contrast, 'has to do first of all with belonging; it is a group of people who belong to one another and to their place. We would say, "We belong to our community," but never "We belong to our public".'[22]

Berry does not deny that under certain circumstances the

---

20. Berry, *Life Is a Miracle*, pp 41-42. Berry's characterisation of science unfortunately too often is accurate, but science can be one of the most exciting disciplines through which to see the beauty of the particulars.
21. Berry, *Sex, Economy, Freedom, and Community*, p 123.
22. Berry, *Sex, Economy, Freedom, Community*, pp 147-148.

public and the community might be compatible, but under the economic and technological monoculture in which we live they cannot help but be at odds. A community is centred on the household, which means it is always concerned with a place and time. The public, when it is rightly formed, is concerned about justice and is centred on the individual. The problem we confront is that the emphasis on individual liberty has made the freedom of the community impossible. Paradoxically, as a result the more the emphasis has been on individual freedom the less liberty and power has been available to most individuals.[23]

In his novel *Hannah Coulter* Berry describes the effects of the university on Caleb Coulter, the son of Hannah and Nathan. Hannah and Nathan are hard working farmers who have managed to create a life from an unforgiving ground. Caleb was the last born of their three children, all of whom went to college. Hannah observes that you send your children to college in order to do the best for them, but neither do you want to burden them with your expectations. Hannah confesses that you hope they will go away and study and learn and then come back and you will have them for a neighbour. However, Hannah observes, while their children were at the university there always 'came a time when we would feel the distance opening to them, pulling them away. It was like sitting snug in the house, and a door is opened somewhere, and suddenly you feel a draft.'[24]

Caleb even became Dr Coulter, a professor, who taught agriculture to fewer students who were actually going to farm. Hannah describes him this way,

> He became an expert with a laboratory and experimental plots, a man of reputation. But as I know, and as he knows in his own heart and thoughts, Caleb is incomplete. He didn't love farming enough to be a farmer, much as he loved it, but he loved it too much to be entirely happy doing anything else. He is disappointed in himself ...

---

23. Berry, *Sex, Economy, Freedom, and Community*, pp 147-155.
24. Wendell Berry, *Hannah Coulter* (Washington DC: Shoemaker and Hoard, 2004), p 120.

Caleb is well respected, and I am glad of that. He brings me what he calls his 'publications', written in the Unknown Tongue. He wants me to be proud of them. And I am, but with the sadness of wishing I could be prouder. I read all of his publications that he brings me, and I have to say that they don't make me happy. I can't hear Caleb talking in them. And they speak of everything according to its general classification. Reading them always makes me think of this farm and how it emerged, out of 'agriculture' and its 'soil types' and its collection of 'species,' as itself, our place, a place like no other, yielding to Nathan and me a life like no other.[25]

The novel *Hannah Coulter* expresses Berry's deepest worry about the contemporary university. Berry's deepest worry about the university is what an 'education' does to people. It is a mistake to accuse him of being anti-technological or against all forms of specialisation. His problem with technology and specialisation arises when they become ends in themselves, producing people with no ends. As he puts it in *Another Turn of the Crank*, he is not '"against technology" so much as I am for community. When the choice is between the health of a community and technological innovation, I choose the health of the community.'[26] Technology, particularly in industrial economies, too easily becomes abstracted from the purposes that it was to serve.

Nor is Berry against science. Science has a proper place in relation to the other disciplines, particularly when all the disciplines are equally regarded and given equal time to talk, no matter what the market may be in 'jobs' or 'intellectual property'. Indeed it is one of the tasks of the university to foster such a conversation between disciplines so that our whole humanity may be embodied in and by the university. So Berry thinks the university has an appropriate task; he is simply doubtful that any university exists which is committed to accomplishing that task.[27]

---

25. Berry, *Hannah Coulter*, pp 131-132.
26. Berry, *Another Turn of the Crank*, p 90.
27. Berry, *Citizenship Papers*, p 189.

That task, moreover, requires that 'a system' exist that secures the conviction that the truth can be known, but never all truth. Such a conviction Berry calls 'religious' to indicate that the world in which we find ourselves is a mystery, making possible accountable speech and behaviour. For I hope it is now clear that Berry's criticisms of the university are but further implications of his concern that we hold one another accountable for what we say. From his perspective the university has become the source of speech determined by abstractions which are no longer accountable to any community of purpose. Berry does not claim that the fate of the modern university is the result of the loss of mystery, but he is sure that all 'answers' put forward in the university

> must be worked out within a limit of humility and restraint, so that the initiative to act would always imply a knowing acceptance of accountability for the results. The establishment and maintenance of this limit seems to me the ultimate empirical problem – the real 'frontier' of science, or at least of the definition of the possibility of a moral science. It would place science under the rule of the old concern for propriety, correct proportion, proper scale – from which, in modern times, even the arts have been 'liberated.' That is, it would return to all work, artistic or scientific, the possibility of an external standard or quality.[28]

Berry's criticisms of the university are clearer than the alternative he offers. That is probably the way it should be. Who knows what a Berry-inspired university might look like? It may well sound too 'artsy' but Berry, I think, would want the centre of a university to be the practice of poetry. For only through poetry, speech tied closely to community, place, and time can we avoid the abstractions that have become our way of life.

Berry reports he was raised by agrarians, but he did not know he was an agrarian until he was a sophomore in college.

---

28. Berry, *Standing by Words*, pp 49-50.

He seems to think it a good thing he was taught he was an agrarian. Indeed to learn he was an agrarian could be considered a poetic development. Learning he was an agrarian meant he was able to distinguish between industrialism, which is based on monetary capital, from agrarianism, which is based on land. Moreover it was partly Berry's education that made it possible for him to trace the lineage of agrarian thought through Virgil, Spenser, Shakespeare, and Pope. According to Berry it is from poets like these you learn you should not work until you have looked and seen where you are, in a manner that honours nature not only as your grandmother, but as teacher and judge.[29]

As critical as Berry is of the university as we know it, and certainly any of us who live in the university recognise that the university exists, he still remains a lover of the university. After all it was in a university he learned to read Virgil, Spenser, Shakespeare, Pope and Jefferson. Yet he seems to hold out little hope that the kind of university he would like to exist could be a reality. No doubt he assumes that his university might exist in pockets of any university, but that such an existence depends on people existing who defy the abstractions that are so tempting. It would be silly to suggest that the church might offer the possibility of making a Berry-like university a reality, but I at least want to explore how we might imagine that possibility.

---

29. Berry, *Citizenship Papers*, pp 118-119. To cultivate and nurture beauty I believe is one of the central tasks of the university. The sheer ugliness as well as the dominance of kitsch in contemporary life is surely an indication that those of us in the university are not doing our job. Andrius Bielskis has argued the culture of kitsch is a correlative of the dominance of liberal democratic societies. Bielskis observes, 'If the role of strong moral judgements and rational deliberation about what it is to live the good life decreases within the public sphere (and the psychological marketing techniques used by politicians illustrate this), then the sphere of democratic politics become dangerously irrational which means we lack the means to resist the sentimentality kitsch represents.' Andrius Bielskis, *Towards a Post-Modern Understanding of the Political: From Genealogy to Hermeneutics* (New York: Palgrove MacMillan, 2005), pp 92-93. Bielskis' argument is shaped by quite interesting readings of Nietzsche, Foucault, and especially MacIntyre.

CHAPTER SIX

3. Why Berry Needs a Church

Christians are a people who worship the God of the Jews. We are a people who worship Jesus, the Messiah, the Incarnation of the Word of God. The God we worship is flesh, so our cardinal action is to eat and drink the body and blood of Christ. The God we worship is, therefore, only known through a story as concrete as 'the old hollow beech blew down last night'. We learn about the old hollow beech by being told by another it was blown down. In similar fashion we know about Jesus by being told by another. Witness is constitutive of the character of what Christians believe. For the Christian witness to be truthful requires that Christians distrust all abstractions not disciplined by the Word that is Christ.

However, well before the development of the kind of abstraction Berry finds so destructive, Christians developed their own form of abstraction. Jesus commanded his disciples to 'Go therefore and make disciples of all nations, baptising them in the name of the Father and of the Son and of the Holy Spirit, and teaching them to obey everything that I have commanded you.' (Matthew 28:19-20) Jesus' command to be a witness to the nations, a task that should force Christians to recognise as well as criticise the infinite and unending forms of abstraction, has also tempted Christians to confuse the pretentious universalism of 'the nation' with the gospel.

The politics of Christian abstraction has taken many different forms. But at least one name for such a politics is called 'Constantinianism.' Constantinianism is the attempt by the church to use the power of the 'state,' and the 'state' is an abstraction, to impose the gospel on others without the vulnerability of witness. Because the church is obligated to be a witness to all nations she has sometimes confused the universalism of the speech of empire, speech that by necessity is shaped by abstraction, with the concreteness of the gospel.

Christians, particularly in modernity, have forgotten that our name for universal is 'Catholic'. The office that enacts the Catholic character of the church is called 'bishop.' The task of the bishop is to ensure that the stories that make a church the church are shared by other churches across time and space, so that our speech is tested by how other Christians have learned they must speak to one another as well as those who do not speak as we speak. Theologians are servants to the bishop, charged with the task of maintaining the memory of the church so that the church may be one. Theologians are, therefore, 'answerable to a specific locality or very often multiple specific localities, such that [their] sense of perpetuating a history must be combined with [their] sense of carrying out an archaeology and mapping a geography.'[30]

If Christians are to support the development of a Berry-like university we will need to be freed of our Constantinian pretensions. That freedom, moreover, will come only by the intensification of the Catholic character of the church. For the abstractions that bewitch our speech as Christians can only be located and resisted by word care, made possible by being challenged by our brothers and sisters across time and place. As John Howard Yoder has observed, the alternative to the confusion of paganism and Christianity so often the result of Constantinianism is 'the concreteness of the visible community created by the renewed message. The alternative to hierarchical definition is local definition.'[31]

---

30. John Milbank, 'The Last of the Last: Theology in the Church,' in *Conflicting Allegiances: The Church-Based University in a Liberal Democratic Society*, edited by Michael Budde and John Wright. (Grand Rapids: Brazos Press, 2004), p 250.

31. John Howard Yoder, 'The Disavowal of Constantine: An Alternative Perspective on Interfaith Dialogue,' in *The Royal Priesthood: Essays Ecclesiological and Ecumenical*, edited by Michael Cartwright (Grand Rapids: Eerdmans, 1994), p 253. Yoder's alternative of localism finds support in the late work of Sheldon Wolin who argues that 'small scale is the only scale commensurate with the kind and amount of power that democracy is capable of mobilising, given the political limitations imposed by the prevailing modes of economic organisation. The power of democratic politics lies in the multiplicity of modest sites dispersed among local governments and institutions under local control and in the ingenuity of ordinary people in inventing temporary forms to meet their needs. Multiplicity is anti-totality politics: small politics, small projects, small business, much improvisation, and fierce anathema to

Modern universities, whether Christian or secular, have been servants of the emerging nation-state system. That nation-state system, moreover, has been the enemy of locality. Local communities are not and cannot be efficient, given the need to organise 'populations.'[32] The abstractions Berry identifies as the enemy are those necessary to legitimate the public organisations that claim to serve our interests. The very language of 'interest,' of course, is but an exemplification of the kind of abstraction Berry deplores.

Berry's appeal to a religious sense of mystery for maintaining some sense of the 'whole' is important, but a sense of mystery cannot be sustained absent a community in which the mystery is materially enacted. A university able to resist the mystifications legitimated by the abstractions of our social order will depend on a people shaped by fundamental practices necessary for truthful speech. In short, without the church, a church capable of demythologising the false idealisms that possess our imaginations, there is no possibility that a university can exist capable of educating a Caleb Coulter who might return home.

These are, of course, highly theoretical remarks. Do they have any implications for what a church-based university might look like? Some are beginning to try to imagine what such a university might entail. For example many of the essays in *Conflicting Allegiances: The Church-Based University in a Liberal Democratic Society* are not content to explore how the contemporary university might be reformed to be more responsive to Christian practice. As Michael Budde puts it: 'The purpose of ecclesially based higher education is to make participants more fully into disciples shaped by the priorities and practices of Jesus

---

centralisation whether of centralised state or of the huge corporations.' *Politics and Vision* (Expanded Edition), (Princeton: Princeton University Press, 2004), p 603.

32. For my analysis of the significance of the creation of the nation of 'populations' see my chapter 'The Christian Difference: or Surviving Postmodernism' in *A Better Hope: Resources for a Church Confronting Capitalism, Democracy, and Postmodernity* (Grand Rapids: Brazos Press, 2000), pp 35-46.

Christ; to help them discern their vocation as members of the transnational body of Christ; and to contribute to the mission of the church – to help the church serve more fully and faithfully as a foretaste of the promised kingdom of God, on earth as in heaven.'[33]

Budde observes this is a difficult task because our imaginations are possessed by what is assumed to be normative assumptions about higher education. Indeed the very language of 'higher' may be misleading just to the extent it presumes that knowing how to milk is not a 'higher knowledge'. Budde however would readily agree that the use of 'higher' to distinguish university subjects from the knowledge represented by 'milking' is part of the problem. Accordingly, many of the essays in *Conflicting Allegiances* challenge the (dis-)organisation of knowledges characteristic of the contemporary university. For example, Therese Lysaught asks what form the life sciences might take if they were organised on the principle that Christians are obligated to love our enemy, even the enemy of death.[34]

The problem is not whether we lack the imagination to begin to think what a university shaped by Christian practice might look like, but rather whether the church exists that can provide the material conditions that can make such an alternative university possible. By material conditions I do not mean only money, but rather whether churches are constituted by the practices, and no practice is more important than the habits of our speech, habits nurtured by worship, that require the development of knowledges that can challenge the abstractions that are legitimated in and by the current university. Have Christians learned to milk non-violently? So, oddly enough, we will not know how to think about the character of the university without thinking about the character of the church.

But we cannot wait. Many of us, as I suggested above con-

---

33. Michael Budde, 'Assessing What Doesn't Exist: Reflections on the Impact of an Ecclesially Based University,' in *Conflicting Allegiances: The Church-Based University in a Liberal Democratic Society*, p 256.
34. Therese Lysaught, 'Love Your Enemies: The Life Sciences in the Ecclesially Based University,' in *Conflicting Allegiances: The Church-Based University in a Liberal Democratic Society*, pp 109-127.

cerning my own life, continue to teach in universities that exemplify the pathologies Berry describes. Should Christians continue to teach in universities, universities that are often identified as 'church-related,' in which students are shaped by abstractions that serve quite a different reality than that of the church? Do Christian academics, in spite of their criticisms of the university, legitimate those universities by our very presence?

Any attempt to justify Christian participation in the university as we know it is an invitation to self-deception. Yet in his 2004 Oxford University Commemoration Day Sermon, Rowan Williams provides some helpful reminders that can point us in a constructive direction.[35] Williams observes that Oxford began as a cell of the Catholic church for the study of canon law, but by the fourteenth and fifteenth centuries Oxford's survival depended on forming people who would govern the kingdom. He notes that this will confirm the worst fears of some that assume that Oxford is primarily an institution committed to serving the elite. Yet Williams points out that it was assumed 'that to govern a kingdom you needed to know how language worked, what difference was between good and bad arguments, and how you might persuade people to morally defensible action.' Accordingly you needed tools of thought that were organised in a hierarchy of learning.

Williams acknowledges that much has changed at Oxford. An abstract understanding of rationality has displaced what many now consider the 'authoritarian' character of the medieval university. Yet, Williams argues, to the extent the university maintains a commitment to disciplined argument, there remains a sense of the capacity to respond with justice and accuracy to the inner structure of creation thus testifying to the divine image constitutive of each of us. Williams, therefore, thinks he is justified to 'insist upon the university's role in nourishing honest and hopeful speech, for the sake of a properly reasonable culture and politics.' He therefore concludes that what the church has to say to the university is:

---

35. Williams's sermon can be found on the Archbishop of Canterbury website.

> Don't be afraid of assuming that your task is to equip people to take authority. In a democratic age, this is not the authority of a royal counsellor or imperial proconsul; it is the authority of the literate and educated person to contribute to the public reason. And don't be afraid in encouraging in whatever way is available the calling both to scientific research and to public service, administration and politics and social care; law and medicine, those ancient and persistent elements in the pattern of public life; the service, in one calling or another of the Body of Christ. Avoid the false polarisation between disinterested research and the world of target setting and assessment; remember that all properly intellectual work can be a form of witness to public values.

I have no idea if Berry would find Williams's understanding of the task of the university compatible with his understanding of what universities ought to be about. However, I suspect Berry might find congenial Williams suggestion that the university's task is to train literate people capable of recognising a good from a bad argument. No doubt the study of poetry helps the development of such a skill, but so can the study of a science. I am sure, moreover, that poets and scientists exist at every university committed to such a task. What remains unclear is whether a people exist who care whether such poets or scientists exist. At the very least, Christians are obligated to care because we believe we have been given the great privilege to stand by the Word.

'To stand by the Word,' moreover, might help us maintain the connection between the labour of the university with those that labour outside the university. Fritz Oehlschlaeger, in a letter responding to my essay, 'Theological Knowledge and the Knowledges of the University,' observes that intellectual work, even at its most strenuous, is not as difficult as physical labour. How then, he asks, can we ever justify those like ourselves who think the work we do in the university is important?

Oehlschlaeger, who teaches in the English Department at Virginia Tech,[36] responds to his question observing:

> It seems to me this requires active memory and recognition by the intellectual of the labour that sustains his/her ability to pursue knowledge. The best way to ensure this is for the intellectual to come into the presence of others, to make offering with them of their labour, and to receive the truly priceless food provided by the One whose love can only be understood as pure gift. Thus we learn that utility in meeting needs can never be a sufficient standard, as we cannot produce the very thing we need most. And the Eucharist perhaps also disciplines the intellectual to recognise his bonds to those whose labours make his work possible – so that any pursuit of knowledge for its own sake carries also the memory of the labour that sustains it. Intellectuals formed within a community nourished by the milk of Jesus seem much more likely to think what they do as requiring a community to receive it ... Maybe there's a role, then, for Christian intellectuals who might mediate among the disciplines and between disciplines and public in ways that would not occur to the market-driven knowledge-producers on today's faculties.

Hopefully, 'maybe there's a role,' is hopeful speech.

---

36. Oehlschlaeger has begun the difficult task of trying to think what a Christian reading of literature might mean in his, *Love and Good Reasons: Postliberal Approaches to Christian Ethics and Literature* (Durham, North Carolina: Duke University Press, 2003).

CHAPTER SEVEN

A Response to Stanley Hauerwas

Patrick Hannon

It is appropriate that an occasion intended to honour Enda McDonagh should include a lecture on the university, given by an internationally distinguished university theologian from another theological tradition. For Enda McDonagh has contributed to university theology internationally and ecumenically; and – as teacher, scholar and administrator – he has contributed to university life in this country and on this campus to an extent unmatched by any peer. It is an honour as well as a pleasure to have an opportunity to contribute to this celebration of an esteemed teacher, colleague and friend, and a pleasure also to welcome Stanley Hauerwas back to Maynooth.

The picture of today's university sketched by Hauerwas will in some of its lineaments seem familiar to an Irish observer, and not least to an observer whose vantage-point is the complexus which our switchboard operators disarmingly announce as the Maynooth campus. Ireland has been touched by several of the ills that have been visited on the universities of North America, and there are aspects of modern Irish university experience that stand indicted under Wendell Berry's strictures too. Enda McDonagh has often spoken and written about the university in Ireland, and a number of his concerns are echoed in Stanley Hauerwas's ruminations on the university in the United States.

There are also unfamiliarities and dissimilarities in Hauerwas's account. The burden of his experience has been in a secular university which has a thriving Divinity School; our nearest equivalent is Trinity College, Dublin. He can speak, in a way that we cannot, of experience of a Christian college and university, for such colleges and universities are still known in North America; and many of the foremost of the now secular universities, the colleges and universities of the Ivy League, as they are called, began as church-related institutions. He is even able to speak of the possibility of the university's being of service to the church, unfearful, it seems, that his audience will take him to mean a church-dominated institution with ecclesiastical purposes, an entity antithetical to the place of wide learning and free enquiry envisioned by leading thinkers from Plato to Newman and beyond.

No doubt it's only to be expected that a North American commentator and an Irish one have some shared concerns about the directions being taken by university education in their respective countries. Our countries both are driven by a capitalist economy, and by economic policies that are interlinked as well as similar. Both countries – ours of course only latterly and as it were microcosmically – are coping with a new multi-culturalism, both contending with all that's comprehended in globalisation. Even if Ireland now looks to Berlin as well as to Boston, it is in any case to see and imbibe an experience that is marked, socially, culturally, economically, by western liberal capitalism.

And it is in the universities' thralldom to certain demands of western liberal capitalism that Hauerwas, following Berry, sees their nature and mission imperilled. One kind of danger lies in a linguistic abstraction which does away with meaning and which, when combined with increasing specialisation, renders communication, or for that matter thought, impossible. And so community becomes impossible, and there is no 'learned community' to which the university is accountable and to which it may speak. A related problem is the drive to 'objectification' in language, which Berry and Hauerwas associate especially with scientists, resulting in a perversion of speech which only 'serves the political purpose of securing the power of those who use it without their being accountable'.

But specialisation of the disciplines is a necessary condition of financial support in a capitalist society, and learning is organised in such away as to preclude interdisciplinary conversation; disciplines rather are 'representatives of competing opposites', and the sciences 'are sectioned off from one another so they might serve their respective corporations'. And, according to Hauerwas, the two questions you cannot ask in the modern university are: 'What is the university for?' and 'Who does it serve?'

Hauerwas and Berry leave us with a bleak picture, though of course we must allow for the conventions both of prophecy and of advocacy, and indeed of poetry; and we can acknowledge the presence of a theme characteristic of Stanley Hauerwas's theology more generally, epitomised in an almost throwaway remark: 'My identity as a theologian means I have always been in the university but not of it'. I shall return to this, but perhaps I might say now that I'm not sure I should like to be a member of (say) the department of Physics whose neighbour in the Divinity School thought and spoke thus.

For Berry, as Hauerwas reads him, the situation is all but beyond redemption: '[Berry] seems to hold out little hope that the kind of university he would like to exist could be a reality. No doubt he assumes that his university might exist in pockets of any university, but that such an existence depends on people existing that defy the abstractions that are so tempting'. Although he thinks it would be 'silly' to suggest that the church might make a Berry-like university a reality, he goes on to explore precisely that idea.

The vision of the church which Hauerwas offers, the church which he thinks Berry needs, is inspiriting and inspiring, but whether it will perform the humanising, community-building task that he envisages for it is another matter. Again, there is an issue of theological emphasis, perhaps I should say of confessional theological import: a robust assertion of gospel values, a vision of a life of witness to these values, and no making terms with what is not of the gospel and can only compromise gospel integrity. But is that how the university is to be redeemed? Again one thinks of the colleague in the sciences or the humanities, and especially one who is not of the household of the faith.

How then is the university to be redeemed? A key problem with the account offered by Stanley Hauerwas as I see it is that it

CHAPTER SEVEN

seems to say that redemption must come from outside. Whoever would participate in its redemption must, it seems, be in the university but not of it. 'A university able to resist the mystification legitimated by the abstractions of our social order will depend on a people shaped by fundamental practices shaped by truthful speech. In short, without the church, a church capable of demythologising the false idealism that possesses our imaginations, there is no possibility that a university can exist capable of educating a Caleb Coulter who might return home'. *Extra ecclesiam nulla salus?*

What I have called the redemption of the university, so far as this is within human competence, is in the hands of those who work and study in the university, and of the communities, local and national, in which our universities find their habitat. *Pace* Stanley Hauerwas, educators and students must be, precisely, of the university in their commitment to truth and, as Enda McDonagh has recently argued, goodness and beauty too.

CHAPTER EIGHT

Enda McDonagh's Dialogue with Vatican II

Charles Curran

The most significant influence on Catholic life and theology in general, and moral theology in particular, in the last fifty years was the Second Vatican Council. Enda McDonagh, like other Catholic moral theologians, found himself in dialogue with the work of Vatican II in light of his own understanding of what transpired there and the developing life of the church and theology after Vatican II.

Vatican II's Major Contribution to Moral Theology
How, in reality, did Vatican II affect moral theology? Its major influence was to make moral theology more theological. Three of the documents of Vatican II illustrate the need for moral theology to become more theological. The *Decree on Priestly Formation* specifically addresses the renewal of moral theology. 'Other theological disciplines should also be renewed by livelier contact with the mystery of Christ and the history of salvation. Special attention needs to be given to the development of moral theology. Its scientific exposition should be more thoroughly nourished by scriptural teaching. It should show the nobility of the Christian vocation of the faithful, and their obligation to bring forth fruit in charity for the life of the world.'[1]

Chapter 5 of the *Constitution on the Church* insists on the call of the whole church to holiness. '[A]ll the faithful of Christ of whatever rank or status are called to the fullness of the Christian life and to the perfection of charity.'[2] 'All of Christ's faithful, therefore, whatever be the conditions, duties and circumstances

---
1. *Decree on Priestly Formation*, n 16, in Walter M. Abbott, ed, *Documents of Vatican II* (New York: Guild Press, 1966), 452.
2. *Constitution on the Church*, 40, in Abbott, *Documents of Vatican II*, 67.

CHAPTER EIGHT

of their lives, will grow in holiness day by day through these very situations, if they accept all of them with faith from the hand of their heavenly Father, and if they co-operate with the divine will by showing every man through their earthly activities the love with which God has loved the world.'³

The pre-Vatican II church had maintained that those who are called to perfection and holiness should leave the world and go off to religious life, but that is now changed. Married couples and Christian parents through faithful love should follow their own proper path to holiness, sustaining one another in grace throughout their lives. In a different way, widows and single people are called to their own holiness. Labourers in the midst of their work, which is often tedious, strive for their own perfection, aid their fellow citizens, and raise all of society, even creation itself, to a better mode of existence. Those who are oppressed by infirmity, sickness, and various other hardships in a special way are united with the suffering Christ for the salvation of the world.⁴

The Pastoral Constitution on the Church in the Modern World declares, 'This split between the faith which many profess and their daily lives deserves to be counted among the more serious errors of our age. Long since, the prophets of the Old Testament fought vehemently against this scandal and even more so did Jesus Christ himself in the New Testament threaten it with grave punishments.'⁵

The first part of *The Pastoral Constitution on the Church in the Modern World* devotes three chapters to the human person, human community, and human activity. In each of these considerations the document insists there must also be a christological understanding of these realities. For example, while the communitarian dimensions of human existence are grounded in creation,

---

3. Constitution on the Church, n. 41, in Abbott, *Documents of Vatican II*, 70.
4. Constitution on the Church, n. 41, in Abbott, *Documents of Vatican II*, 69-70.
5. The Pastoral Constitution on the Church in the Modern World, n. 43, in Abbott, *Documents of Vatican II*, 243.

'this communitarian character is developed and consummated in the work of Jesus Christ.'[6] The second part of the Pastoral Constitution claims to discuss five particular issues facing human life and society 'in the light of the gospel and of human experience.'[7]

McDonagh's Development of Vatican II Themes
McDonagh rejoiced in the work of Vatican II that called for a new approach to moral theology away from the older manuals. He describes the stony atmosphere of Maynooth in the 1940s and 1950s when he was a student there in this premier Irish seminary. 'The fortress church with its stone ramparts of precise teaching and Latin liturgy, and with its granite doctors of divinity, enjoyed (if that be the word) its most powerful period from the 1860s to the 1960s.'[8] In his writings McDonagh developed four significant Vatican II themes: 1) the demise of the manuals of moral theology; 2) the theological dimension; 3) the connection of morality with spirituality and liturgy; 4) the ecumenical dimension.

1. Demise of the Manuals
The manuals of moral theology, the textbooks of the discipline of moral theology in the pre-Vatican II church came into existence in the post-Tridentine church to train confessors for their role as judges in the sacrament of penance. These texts dealt primarily with Christian misconduct (not its conduct), following the approach of the Ten Commandments. Natural law obligations were primary, and they were increasingly supplemented if not altogether overshadowed by the provisions of canon law. The approach of the manuals was act-centred, legalistic, minimalistic, and casuistic. There were no attempts to connect these

---

6. The Pastoral Constitution on the Church in the Modern World, n. 32, in Abbott, *Documents of Vatican II*, 230.
7. The Pastoral Constitution on the Church in the Modern World, n. 46, in Abbott, *Documents of Vatican II*, 248.
8. Enda McDonagh, *Faith in Fragments* (Dublin: Columba Press, 1995), 36.

many laws describing what is sinful and the degrees of sinfulness with the primary biblical injunction to love God with your whole being and your neighbour as yourself.[9] This theology tended to indoctrinate rather than inspire.[10] Moral theology, supposedly the most practical of theological disciplines, was interested primarily in categorising personal sins for confessional practice. Personal moral development and social justice issues were not even discussed.[11] Looking back thirty years later McDonagh admits it is difficult to recall and relive the excitement of Vatican II's convening and concluding. The stones were rolled back. The petrified church became flesh and blood once more. A new approach of a life-centred moral theology replaced the narrow and limited scope of the manuals.[12]

In his latter writings, reflecting on the change of moral theology, McDonagh points out that the work of renewal had begun before Vatican II. Fritz Tillmann, the Bonn scripture scholar in the 1930s, called for a more theological and scriptural approach to moral theology. Bernard Häring's *Law of Christ* attempted a new moral manual with the broader purpose of elucidating the moral life of the Christian called by God in baptism to be a follower of Jesus. The call for renewal in moral theology even before Vatican II came in the context of other renewal movements then going on in the church. The biblical renewal developed the biblical basis for the Christian moral life in the work of scholars such as Rudolf Schnackenburg and Ceslaus Spicq. The theology of the church with the emphasis not on the juridical structures of the hierarchical church but on the church as the body of Christ and the people of God called for a different approach to moral theology as reflecting on the life of discipleship in the body of

---

9. Enda McDonagh, *The Making of Disciples: Tasks of Moral Theology* (Wilmington, Del: Michael Glazier, 1982), 22-24; McDonagh, *Invitation and Response: Essays in Christian Moral Theology* (New York: Sheed & Ward, 1972), 16-19.
10. McDonagh, *Faith in Fragments*, 34.
11. Enda McDonagh, *Vulnerable to the Holy in Faith, Morality, and Art* (Dublin: Columba Press, 2004), 35.
12. McDonagh, *Faith in Fragments*, 36.

Christ. The liturgical renewal called for the active worshipping community of all the baptised who were called to live out a Christian life of service within the church and world. The ecumenical movement made Catholics more aware of the narrow legal focus of their moral theology and the need for more biblical, Christ-centred, and charity-inspired developments of the Christian moral life.[13]

Even before Vatican II, McDonagh himself was aware of the need for a new approach to a life-centred moral theology, away from the narrow scope of the manuals. Even in the 1950s he had been discontented with the existing manuals of moral theology and in his readings and interests strayed beyond the confines of 'pure' theology. Moral theology, as mentioned, was closely associated with canon law. In keeping with that understanding, McDonagh in the late 1950s was sent to the University of Munich to get a second doctoral degree in canon law. But, rather than work on a canonical and casuistic topic, his 1960 dissertation discussed church/state relations.[14] McDonagh's creative and imaginative intelligence, even in the pre-Vatican II days, anticipated the need for change in the focus of moral theology that Vatican II ultimately proposed for the whole church.

2. Emphasis on the Theological Dimension

McDonagh, in keeping with this important Vatican II emphasis, has insisted on the theological aspect of his understanding of morality and social ethics. No Catholic moral theologian of this period has emphasised the theological aspect as much as McDonagh. Even immediately after Vatican II, he believed the various divisions of theology (e.g. dogmatic, moral, and scriptural) had not been helpful in practice to bring together an integrated theology that brings Christian theory and practice together. The end of all Christian theologising is the making of disciples. For this reason he does not even want to call himself a moral theologian. The end of moral theology, accompanied by the end of

---

13. McDonagh, *Invitation and Response*, 18-21; *Making of Disciples*, 22-24.
14. McDonagh, *Vulnerable to the Holy*, 36.

CHAPTER EIGHT

the self-enclosed dogmatic theology, could prepare the way for a rebirth of an integrated theology. The end of moral theology (also including the notion of purpose) is the making of disciples and the remaking of theology itself.[15]

The essays collected in *Between Chaos and the New Creation* (1986) and the *Gracing of Society* (1989) continue the emphasis on a more integrated theology, centred on the community of the disciples of Jesus, announcing, discerning, promoting, and bearing witness to the reign of God which is the new social existence of human beings. The earlier volume deals with the deep dialectic of Christian existence struggling between chaos and new creation.[16] The gracing of theology or a theology of society follows the method of faith-hope-love seeking understanding.[17] McDonagh in the 80s was teaching more in the area of social ethics, but he entitled his course 'A Theology of Society' for two reasons. First is his continuing interest in developing an integrating moral theology into the one science of theology. Second, he wanted to underscore the social nature of God, grace, salvation, and humanity itself.[18]

His last collection of essays uses the metaphor of 'Vulnerable to the Holy' to bring together faith and daily life. Here it seems to me that McDonagh is employing what is perhaps the most distinctive characteristic of the Catholic theological tradition – the concept of mediation which understands the divine as being mediated in and through the human. Thus, all the essays in this collection maintain that in the central areas of Christian living discussed in the volume, from the very personal areas of friendship, sexuality, and marriage, to the great contemporary social issues of HIV/AIDS and peace and war, openness and vulnerability to others is crucial, cruciform, and Christian.[19]

---

15. McDonagh, *Making of Disciples*, 2-8.
16. Enda McDonagh, *Between Chaos and New Creation: Doing Theology at the Fringe* (Dublin: Gill & Macmillan, 1986), 9.
17. Enda McDonagh, *The Gracing of Society* (Dublin: Gill & Macmillan, 1989), 1-7.
18. McDonagh, *Gracing of Society*, 48-80.
19. McDonagh, *Vulnerable to the Holy*, 9.

3. *Spirituality, Liturgy and Morality*

Vatican II insisted that spirituality and morality cannot be separated. McDonagh throughout his search for an integrated theology has tried to bring together the aspects that have too often been separated – theory and praxis, faith and life, spirituality and morality, holiness and the apparently secular. Again, *Vulnerable to the Holy* connects morality and spirituality especially in the form of prayer. McDonagh insists on a deep relationship between prayer and poetry. Prayer is awareness of and response to God, the ultimate reality. Poetry is the human expression of reality, often in its tragic mode. Prayer and poetry deal with mystery, inspiration, and the search for adequate and beautiful form. Not only in poetry and in literature, but also in other art forms such as painting and sculpture, one becomes vulnerable to a deeper beauty and otherness.[20] Yes, art work has to be appreciated for what it is in itself, but the believer sees in the work of art the creator and redeemer God.[21]

Probably many believers see some connection between art and prayer but McDonagh also insists on a connection between politics and prayer. Again, most Christians would probably recognise that prayer should lead to political involvement in working for a more just human society. But for McDonagh the relationship between prayer and politics is a two-way street. Objections to this understanding easily come to mind. For many politicians there is absolutely no connection between political involvement and prayer. Even for most believers political involvement does not lead to prayer. But McDonagh insists on the movement from politics to prayer. In political involvement we open ourselves to the transforming mystery of the other with attitudes of wonder, awe, thanksgiving, humility, and forgiveness. These are the same basic characteristics of prayer. The openness to the other in politics by its inherent dynamism leads to openness to the transcendent God as the one who is mediated in and through the political involvement with the other and es-

---

20. Ibid., 137-190.
21. Ibid., 9.

pecially the other in need. Social and political activity for the Christian should lead to prayer.[22]

In his striving for a more integrated theology, McDonagh brings together morality and liturgy. Liturgy and Christian life go together. In so doing, he goes beyond Vatican II, which, while it called for a renewed moral theology, failed to explicitly recognise the important relationship between liturgy and moral theology. According to *The Constitution on the Liturgy*, liturgy should be a major course in the seminary. Professors of dogmatic, spiritual, and pastoral theology as well as of sacred scripture, should bring out the connection between their subjects and the liturgy.[23] No mention is made of moral theology – a fact that illustrates the hold of the manualistic approach to moral theology even on the participants of Vatican II. But from his earliest writings McDonagh recognised the close relationship between liturgy and moral theology. An early essay shows how both liturgy and Christian life have Trinitarian, covenantal, and community aspects.[24] A later essay on society and the sacraments tries to bring together the first document on Vatican II on the liturgy with the last document on the church in the modern world. Too often the emphasis on sacraments and liturgy has been too personal and has failed to recognise the important relationship to the community and the broader society. This particular essay brings together political and liberation theology with liturgical and sacramental theology.[25]

In light of his previous publications, one can readily understand why Enda McDonagh was invited to write the article on liturgy and Christian life for the *New Dictionary of Sacramental Worship* published in 1990.[26] A large part of this article probes

---

22. McDonagh, *Making of Disciples*, 99-111.
23. Constitution on the Liturgy, n. 16, in Abbott, *Documents of Vatican II*, 144-45.
24. McDonagh, *Invitation and Response*, 96-108.
25. McDonagh, *Between Chaos and New Creation*, 76-88.
26. Enda McDonagh, 'Liturgy and Christian Life,' in Peter E. Fink, ed., *New Dictionary of Sacramental Worship* (Collegeville, MN: Liturgical Press, 1990), 742-53.

the connection of the liturgy and the sacraments with the kingdom values or virtues. The primary kingdom values or virtues, as mentioned above, are faith-hope-love which bring about our entry into the reign of God and support our continuing involvement in the reign of God. The essay then considers four more particular kingdom values – truth, liberation and freedom, justice and equality, and solidarity and peace. With his emphasis on the community, McDonagh relates all of these to the community of the church and the community's role in making the reign of God more present in our world. Liberation calls us to renounce the demons of sin, oppression, and exploitation in the Christian community and in the world in which we live. Justice and equality in the reign of God give special place to the poor, the marginalised, and the needy. Solidarity and peace call for reconciliation and a flourishing in community.

The liturgical and sacramental symbol and reality of communion confront the sacramental community with the problem of consumption and consumerism in our world. The rich consume the poor, the powerful consume the powerless, we consume our environment. Jesus was consumed by the political and religious leaders of his time – *consummatum est*. In contrast, the communion of the sacraments in general and of the Eucharist in particular as a sharing in the bread of eternal life and the cup of salvation, brings about a sharing in the love and the life of the triune God. The symbol and reality of the communion celebrated in the sacraments radically confront the consumption so prevalent in our society.[27]

4. Ecumenical Dimension
Vatican II with its *Decree on Ecumenism* brought the Roman Catholic Church into ecumenical dialogue with other Christians and into interfaith dialogue with other religions. McDonagh's life and work have had a strong ecumenical dimension. In his writings he has been in dialogue with many Protestant moral theologians throughout the world. The participation of Stanley

---

27. McDonagh, *Faith in Fragments*, 104-07.

Hauerwas in this conference testifies to their dialogue over many decades, with their agreements and disagreements. In more practical activities, McDonagh has worked ecumenically in Ireland in dealing with the issues arising in Northern Ireland, and also with regard to the social issues and church issues facing the Republic.

In his writings he has made some creative suggestions for how the ecumenical dimension might be more present in the life of the Catholic Church, but unfortunately his suggestions have not been accepted by church authorities. One of the positive results of ecumenical dialogue is the full restoration of the mutual acceptance of baptism done in other churches and communions. By their baptism all different Christians are called to work for the unity of the church, and for a greater presence of the reign of God in our world. In certain societies where Christianity is a source of division, as in Bosnia and Northern Ireland, interchurch celebration of baptism creatively demonstrates the unity of all the baptised and challenges the destructive divisions that religion has brought about. In such situations, the joint celebration of the entry rite into the body of Christ would put flesh and blood on the ecumenical understandings we accept in theory. Ecumenical dialogue has also made great progress, in that Orthodox, Roman Catholics, and many Reformed churches agree on both the memorial and sacrificial aspects of the Eucharist. In light of this, McDonagh sees the possibility and even the need for some inter-communion after due preparation. One suggestion calls for the Church Unity Octave Week to be a week of penitential preparation for a shared Eucharist on the final Sunday.[28]

McDonagh's Differences with Vatican II
McDonagh's theology developed in the years since Vatican II, and in five areas in particular his later approach differed from the Vatican II approach: 1) a more theological approach especially to social morality; 2) the need for a local theology; 3) a challenge

---

28. McDonagh, *Vulnerable to the Holy*, 51-59.

to the more optimistic view of historical progress found in Vatican II; 4) an emphasis in anthropology, not primarily on the person, as in Vatican II, but on the other; 5) the doing of theology from the fringe and not from the centre as in Vatican II.

A more theological appraoch to social morality
As mentioned earlier, perhaps the primary emphasis of Vatican II was to make the discipline of moral theology more theological, and perhaps no Catholic theologian has developed the theological aspect of moral theology as much as McDonagh has. His primary criticism is that post-Vatican II Catholic social morality does not emphasise enough the theological character of its method and approach.[29]

McDonagh explicitly criticises *Gaudium et spes* itself. As noted earlier, *Gaudium et spes* certainly calls for a more theological approach, but this emphasis exists especially in the first part of the document dealing with more methodological and generic understandings such as the person, human action, the human community, and the role of the church in the world. The second part deals with five more specific issues of marriage, culture, socio-economic life, political life, and the fostering of peace in the community of nations. There is no doubt that the second part dealing with these five specific issues is much less theological. A primary reason for this comes from the fact that the two parts were drafted as two very different sections. In fact the original idea was simply to publish the second part only as an appendix because according to some it was not theological enough.[30] Only late in the Council deliberations was it decided to publish both parts in the one document, but in a sense the second part was never developed and integrated into the approach of the first.[31]

---

29. McDonagh, *Gracing of Society*, 20-21.
30. Enda McDonagh, 'The Church in the Modern World (Gaudium et Spes),' in Adrian Hastings, ed, *Modern Catholicism: Vatican II and After* (New York: Oxford University Press, 1991), 100.
31. M. G. McGrath, 'Note storiche sulla Costituzione,' in Guilherme Baraúna, ed, *La Chiesa nel Mondo di Oggi* (Florence: Vallecchi, 1966), 155-56.

CHAPTER EIGHT

The official hierarchical teaching on social morality or ethics is often called Catholic social teaching and it includes the post-Vatican II social encyclicals – Pope Paul VI's *Populorum progressio* and the three encyclicals of Pope John Paul II – *Laborem exercens*, *Sollicitudo rei socialis*, and *Centesimus annus*. All of these documents, in keeping with the practice introduced by Pope John XXIII in *Pacem in terris* in 1963, are also addressed to all people of good will.

By definition, therefore, these documents are not going to emphasise only the distinctive theological aspect of Catholic teaching, but rather an approach and proposals that can be accepted by all people of good will. McDonagh criticises these encyclicals as not being theological enough.[32] But McDonagh has to respond to the question whether he also wants to address all people of good will and whether or not his theological approach will be able to accomplish that. A more explicitly theological approach to social morality easily appeals to a less heterogeneous society, but in a more heterogeneous and pluralistic society such an approach will not appeal to all people of good will.

Be that as it may, there is no doubt that McDonagh himself has attempted to develop a more theological approach to society, and he has pointed out that the central doctrines of God, church, the Holy Spirit, salvation, grace, and sacraments have not been vital sources for the development of Catholic social morality.[33] One example of the impoverishment of post-Vatican II moral theology in this area is the concept of justice. The Aristotelian and Thomistic notion of justice reigned before Vatican II, and it still continues to influence heavily even post-Vatican II Catholic social morality. Liberation theology has taken a different course. The biblical approach as distinguished from the philosophical approach sees justice as a characteristic of God and his/her dealings with the covenant people of Israel. The primary criterion of biblical justice is the treatment of the poor, the needy, the disabled, the marginalised, the sick, and the

---

32. McDonagh, *Gracing of Society*, 21.
33. Ibid., 34.

stranger. In keeping with the essay genre that he uses to develop his thoughts, the concept of this justice is not fully developed by McDonagh, but he concludes that transformative justice could offer a way into a genuinely theological moral theology.[34]

A rather long essay is a reflection on his course which is not entitled social ethics but rather 'Theology of Society.'[35] Theology is a multicoloured reality – a science, an art, a praxis. Faith-hope-charity (a favourite description of his Christian theological starting point) bespeaks engagement for the Christian in the service of God and neighbour. Society is simultaneously the context, the subject, and the object of theology. Here he stresses the kingdom values of freedom, justice, peace, and truth. (Interestingly enough, Pope John XXIII in *Pacem in terris*, on the basis of a natural law methodology, insisted on the four virtues or values of love, justice, truth, and freedom as the way to bring about peace.) McDonagh, however, develops these virtues or values from a theological and biblical perspective.[36]

A Local Theology
Vatican II conceived of Catholic theology as a universal theology for the whole church throughout the world. The universalising tendencies of Catholic life and thought had become even more pronounced in the nineteenth and twentieth centuries. But as McDonagh points out, the seeds of differentiation were also present even at Vatican II. Shortly afterwards, Latin American liberation theology led the way toward more particular theologies, but the particularisation of theology soon embraced many different aspects – regions, social differences, culture, race, and gender. Writing in 1986, McDonagh claims that the move to particularity constitutes the greatest single change in theology since Vatican II. The recognition of historical consciousness was behind this move to particular theologies.[37]

---

34. Ibid., 27.
35. Ibid., 48-80.
36. Pope John XXIII, *Pacem in terris*, n. 35, in David J. O'Brien and Thomas A. Shannon, eds, *Catholic Social Thought: The Documentary Heritage* (Maryknoll, NY: Orbis, 1992), 136.
37. McDonagh, *Between Chaos and New Creation*, 91-95.

CHAPTER EIGHT

McDonagh wants to hold on to both the universal and the particular aspects of Catholic theology. The danger of the claim to universality is that this claim is really a particular theology at work thus involving in its own way a theological imperialism. There remains, however, a need for the universal. After all, Catholic by definition means universal. We need particular theologies, but theology must communicate across the boundaries of geography, culture, history, social class, race, economic differences, and gender. The many particular Christian communities share considerations of faith, understanding, and practice that are common to all Catholics.[38]

From his earliest writings McDonagh recognised his own social location. The very first collection of his essays refers to the inescapably autobiographical character of theology. One does theology in response to particular situations and demands and in light of one's own concerns, interests, and abilities.[39] His subsequent work described theology as socio-biography in light of recognising the important social dimensions affecting the world, the church, and the theologian.[40]

In his 1986 collection, *Between Chaos and New Creation*, he brings together six essays under the heading 'Constructing of a Local Theology.' The social context of this consideration is the world in crisis with Ireland sharing in that crisis but in its own ways.[41] The whole world has been aware of the problems of Northern Ireland and especially the role that religion has played there. But the Republic has faced its own problems. Scandals have racked the church. The hierarchical leadership has been slow to act and has not responded to the many problems facing the church. There is a growing lack of credibility, and a move by many people in Ireland away from the church. Truly the church in Ireland is experiencing its winter. The church itself has not

---

38. Ibid., 91-122.
39. McDonagh, *Invitation and Response*, viii.
40. Enda McDonagh, *Doing the Truth: The Quest for Moral Theology* (Notre Dame, Ind: University of Notre Dame Press, 1979), 1-13, 187-207.
41. McDonagh, *Between Chaos and New Creation*, 3.

dealt creatively with the problems it is facing internally and with the growing secularisation in Ireland. Despite the recent economic success in Ireland that is so often mentioned, the country is faced with continued poverty and a growing gap between the rich and the poor. Individualism seems to have become ever more significant as a cultural phenomenon and there is much less concern about the community and especially the needs of the poor, the marginalised, and the oppressed.[42] These have been difficult times of crisis and McDonagh has proposed some creative and imaginative ways of helping the fragmented community of Ireland and the church in Ireland to struggle with them.

A move away from the overly optimistic of Vatican II
McDonagh perceptively points out, in an article written twenty-five years later on *The Pastoral Constitution on the Church of the Modern World*, that this document shows an insufficient awareness of the tragic dimension of human existence. The understanding of history and progress is much too optimistic, and the document fails to recognise the eschatological aspects, especially the apocalyptic aspects of eschatology.[43]

McDonagh recognises that the 60s were optimistic times.[44] By changing the Catholic Church quite dramatically, and calling for a reform of the church which had not been experienced in the Catholic Church in the last four centuries, Vatican II itself thus contributed to the optimism that many Catholics experienced. In my own country, Catholics lionised the work of the two Johns – John XXIII and the Second Vatican Council and John F. Kennedy who proclaimed that the torch now had been passed to a new generation born in this century. We were overly optimistic and even naïvely optimistic about both the church and the world.

McDonagh maintains that the optimistic aspect of *Gaudium*

---
42. McDonagh, *Faith in Fragments*, 7-89.
43. McDonagh, 'The Church in the Modern World (Gaudium et Spes),' 102-03.
44. Ibid., 102.

et spes comes from the failure to recognise enough the presence of sin in the church and the world and the fact that the fullness of the reign of God will only come at the end of time.[45] The theological and historical context of the document helps to explain the problem. This document rightly tried to overcome the separation between faith and daily life, the separation between the supernatural and the natural. In a pre-Vatican II theology the world was seen as the realm of the natural governed by reason and natural law. The document emphasised that faith, grace, and Jesus Christ were now present in the world and trying to transform it. Just as there had been a great impetus for reform and change in the church because of Vatican II, many Catholics in the light of Vatican II began to think that progress and development would readily take place once we realised the role of grace and faith in transforming the world. From a theological perspective this approach forgot the presence of sin in our world and the fact that the fullness of the reign of God will only come at the end of time.

In the pre-Vatican II understanding, Catholic theology was often guilty of a natural law optimism that failed to recognise the presence and power of sin in the world. Even a Vatican document issued on the tenth anniversary of *Pacem in terris* recognised that the famous encyclical of Pope John XXIII needed another chapter entitled *Bellum in terris* in light of the violence and the wars that have marked human history and are still in existence at this time in many parts of our world.[46] The danger of not recognising enough the presence of sin in the world became even more grievous in light of the attempt to see faith, grace, and the redeeming love of Jesus transforming the world.

McDonagh has pointed out the lack of an eschatological perspective in the document. An analysis of the document clearly

---

45. Ibid., 102-03.
46. Cardinal Maurice Roy, 'Reflections on the Occasion of the Tenth Anniversary of the Encyclical *Pacem in Terris* of Pope John XXIII,' in Joseph Gremillion, ed, *The Gospel of Peace and Justice: Catholic Social Teaching since Pope John* (Maryknoll, NY: Orbis, 1976), 548.

shows this lack of the eschatological future. The first two chapters of part one deal with the human person and the human community, and both chapters neglect the eschatological aspect. The first chapter ends with a section on 'Christ and the New Man,' while the second chapter ends with a section on 'The Incarnate Word and Solidarity.'[47] Only the third chapter on human activity brings in the eschatological aspect with a final section 'A New Earth and a New Heaven.'[48] The theological problem here is a collapsed eschaton that results in a too optimistic approach to history and human progress.

Historical events influenced McDonagh and all of us in the realisation that *Gaudium et spes* was too optimistic in its view of human history and its progress. Experience in the church universal and the local church reminded believers of the sinful nature of the church, and the fact that the church is only the sacrament and sign of the reign of God which will only come about fully at the end of time. We are a pilgrim church, always in need of reform.

In the church *Humanae vitae* provided a great shock, and in the intervening time the failure of the institutional church to hear the needs of the divorced and of gays and lesbians has disillusioned many. The most alienated people in the church today are women who are denied any true leadership roles in the church. The emphasis on authority and centralisation, and the lack of creative leadership, have frustrated many Catholics. Mc Donagh points out that the church in Ireland has suffered from these same realities compounded by problems indigenous to the Irish Church.[49]

We have also become much more conscious of the problems facing our world. Violence, war, injustice, ecological devast-

---

47. Pastoral Constitution on the Church in the Modern World, nn. 22 and 32, in Abbott, *Documents of Vatican II*, 220-22 and 230-31.
48. Pastoral Constitution on the Church in the Modern World, n. 39, in Abbott, *Documents of Vatican II*, 237-38.
49. McDonagh, *Vulnerable to the Holy*, 22-83.

CHAPTER EIGHT

ation, and poverty in all its many forms of hunger, homelessness, and illness are all very prevalent on our earth. Instead of overcoming the gap between the rich and the poor, the last few years have seen a growing gap, not only between the various parts of the world, but also in practically all of our countries. In McDonagh's words, there are many crises facing our world and our church today.[50]

The danger of over-optimism shows itself today in a poor understanding of the meaning of the Christian virtue of hope. Very often today I hear the question: Is there any hope for the church? Paul's understanding of hope in the Letter to the Romans reminds us of the true meaning of hope. If you can see the goal, there is no space for hope. Hope is hoping against hope. Hope sees light in the midst of darkness, joy in the midst of sorrow, and life in the midst of death. One who does not know how to suffer does not know how to hope. Yes, there have to be some positive signs that are present, but hope does not depend on what we can feel, see, or touch. McDonagh's writings have attempted to provide hope for the church in Ireland in the midst of the many crises it faces.[51]

McDonagh explicitly reflects on the good number of friends and others who have left the church while he and others choose to remain. Unfortunately, now as in the time of Jesus, cowardice and power seeking have prevented the church community and its leaders from recognising their mediating-reconciling role proclaimed by Jesus. Structural change in the church is necessary but it will never solve all our problems. The community of the church experiences the presence and power of the divine within the created, human, pilgrim, and sinful community of the church. The pilgrim and sinful church lives in the betweeness of Good Friday and Easter, the half-life and half-light between the death of Jesus and the resurrection of Christ. Faith and sacrament only partially remove the darkness and doubt of our medi-

---

50. McDonagh's writings from the mid-eighties have pointed out all these problems.
51. McDonagh, *Faith in Fragments*, 20-89; *Vulnerable to the Holy*, 22-83.

ated access to God's loving presence. Life for all in the church, leaders and members alike, is by times illuminating and disillusioning, transforming and frustrating. The pilgrim community of the church should be generous in the boundaries and welcoming of the gifts of all the faithful, not just of the 'party faithful' but of the partly faithful which in reality includes all of us, members and leaders, always in need of being sustained, forgiven, and transformed by the inbreaking God. The recent essay that develops these ideas is entitled 'A Communal Hope.'[52]

Less emphasis on person and more on community and the other
McDonagh appreciates the renewed anthropology of *Gaudium et spes* with its attempt to recognise both the personal and the social dimensions of the human person but in the end this document puts more emphasis on the personal than on the social and the communitarian. The individual person remains dominant while the social aspects seem subordinate. In reality the person is only a person-in-relationship-in-structures, as person-in-community, and as in an immediate dialectic with a community-of-persons.[53]

From his earliest writings McDonagh emphasised the importance of community. One becomes a person only in and through community.[54] Just as the community forms the person so the person forms and changes the various communities of family, school, neighbourhood, city, nation, and world. Only such a community can deal with the problems facing our society today – waste, pollution, devastation, injustice, poverty, and war.[55] Community is in many ways the central theme in the essays found in the *Gracing of Society*.

More than any other Catholic moral theologian McDonagh has emphasised 'the other.' The scriptural connection between otherness and holiness, as well as the philosophical work of Emmanuel Levinas, has influenced him.[56] His early emphasis

---

52. McDonagh, *Vulnerable to the Holy*, 73-83.
53. McDonagh, 'The Church in the Modern World (Gaudium et Spes),' 102.
54.. McDonagh, *Invitation and Response*, 6-8.
55. McDonagh, *Making of Disciples*, 77-79.
56. McDonagh, *Vulnerable to the Holy*, 8-9.

on the Christian life as gift and call sees the moral obligation in terms of a call that has an unconditional character about it. The source of the call-obligation is another person or a group of persons. In transcending self to reach out to the call of the other a certain disintegration of the subject occurs followed by a reintegration of the subject in relationship to others and other communities. But in keeping with his recognition of the sinful and tragic dimensions of human existence the other constitutes not only a gift but also a threat. The twofold aspect of gift and threat calls the person to conversion, true liberation, and proper relationships.[57]

The emphasis on the other has continued to grow in McDonagh's later writings. An essay in *Faith in Fragments* recognises that the recovery of the other/stranger 'both human and divine' is at the heart of the renewal of ethics and of God's place in it. God is the stranger God and we who believe the stranger God has come to us must also accept and bring into relationships the human strangers both in the form of individuals and groups. Such an approach challenges the exclusiveness so often present in our world based on economic, cultural, political, and gender factors.[58] This essay became seminal for the development of the theme of the other, ethics, and holiness in *Vulnerable to the Holy* published in 2004.

In this last collection of essays both the attraction and the threat of the other, the beauty and the horrors of every body, every where, and every when render us vulnerable to the Holy. Encounter with the other requires for us a letting be that has both passive and active aspects. Passive letting be calls for patient and loving acceptance of the different other. The active aspect of letting be means that letting be is not merely a toleration of the other but a loving acceptance and enablement of the other. The same call to let be also serves as the criterion for the proper relationship of human beings with the environment and opposes

---

57. Enda McDonagh, *Gift and Call: Toward a Christian Theology of Morality* (Dublin: Gill & Macmillan, 1975), 39ff.
58. McDonagh, *Faith in Fragments*, 137-45.

the utilitarian ethic that sees the environment merely as a means for the satisfaction of human individuals. *Letting be* in the passive and active senses of accepting and enabling requires for its completion a *letting go*. This calls for respectful acceptance of the other's privacy and freedom and reaches its height in the willingness to forgive our enemies – the most painful aspect of letting go.[59] In the essays in this book McDonagh develops our relationships to others, to art, to the natural environment, and even to our other self as making us vulnerable to the ultimate other – the Holy.

Theology from the Fringe
The recognition of the tragic dimension of human existence, the emphasis on the other, and the influence of liberation theology brought McDonagh to realise that we live between chaos and new creation, calling for doing theology from the fringe. Vatican II's theology was a universal theology primarily emanating from the centre. McDonagh now does theology from the fringe, in accord with the liberation emphasis on the privilege of the poor, the oppressed, and the marginalised. Human history shows forth the biblical dialectic between destructive human chaos and new divine creation slipping again into chaos that reached its pinnacle in the Paschal Mystery of Jesus. Human suffering and human destructiveness continue to encounter the co-suffering, inexhaustible, and creative God in life, liturgy, and literature.[60]

In this context McDonagh again acknowledges the positive approaches put into place by *Gaudium et spes* but also points out the danger of theology that is not done from the fringe. Latin America and the Third World face great poverty and privation. The economic form of liberalism with its centre and periphery, the powerful and the powerless, and dominating and the dominated, becomes an instrument of oppression for the powerless, the peripheral, and the marginalised. From a theological per-

---

59. McDonagh, *Vulnerable to the Holy*, 12-20.
60. McDonagh, *Between Chaos and New Creation*, 1-9.

spective the theology of the West, the North, and Europe no longer provide the churches in the Third World with the Christian inspiration and theological analysis they need. Despite its many positive contributions even for the deprived, *Gaudium et spes* must be supplemented and even transformed in these very different worlds.[61] In reading the signs of the times *Gaudium et spes* gave insufficient attention to the tragic aspects present even in Europe, to say nothing of the problems of the two-thirds world. Hope can only be hope by arising in, through, and beyond failure and the tragic.[62]

McDonagh's local Irish theology makes the same point. Ireland has its share of poverty, violence, and even fratricidal killing. The Irish church and people cannot really be people of hope unless they first acknowledge and recognise their participation in the grief and anguish (*luctus et angor*) of the times and their complicity in all of this. Theology at the fringe puts the spotlight on the chronically and terminally ill, travellers, the homeless, the handicapped, the unemployed, prisoners, gays and lesbians, and all other deprived minorities.[63]

The Maynooth professor uses the same theology from the fringe in dealing with the Irish church. The church is not the reign of God but its herald or servant. The church always stands under the challenge and judgement of the reign of God. The pilgrim church is always a sinful church in need of reform. The leadership of the Irish church has, unfortunately, held onto a triumphalistic notion of the church with its power in and over society, even though it has been widely recognised from verifiable evidence that this approach has not worked. Look at the precipitous decline in the number of religious and priestly vocations and the growing number of people who do not participate in the Eucharist, and then the problems created by clergy sex abuse and their cover-up by church leadership. McDonagh in his gentle way has challenged the Irish church in the way it treats gays and

---

61. Ibid., 191.
62. Ibid., 192-93.
63. Ibid., 193-94.

lesbians and women. A church which recognises and confesses its own sinfulness and complicity in the problems could become a source of hope and light for a suffering and tragic world looking for light and hope.[64]

Conclusion
The focus of this paper has been an analysis of Enda McDonagh's writings in light of Vatican II and has concentrated especially on methodological approaches to moral theology. As a result this paper does not pretend to cover all that McDonagh has written in his long and productive career. Some aspects such as his developing positions on non-violence have been discussed at great length elsewhere and are not mentioned here.[65]

In addition, since Vatican II, McDonagh has been cognisant of, and dialogued with, other approaches and positions that have emerged both in the academy and in the life of the church. Mention has already been made of his learning much from political and liberation theologies. He is also familiar with many other approaches – biblical approaches to morality, feminist theology, narrative theology, metaphorical theology, as well as praxis theology. Few theologians have the breadth of interest and vision that McDonagh has brought to his work. The festschrift in his honour, so ably edited and put together by Linda Hogan and Barbara FitzGerald, is aptly entitled: *Between Poetry and Politics*. But his interests are even broader than this. He is in dialogue with many aspects of art. Ethics, aesthetics, and Christian faith are natural companions for him.[66]

A concluding word should be said about the essay genre of his work. He has not written a systematic approach to moral

---

64. McDonagh, *Faith in Fragments*, 18-39; *Vulnerable to the Holy*, 22-83.
65. Stanley, Hauerwas, 'Reflections on the 'Appeal to Abolish War' or What Being a Friend of Enda's Got Me Into,' in Linda Hogan and Barbara FitzGerald, eds, *Between Poetry and Politics: Essays in Honour of Enda McDonagh* (Dublin: Columba Press, 2003), 135-47; Patrick Hannon, 'Theology, War, and Pacifism,' in Hogan and FitzGerald, *Between Poetry and Politics*, 117-34.
66. McDonagh, *Vulnerable to the Holy*, 9.

theology nor a monograph exploring in depth a particular approach or position. McDonagh obviously is very much at home with the genre of the essay and has in many ways become a master of this genre. But the essay format also has its limitations. Approaches and issues cannot be developed in depth. Comparisons and contrasts can only be hinted at. He makes many creative suggestions but by definition they are not blueprints for what should be done. For example, in his significant emphasis on doing theology from the fringe, he disagrees with the methodology of *Gaudium et spes*, while at the same time he acknowledges that there is still some place for that methodology, though without developing exactly how the two fit together.[67]

The essay approach obviously also fits with his own temperament and skills. Here again we have proof of his own insistence that theology is autobiographical. But there also are other reasons explaining the genre he has used. By definition one dealing with morality from a Christian perspective (recall his continued unwillingness to speak of himself as a moral theologian) must be in dialogue with what is happening in the church and in the world. His broad and catholic concerns and interests have put him in dialogue with many other disciplines and with many of the issues facing church and society today. There has been no time to write monographs. In retirement he had planned to write a manuscript on the *Risk of God*, but even in retirement the many demands and calls on his time have prevented him from writing such a book.[68] In addition, the times in which we live, as he insists, are dark and fragmentary. These times do not call for systematic approaches or for in-depth monographs.

The essay format also fits well with his understanding of the role and function of the theologian dealing with morality. The pre-Vatican II moral theologian was the answer man (this is not a case of exclusive language) who provided answers for all the people of God. In today's church and world, the theologian enters

---

67. McDonagh, *Between Chaos and New Creation*, 191
68. McDonagh, *Vulnerable to the Holy*, 7.

into dialogue with others. In fact, in many cases there are no easy answers. The essay format is well adapted for such a suggestive and creative dialogue with other pilgrims in the church and the world.

The most important influence on Catholic moral theology in the last fifty years was Vatican II. This essay has attempted to show how McDonagh has dialogued with Vatican II in light of the ongoing life of the world, the church, and theology. He has developed some of Vatican II's themes, but also moved away from other approaches to moral theology that are found in the conciliar documents.

CHAPTER NINE

A Response to Charles Curran

Vincent MacNamara

It is a particular privilege to speak here on this occasion. Because, happily, it brings together two people to whom post-Vatican II moral theology in the English-speaking world is greatly indebted, Enda McDonagh and Charles Curran. Thank you Enda and Charles for that. And thank you, Charles, for tonight – as we expected, a lucid, perceptive, knowledgeable account of moral theology since Vatican II.

Forty years ago this year Enda McDonagh edited a book, *Moral Theology Renewed* in which he himself had two essays: 'Moral Theology, the Need for Renewal' and 'The Primacy of Charity' – essays that were to be influential in his own life and in ours. That renewal, not quite initiated by but furthered by Vatican II, as we have heard, was largely about a theological, christological, scriptural approach to the business of morality. It presaged a new dawn of light and hope after the dreary days of neo-scholasticism. We have seen tonight something of the fruits of that renewal in the work of Enda McDonagh. There has been a Christianising of moral life, to which he has notably contributed, and in which he has encouraged others. But we do not cease from exploration. It is worth saying that the renewal is still work in progress.

Things proved more difficult than that first fine careless rapture of the Council might have suggested. Charles Curran and Enda McDonagh have both pointed out shortcomings and concerns. The conjunction of religious faith and moral concern is a delicate matter and it is of interest beyond the theological community. Questions arise about how one is to proceed, about method. To engage the world of morality with biblical or theological themes is obviously a subtler approach than what we had been accustomed to – the derivation or entailment of rules from some general moral theory. And a more confined one than, say, a natural law approach, which purports to be in principle available to all serious seekers of truth. Questions then arise for the moralist about how one justifies moral conclusions, about how exactly faith bears on ethics – there is a danger of naïve and facile moves. And wider questions about how a faith-community relates to those of different or no religious perspective, of how it comports itself in society. Whether it becomes a ghetto retreating into positions that make no sense to others, or whether it can hope to claim a place in society.

Certainly, our colleagues in moral philosophy have been less than impressed by all this talk of renewal: what we have ended up with, one of them has told us is, 'rich mines of fallacious argument and unexamined assumptions'. And, even within Roman Catholicism there has been debate about whether all the fine talk about theology and scripture yields anything in the end but rhetoric and decoration. Some theologians have even suggested that the question of a Christian ethic is a non-question. But it seems to me that what the renewal initiated, and what has been so carefully developed by people like Enda and Charles, needs to be pursued more rather than less intensely in these days. What it means to do morality as a Christian or analogously as a Jew or a Muslim or Buddhist or Hindu – the logic of it – has become more important than ever, not only for a tradition's understanding of itself and its own way, but in terms of inter-religious dialogue and of the role, if any, of religious morality in the market place. We haven't had much of that debate in this country but both the Taoiseach and the Archbishop of Dublin have recently suggested that we need to rethink the relationship between church and state. That will be interesting: tensions in the past have been largely about issues of morality. If there is to be a rethink, it cannot escape an engagement with this very issue of the role, logic and legitimacy of religious moralities in an increasingly pluralist society.

So much for that issue. I thought it might be interesting to point to another issue, a different kind of renewal, I would argue, which has been driven not only from within theology (the acknowledgement of the centrality of charity-love) but from without. It is what I can only call a return to the subject, the one who does or wrestles with or lives morality. It is about consciousness and perception. (Feminist ethics, to take an example, is not about applying trusted principles to new issues – a necessary and increasingly difficult concern for morality – but is about a distinctive mode of consciousness, an experience that issues in a different way of reading the moral landscape.) The moral subject, you and I, in the traditional textbook was a bland, disembodied entity, thoroughly describable and definable, unchanging through time and place and circumstance and cultures – the easy subject of moral universals or absolutes. There was no room for differentiation: everyone was measured against the same general template – the 'one size fits all' approach.

Many world influences have conspired to nudge us towards a more nuanced view, and that has had or ought to have had its effect on our thinking and on our moral conclusions. I think of influences such as the pervasiveness of a personalist philosophy, a greater historical consciousness, an awareness of the social construction of reality. I think of questions about the very notion of a human nature, about the comparative study of cultures with their different perceptions of key concepts like 'ethics' 'rationality', 'moral justification', 'flourishing', (and need I say in the light of the present world conflict) 'freedom', 'democracy', 'justice', 'rights'. I think of the contribution of psychology and psychoanalysis to a richer understanding of the emergence of the personality, of the mysterious origin of our desires, of the significance of the unconscious for ethics, of the limits of freedom, of our uneven human and moral development, of the inescapable fragmentation of our lives. I note the wider recognition of the bearing of context and gender and worldview, including religious worldview, on moral perception.

In the traditional textbook the moral act stood in splendid isolation, untroubled by any of these awkward considerations.

But human beings do not stand isolated from time and place and story. Post-Vatican II theology has moved into a more realistic analysis of the moral act, of what it means for any of us to choose morally, of how to evaluate choice, of the significance of our intentions, motives, meaning and circumstances for our actions. We have had to look more understandingly at the moral capacity of individuals, at the condition and story of each one's life. To give weight too to the bearing of structures on possibilities and choice. To be more sensitive to difference, more tentative in judgement, more wary of absolutes, more ready to honour individuality and complexity, refining even what we mean by objectivity in morals. There are those who brand all that as theological softness, when I hope it is rather theological acuteness. It often seems to me that theologians labour long on such matters but that the instinctive wisdom of the community more readily senses the need for re-assessment. We have heard at this conference about anger, especially among women, at the rigidity that has stunted lives: Christians have been looking longingly for a more human face to moral teaching.

I see it as a kind of renewal, as a humanising of moral theology, and it runs through much of what Charles Curran has pointed to in his exposition of the story since Vatican II. Perhaps the heart of it was a simple return to the fundamental question: what is morality about? Or better, who is morality about? And, centrally, it is about the mystery of the claim of the other on us, in all its implications, about reverence for the inviolability of the human subject, about hope for a society that enhances human flourishing. It is a reverence that is enriched by, though not confined to, the Christian story and that, amazingly, aspires to be unlimited, unconditional, asymmetrical, embracing even the least endowed and the most ungrateful.

No one has done the humanising better than Enda McDonagh – and nowhere does he do it better, as many people have gratefully experienced, than in situations of life and love and faith which appear to smaller minds to be intractable. And in his brave concern for the outsider, the marginalised individual or

CHAPTER NINE

group. The title of this conference in his honour is appropriately *The Risks of Theology*. I take him both as an illustration of the best of post Vatican II theology and as an encouragement. He has led us, to use John McGahern's words, from a fortress church of edicts, threats and punishments to a church of spires and brilliant windows that go towards love and light.

Forty years ago he laid down the foundation in 'The Primacy of Charity', not in the old sense of charity as almsgiving but as a sensitive concern for the integral well-being of the other and for the reform of the structures that cripple lives. He has liberated us to recognise that moral thinking is not about religious control of the lives of people, not about tomes of casuistry, not about the shadow of Satan in the dark corner of every church, nor about giving Eros poison to drink. But, as you find in the extraordinary range of his writings, about the great humanly resonant issues of love and relationship, of hope and vulnerability, of Eros and Thanatos, of suffering and failure, of pain and disappointment, of darkness and the small hours of unbelief, of peace and war, of symbol and sacrament. Of our immortal longings.

It comes as no surprise then that for a long time he has been fascinated by and as theologian has made friends with the worlds of literature and art – it has been noted tonight that his Festschrift is rightly entitled, *Between Poetry and Politics*. I think of Karl Rahner's essay on the priest and the poet – both engaged, I suppose, in the one search, making 'raids on the inarticulate'. In the domain of moral theology this has meant for him, and must mean for all of us, trying to touch into the meaning of the human person, honouring the mysterious and unsayable otherness of the other and the strange ways of human becoming.

It is sometimes said that doing morality is about imagining. For Enda McDonagh it has been such and it has been a Christian imagining. He hasn't just written theory; he has imagined what it means to be a Christian in society in all its colourful and demanding complexity.

There are many, many things that could be said about Enda McDonagh the theologian and I think I know most of them. If I had to choose one, I would settle for a remark of Chekhov about one of his characters, who, he said, had a talent for humanity. No bad thing for a theologian.

CHAPTER TEN

Respect for life and the problem of scriptural violence

Joseph O'Leary

'Respect for life', *Ehrfurcht vor dem Leben*, is a phrase that occurred to Albert Schweitzer in September 1915. He saw it as the value to be cultivated in order to reverse the decline of humankind toward barbarity. Schweitzer's language is rather cloudy, demanding a sympathetic intuition from its hearers: 'What is respect for life, and how does it arise in us? The most immediate fact of human consciousness is: "I am life, that wants to live." In every moment in which the human being considers himself and the world around him, he grasps himself as will to life amid will to life.' This brings a sense of unlimited responsibility to the totality of the biosphere, the duty to foster all life in its development and to resist all that thwarts this development.

Respect for life, in this sense, is still not a widely approved virtue. Making a distinction based on the two Greek words for 'life' one may say that selfish humans cherish the life they are leading – their *bios* –, but not the life by which they live, the *zôê* of the cosmos. Full of the arrogance of life, *hê alazoneia tou biou* (1 Jn 2:16), they see the life of others as an encroachment on their space. Rather than a communion of *zôê* we have a rivality of *bios*, leading to violence. To revel in our own lives, as a possession, is to disrespect the lives of others. Instead, Schweitzer would urge, we are to tune in to the life of the cosmos, in a dying to self, on the model of the Johannine Jesus who 'lays down his life' (*tên psychên autou*, Jn 15:13; cf. Jn 10:15-18) 'for the life of the world' (*kai zôên didous tô kosmô*, Jn 6:33; cf. Jn 10:10).

Another reason why the holistic ideal of Schweitzer fails to enchant is that we find morally objectionable its apparent implication that an individual life is not absolutely sacred. To insist on preserving an individual life at the cost of the biosphere or of the life of the community is immoral in Schweitzer's eyes, but such a scruple never occurs to those who have an individualistic conception of the sacredness of life, a conception no doubt rooted in a self-centred clinging to life, to *bios* as an imagined possession of our imaginary ego. Ancient religious texts challenge this absolutisation of individual life by their glorification of martyrdom and of mortification and renunciation. Even texts we find morally shocking, wherein parents are commanded to slay their children (Genesis 22) or to offer their enemies in battle as a holocaust to God (Deut 13:16; Is 34:6; Jer 50:27) or as the warrior's equivalent of the brahmin's sacrifice (*Bhagavad Gîtâ*) can serve to shake us out of a blind clinging to life that we confuse with high moral principle.

There is an idolatry of life that is in reality opposed to respect for life, and that has more to do with *hê alazoneia tou biou* than with having life in abundance. One sign of this is that it prizes life selectively. Thus the life of an embryo – which is a full individual human life in potency, but not yet in act – becomes more sacred than the life of mothers, or of the doctors targeted by zealots. The collateral casualties of war, children lured by the cute-looking bomblets packed in cluster bombs, and maimed, blinded or killed by them, count for little, as do the lives of the criminal underclass. The tortured bodies of people in a permanent vegetative state are kept alive by families who cannot let go and who ritually denounce as murderers those who follow common sense and classical Catholic moral tradition in this matter.

The 'seamless robe' ethic that would cherish all life cannot be merely the automatic application of the rule, 'Thou shalt not kill'; it must also be prevenient, labouring primarily to undo those conditions that give rise to the taking of life – poverty, war, aggression, vengefulness – and to replace them with conditions that make for respect for life – equality, peacefulness, forgiveness.

In the economy of older Japanese society it was often thought necessary to send newborn infants 'back to the gods'[1] and old

---

1. See William Lafleur's thought-provoking book, *Liquid Life: Abortion and Buddhism in Japan* (Princeton University Press, 1994).

people would likewise go away to die;[2] suicide, too, in a wide range of circumstances became virtuous. Morally unacceptable as this may be, it bespoke a serene recognition of the limits of life, an ability not to cling to it in aggressive self-assertion. To condemn it as merely a 'culture of death' would miss the distinction between a mode of living rooted in respect for the total biosphere and one based on territorial aggression that refuses to take the wider context into account at all.

Leaving these delicate topics to the expert hands of the moral theologians, I should like to look again at the scandalous scriptural texts mentioned above. For centuries the church was not very keen on allowing the laity to read scripture.[3] After Vatican II many pious Catholics found themselves repulsed by the contents of the Bible now thrust into their hands. The same reaction is seen among diligent lay readers of scripture in the Renaissance. Lucien Febvre recounts the reaction of Marguerite de Navarre:

> Hélas! mon Dieu, mon frère et vrai Moïse,
> J'ai estimé vos oeuvres estre vice

she cries in the *Miroir*, after a reading of the historical books of the Old Testament, filled with wars, massacres, cruelties, gleefully perpetrated:

> Vous nous faites de mal faire défense,
> Et pareil mal faites sans conscience.
> Vous défendez de tuer à chacun,
> Mais vous tuez, sans épargner aucun
> De vingt-trois mil, que vous faites défaits.

And again:

> … Je venais à douter

---

2. See Shohei Imamura's film, *Ballad of Narayama* (1982), for a bleak view of such a world.
3. See the condemnation of Wycliffe's Bible in 1408 and of all unauthorised translatiosn in 1559; in *Quellen zur Geschichte des Papsttums und des römischen Katholizismus*, ed. Carl Mirbt and Kurt Aland, I (Tübingen: Mohr, 1967), 476, 587.

> Si c'estoit vous, ou si par aventure,
> Ce n'estoit rien qu'une simple escriture.[4]

Note, however, that is it not the cruelty of biblical wars that offends Marguerite, but the extreme punishment meted out by God for fornication. The 23,000 to whom she refers are the victims of the plague caused by Israelites having intercourse with Moabite women, a plague stopped by Phinehas's spearing of one such couple; the number is given as 24,000 in Num 25:9 but 23,000 in 1 Cor 10:8. Older periods had not cultivated our scandalised reaction to the exterminating warrior-God of the Pentateuch, since their own war ethic was hardly more refined. The unconsciousness with which the Inquisition and the massacres of the Crusades were accepted scarcely prepared people to be scrupulous about biblical stories of bloodshed in war. Even today, to take offence at these stories is the privilege of the left.

Phinehas, by the way, was glorified for his noble deed. His priestly lineage was held in high esteem. He provided inspiration for Mattathias in the Book of Maccabees. Along with Samson, slayer of Philistines, and Jephtha, sacrificer of his daughter, he is recalled as a hero of faith in Hebrews 11:32. What strikes us today is the hatred of sexuality underlying his deed. Warnings against *porneia* as not making for holiness or for human flourishing are one thing (1 Thess 4:3); but a zeal for holiness that expresses itself in hatred is another. We have not even begun to analyse, or to psychoanalyse, this murky dimension of scripture. Of course it is urged that the zeal of Phinehas was directed not against sex but against idolatry. But hatred of idolatry often takes on a sexually phobic hue in scripture, as in the rage against the feminised religion of Canaan or Paul's view of lesbianism as punishment for idol-worship. The question arises

---

4. Lucien Febvre, *Amour sacré, amour profane* (Paris: Gallimard 1944, 1996), 201-2. 'Alas, my God, my brother and true Moses, I esteemed your works as vice ... You forbid us to do evil and do the same evil without conscience. You forbid anyone to kill, yet you kill, without sparing anyone, twenty-three thousand whom you cast down ... I came to doubt whether it was you or whether perchance it was only a mere piece of writing'.

whether monotheism can avoid the traps of such patriarchal rigidity and intolerance.

Apologetic responses
It is perhaps only today that the violence of scripture has become truly scandalous to us. For reasons that are obvious, including the extermination practices of the last century, the bloodthirsty aspect of scriptural texts, Jewish, Christian and Islamic, has become a neuralgic point in current religious reflection. Ancient Israel rejoiced in the gift of life, but regarded rival tribes as encroachers to be eliminated. There was no thought of celebrating a communion of life with them. Wars of extermination were as intrinsic to the religion, polity, law, culture and spirituality of ancient Israel as crusades and inquisitions were to those of the Catholic Church for centuries. The latter also are phenomena that we used to gloss over, despite the efforts of Protestant and Enlightenment critics to rub our noses in them; now we feel a duty to gaze on 'the unacceptable face' of church history and draw what lessons we can from it.[5] One need look no further than the tortured efforts of fundamentalists to justify this violence to see how dangerous these ancient texts still remain, at least to the degree that they dull the intellectual and moral integrity of such apologists and the numerous believers they represent.

Even though the enlightened conscience of humanity today cannot be squared with a God who commands the slaughter of women and children, and the abduction of virgins as war booty (Numbers 31), these tales hold a morbid fascination for us. Their sublime, sacral style, the sanctification of violence they enact, comes from a primitive stratum of human history, like voices from an exotic other planet. This aura has led biblical inerrantists to glorify the genocidal activities, blaming their victims:

> This action/atrocity by the Midianites is an intensely sordid

---

5. See John Kent, *The Unacceptable Face: The Modern Church in the Eyes of the Historian* (London: SCM, 1987).

and depressing tale, of greater scale than even that of Sodom and Gomorrah, and of greater anti-Hebrew malice and calculating treachery than even that of the Amalekites. The removal of this exact sub-culture (without impacting the Moabites or the rest of the Midianites—for good or ill), while mercifully sparing a very large number of innocent young girls, yet without sparing the guilty Israelites, seems neither cruel nor unfair nor unwarranted, given the horrendously dehumanising character of this crime, and given the unavoidable consequences of conflict upon children in the ancient world.[6]

This seems quite perverse. Yet a lot of biblical violence still fails to stir any unease even in Christians who are far from fundamentalism. The discomfiting of the Egyptians, for example, the drowning of Pharaoh and his host in the Red Sea, has been so well integrated into our Easter typology that it hardly troubles us as the fate of the Midianites does. We jauntily sing: 'Kings in their splendour he slew, for his great love is without end' (Ps 135). But maybe even in such cases some belated scruples might not be out of place.

Virgins are again taken as booty in Judges 21:11, in a war of extermination against fellow-Israelites, punished for not taking part in a previous war of extermination against the Benjamites, who had refused to extradite the gang-rapists of a certain concubine. The four hundred virgins are given to the six hundred Benjamite males who are the sole survivors of that war so as to keep the tribe of Benjamin from disappearing entirely; an oath prevents the Israelites from giving the Benjamites their own daughters; but the requisite two hundred virgins are nonetheless supplied by allowing the Benjamites to abduct them at the festival of Shiloh. Exegetes seek to give an edifying gloss to all these rather barbarous doings. They discern that the war against the Benjamites was entered on hastily, on the basis of a distorted report and without a divine command, so that God allows Israel

---

6. Glenn Miller, http://www.christian-thinktank.com/midian.html (May, 2001).

to be twice defeated – giving ambiguous responses in the manner of a pagan oracle – before giving them victory on the third attempt (before which they consult him more humbly than on the two previous occasions).[7] As for the abduction of the virgins at Shiloh, it allowed Israel to provide wives for the Benjamites without forcing the girls' fathers to transgress their oath. In any case the girls deserved their fate: 'At Shiloh the venerable covenant sanctuary had reverted to older Canaanite patterns of celebration. But even the evil that men do, the redactor seems to be saying, could be providentially exploited on that occasion, thanks to the quick-witted reasoning of Israel's elders'.[8] Such attempts at edification are themselves disedifying. But they also shield us against the full force of the texts. Magical consultations of Yahweh belong to a world in which to be seized by the Spirit of God is to become a frenzied killer, as in the case of Samson (Judges 14:19). A good literary critic will seek to feel the full archaic power of such representations, so foreign to the modern mind.

Is the Samson-mentality really a thing of the past? It is kept alive at least on the plane of fantasy by biblical inerrantists. Tackle them, say, on the bashing of innocent babies' heads against the stones (Ps 137), and they will reply: 'First, who says they were innocent? Second, can you deny that God appoints humans as agents of his vengeance? Third, who are you, a corrupt sinner, to criticise the Word of God?' That dogmatic rhetoric may be old-fashioned, but it is intoxicating, and can be reactivated at any time. In the past, at least, such attitudes translated into deeds. The English Puritan revolutionaries 'saw themselves as "Saints of the Most High", commissioned to execute judgement on kings and nobles. Oliver Cromwell drew a parallel

---

7. See Robert Boling, *Judges* (New York: Doubleday), 288.
8. *The Interpreter's Bible*, ad loc. The second, homiletic column in *The Interpreter's Bible* must often resort to ad hoc comments, embarrassed and desperate efforts to wring edification from the text at any cost; its comment on Numbers 31:22, for instance, grasps at the straw of a spiritual significance in the reference to the purging of anything that will stand fire.

between his revolution and the Exodus and proceeded to treat the Catholics of Ireland as the Canaanites. He even declared that "there are great occasions in which some men are called to great services in the doing of which they are excused from the common rule of morality".'[9] This is an example of what Karen Armstrong calls antinomian fundamentalism.[10] The genocide of Indians in America was based on similar biblical imagination. The obsession with inerrancy is peculiar to America today, and does not seem widespread in Europe. It goes hand in hand with a readiness to see even the most ill-thought-out and illegal military aggressions as somehow commanded by God. The inerrancy of scripture translates into *my* inerrancy and *my country's* inerrancy, and inspiration, as it reduces the word of God to a magic oracle, letting it lead them into one catastrophic misadventure after another.

One apologetic tactic is to claim that Israel's practices of extermination differed from those of its ancient neighbours in that here God used the weak human proclivity to violence and channeled it for a divine purpose as opposed to a merely tribal one. Thus the violent texts can be read with an eye to this divine purpose, as testifying to divine holiness, while we overlook the unsatisfactory ethical understanding of the time as a limited, culture-bound aspect. But this forestalls a more disturbing question: What if the sense of divine purpose made the Israelites not less, but more ruthless in their ideology of extermination?

Ben Witherington, asked about inerrancy on his website, engages in a characteristic apologetic shuffle.

> Inerrancy is a negative word which leads one to have to define (or redefine) what amounts to an error. I prefer saying that the Bible is totally truthful and trustworthy in what it asserts ... Its provenance is telling the truth in the main about history, theology, ethics and those sorts of

---

9. John J. Collins, 'The Zeal of Phinehas: The Bible and the Legitimization of Violence', in J. Harold Ellens, ed, *The Destructive Power of Religion* (New York: Praeger 2004), I, 11-33; here, 13.
10. Karen Armstrong, *The Battle for God* (New York: Knopf, 2000).

subjects ... The sun doesn't rise or set, but it certainly appears to do so, and truthful phenomenological language is found in many places in the Bible ... I see no reason to doubt the veracity of the Bible on what it tries to teach us, so long as it is rightly understood taking into account genre of literature and the like.[11]

Phenomenologically, the Israelites no doubt understood God to be on their side in wars of extermination; but for us it is a fallacy deriving from their general sense of having God 'on tap'.

Pious hermeneutical principles, such as Luke Johnson's claim that 'God's wisdom is somehow seeking to be communicated even through the impossibilities of the literal sense' and that we must wrestle with apparently difficult texts instead of condemning them 'until they yielded a meaning "worthy of God"' prevent one from reading the texts with full sensitivity to their literary texture. They prescribe in advance that the texts must have an edifying sense. This approach is theologically as well as literarily objectionable. When John J. Collins proposes that 'this material should not be disregarded, for it is at least as revelatory as the more edifying parts of the biblical witness', what he means is that it is revelatory of the all-too-human, culture-bound roots of the construction of monotheism: 'The power of the Bible is largely that it gives an unvarnished picture of human nature and of the dynamics of history, and also of religion and the things that people do in its name.' I would say that the power of the Bible is primarily that it corrects these evils, offering a medicine-chest for the religious pathologies of humanity (as Gregory Baum once remarked). But the evils do show themselves clearly, and are not entirely controlled, analysed and overcome by scripture itself, even at the last redactional level, though perhaps they are if we take into account at every step the total vision of the entire canon. If the Bible tells us something about the divine it tells us much about the human, and in the

---

11. http://benwitherington.blogspot.com/2006/02/2-tim-316-on-inspiration-and-authority.html

end the divine is best revealed in the process of humanisation that the Bible attests.

Official Catholic statements on this question are often unsatisfactory as they tone down the literal force of the scandalous texts. 'No one who has a proper idea of biblical inspiration will be surprised to find that the sacred writers, like other men of antiquity, employed certain techniques of exposition and narrative, certain idioms characteristic of the Semitic language, certain exaggerated, often paradoxical expressions designed for emphasis' (*Divino Afflante Spiritu*, 1943). This rejects crude ideas of what inspiration entails, but does not meet the problem of massacres presented as divinely sanctioned. This problem is addressed head-on in the 1994 document of the Pontifical Biblical Commission (no longer an organ of the Magisterium) on 'The Interpretation of Scripture in the Church', where we read:

> The Bible reflects a considerable moral development, which finds its completion in the New Testament. It is not sufficient therefore that the Old Testament should indicate a certain moral position (e.g. the practice of slavery or of divorce, or that of extermination in the case of war) for this position to continue to have validity. One has to undertake a process of discernment. This will review the issue in the light of the progress in moral understanding and sensitivity that has occurred over the years. The writings of the Old Testament contain certain 'imperfect and provisional' elements (*Dei Verbum*, 15), which the divine pedagogy could not eliminate right away.

This remains evasive, for it suggests that extermination of civilian populations is not intrinsically evil but had validity under the circumstances of pentateuchal times. Concern to safeguard scriptural inerrancy seems here to be opening the doors wide to an extreme moral relativism.

The *herem* or ban was a common institution of antiquity and is clearly blessed and commanded by God in scripture. These texts reflect a real-life violent world. John J. Collins cites a ninth century parallel, the Moabite stone : 'And Chemosh said to me, "Go, take Nebo from Israel." So I went by night and fought against it from the break of dawn until noon, taking it and slaying all, seven thousand men, boys, women, girls, and maidservants, for I had devoted them to destruction for (the god) Ashtar-Chemosh' (I:13)'.[12] Biblical texts as late as the seventh century BCE glorify the *herem*, and its spirit lives on in much later texts. The four volumes on *The Destructive Power of Religion*, edited by J. Harold Ellens,[13] offer an airing of this nightmare history, though the healing response it proposes is sometimes short on theology and too facile in its psychological generalisations. The church still wants to hold that it has no authority to deplore this tradition, but the question of moral judgement is forced on us again and again, and there is a sense that to fudge it out of respect for the archaic but inerrant texts is to have lost the legitimate freedom of Christians in their handling of scripture.

Perhaps the root of all the forms of violence scripture harbours, or at least of their perpetuation, is the violence of the claim whereby scriptures impose themselves as having divine authority. Churches that make peremptory use of scriptural proof-texts, or who use their own official statements as even stronger proof-texts and criteria of truth, as well as fundamentalists who build castles of closed-mindedness on rigid understandings of literal inerrancy, are all building on a foundation laid in the sacred texts themselves.

But here again, one can go beneath the dogmatist layer and discover a more gracious sense in such declarations as, 'This is the word of the Lord.' When the prophets use that expression, it is in the context of a concrete intervention in some troubled situation. They are claiming that the word of God has come to them – the biblical God is always a 'God who comes'. He has given them a burning word to be uttered here and now, not one to be used to bully people three thousand years later.

---

12. Collins, 20.
13. For comment see D. Andrew Kille, SBL annual meeting, Nov 2005; http://psybibs.home.att.net/2005/kille.destructive_power.pdf.

Biblical triumphalism is at the root of the evils of sectarianism that have blighted Christian history. A scruple holds us back from sharing in it today, and notably in the case of New Testament passages directed at various parties in Judaism or at the Jewish people itself. Beyond this, the bullying tone of scripture is no longer something we are ready to accept as 'good for us'. Rather we detect here a root of the violence that emerges in more scandalous forms in texts advocating murder or genocide. We resist what we perceive as moral blackmail, as scripture laying a guilt-trip on us. The resistances expressed by the critics of Christianity since the Renaissance are now knit into our own contemporary sensitivity. We are suspicious, as well, of the authoritarian attitude that discourages the mind from searching after truth and discourages society from developing a democratic culture of debate and consultation.

Biblical conservatives may rail at those who dare to stand in judgement over the Word of God, yet increasingly their rhetoric is losing its power, as we see the role such biblical conviction has played in the wars of the new century. Christians do in fact stand in judgement on the Bible, and they also devoutly wish that Muslims would do the same for the Qur'an. Biblical authority as traditionally understood is increasingly being unmasked as an imposition and as an obstacle to human progress.

How scripture corrects itself

Scripture is always correcting itself. An obvious way it does this is when later redactors take some old text and modify it or join it with other texts in such a way as to make it more acceptable as an expression of Israel's faith. These redactional efforts to impose an edifying reading offer a clue on which exegetes may build. The old allegorical method of finding an edifying spiritual sense – taking Samson as a type of Christ, for example – has lost authority. But attention to the theological vision of the Book of Judges as a whole may discover an initial theological reaction against the Samson lore in its primitive original form,[14] and ref-

---

14. See Dieter Böhler, 'Was macht denn Samson in der Bibel?', *Theologie und Philosophie* 80 (2005), 481-9.

erence to the wider canon may discern here a pointer to values worked out more fully further along the Bible's trajectory of moral reflection. Scripture is *sui ipsius interpres* and also *sui ipsius critica*. But, against Luther, it is when it is read by the church that scripture best effects its own self-critique, the Spirit overcoming the letter that kills.

Vatican II seeks to edulcorate an earlier stress on literal inerrancy, monumentalised in the embarrassing decrees of the Pontifical Biblical Commission early in the twentieth century: 'the books of scripture, firmly, faithfully and without error teach that truth which God, for the sake of our salvation, wished to see confided to the sacred scriptures' (*Dei Verbum*, 11). Such inerrancy does not entail that scripture must be free of all historical inaccuracies, or even failures of moral insight due to a less developed state of reflection. Even the New Testament points beyond itself to deepening insights that will unfold in the future: 'I have yet many things to say to you, but you cannot bear them now. When the Spirit of truth comes, he will guide you into all truth; for he will not speak on his own authority, but whatever he hears he will speak, and he will declare to you the things that are to come' (Jn 16:12-13). This suggests that there is room for a broadening of moral vision beyond the conventional accounts of vice and virtue that the Pauline literature picked up from its environment. One may take it that the total effect of the biblical record, in the dialectic of its inner development and subsequent interpretation as enfolded in the church's canon, is to transmit that saving truth. This allows a wide space for letting the texts in their original historical texture be what they are. Factual error is hardly a problem if it is recognised that the literary genres of scripture, even in the historical books, do not aim at literality. But moral error is another matter. And it seems that humanity progresses to truth through a process of trial and error, a process that is going on within the pages of scripture as well.

We could reinterpret inerrancy as a regulative ideal. It means that 'the Bible cannot be wrong', that is, it urges us to use the Bible in an 'inspired' way, so that we draw from it only healing truth, while leaving in obscurity texts that could create attitudes incompatible with the Bible as the church now interprets it. The Bible stands over against the church and judges it, to be sure, but only insofar as it can be actualised as a living word. To take dusty passages from little-known corners of scripture and jump them on people as the Word of God would be a bizarre parody of effective scriptural authority, which depends on the Bible being voiced in a church context of spiritual discernment. It is a fundamental abuse of the Bible to make it an arsenal for polemic purposes. Its authority never comes from outside, from an unexpected lateral angle, but from within the life of the church and the vital role it fulfils within the life of the church. It is interesting that the stories of Sodom and Gibeah, some obscure verses of Leviticus, and a little-regarded *obiter dictum* of Paul in Romans 1, skipped over in the ancient commentaries, are the main scriptural ammunition of anti-gay Christian voices – texts that have never lived and breathed in the church's worship.

The Bible corrects itself but it is also corrected by the wider revelation of the divine that is coterminous with the spiritual history of humankind. If it is cut off from that background even the New Testament becomes a sectarian and violent text. A more nuanced attitude to inerrancy – which distances the church from fundamentalist literalism – allows us to take on board the genuine insights of the Enlightenment critique of religious scriptures, while allowing the scriptural texts to speak to us anew with power. The trajectory of scripture encourages us not to put our faith in authorities but to trust the instinctive reaction of reason and conscience. There is nothing to apologise for if we find biblical language barbaric and intolerable. We need to discover this freedom of discernment, within a general respect for the overall message of scripture. The values of the Enlightenment often clashed with biblical and ecclesiastical orthodoxy. But insofar as those values were based on reason and conscience, they have triumphed, and force a rethinking of biblical and ecclesiastical tradition. The enlightened conscience of humanity has its authority too, a divine authority. Our appeal to it can find a warrant also in the radical texts of the prophets and St Paul that speak of the law written on our hearts. 'And they shall all be taught by God' (Is 54:13; Jn 6:45). The rebellion of modern poets and thinkers against an abusive God is thus in large part divinely inspired.

Critique of scripture can proceed 'from outside', laying bare dangerous strands in scriptural culture and the *Wirkungsgeschichte* of scriptural texts. Such cool, rational critique of past moral attitudes will take on board all the perspectives of a hermeneutic of suspicion (Feuerbach, Nietzsche, Marx, Freud) while going forward to a rational reappropriation of the sense of the text as an anthropological document. There is nothing wrong with this. But it will not disclose the full depths of the scriptural text.

To a disillusioned secularist gaze scriptures are at best products of religious experience and speculation, to which an undue authority has been given by communities that have taken them up as texts enjoying sacred authority. This conferral of intrinsic authority is seen as spoiling the original value of the writings, removing them from the milieu of free critical judgement to which any human writing should be exposed.

Scholarly hermeneutics without a faith-investment will seek to grasp the historical and literary texture of the scriptural writings in all its richness. It will reap the anthropological insights these texts contain just as it draws out the anthropological vision of Greek classics. When it comes to ethical judgement, the secular scholar will argue freely with the scriptural text, assessing its codes without respect for their hallowed status in still living traditions. Differentiation between what is viable and what is unacceptable in scriptural ethics will emerge in this process, and the Bible will become a repertoire both of classical ethical mistakes, or primitive bypaths in the genealogy of morals, on the one hand, and of seminal ethical breakthroughs of the Axial Age on the other. This critical reappropriation of sacred scriptures as part of the heritage of secular humanity provides a broad basis to which the specifically religious retrieval of this heritage would do well to attend.

The critique of scripture can also proceed 'from within,' in a broad hermeneutic sympathetic to the religious texts that may play off their religiously significant aspects against other aspects that seem to clog that significance or to be in contradiction with it. The task demands a balance of empathy and critique, ripening into the position where the critique becomes the natural supplement or outflow of the empathy.

But the fullest form of critical overcoming and reappropriation occurs when an engaged faith-community uses the text as an occasion of potential revelation, or enlightenment for present action. The sacredness of scripture lies then primarily in its unexhausted capacity to produce effects of liberation and enlightenment in the present.

The naturalistic outlook on scripture has entered theology through the critical-historical study of scriptures, which recovers their human, historical texture, reconstructing the real motivations of the authors in their contexts. Such demystified reading of scriptures is a resource for liberation from the many oppressive effects of scriptures whose authority has been swallowed hook, line and sinker. Liberal theologians believe that it can also be a resource for the demystified reappropriation of scriptures by religious communities, empowering them to use the texts with creative freedom rather than being shackled by their archaic letter.

None of this honesty in exploring the human, historical texture of scripture entails a denial of the holiness, inspiration and inerrancy of the biblical message. Indeed, as we confront residues of evil in the mentalities of the scriptural world, we discern within scripture the prophetic values that overcame this evil in the past, at least in principle, and that in the spiritual reading of the church continues to overcome it in new ways here and now.

Scripture records a divine pedagogy, a growth in awareness of the divine and the values it entails. If one wants to square this with the traditional doctrine of *inspiration*, something like the following picture may emerge. The locus of inspiration is the people of Israel, in their ongoing quest to understand and be faithful to the God of the Covenant (as Karl Rahner argued). Their scriptures are inspired as part of this graced effort.

Israel was a people who opened themselves to God, came before the Holy One and experienced their own wretchedness and sin under his gaze. But as they persisted in their quest for, and orientation to the divine they found also a God who was attested in respect for the life and rights of one's neighbour, a God of justice. Biblical holiness is more a matter of justice than of spirituality or mysticism. The phrase 'I, the Lord, am holy' is appended to commandments concerning social justice (Lev 19). Further acquaintance with the God of justice revealed that he was also a God of mercy and forgiveness. A culture of justice could not come to fruition without becoming a culture of mercy and forgiveness as well, something we still need to learn. In the Christian dispensation we bring our sin to Christ and receive in exchange his righteousness, and in this more intimate exchange of human and divine all the rougher earlier projections of a fearful God of vengeance are allegorised or integrated as lower stages or, with Luther, as an 'alien work' of God, preparing his 'proper work' of forgiveness and redemption.

That is the general direction of the biblical trajectory, but in practice elements of the older projections persist unchanged even in such summit documents as the gospel of John, with its insidious polemic against 'the Jews'. Human nature shows its violent side even as it confides itself to the mercy of Christ, and the God it projects remains a barbaric killer or torturer. In defusing the notion of Christ's sacrifice of the idea than an angry God is calling for blood we might draw on the softer soteriology of Luke, for whom the death of Christ has a saving impact due to the remorse and conversion it inspires rather than as a blood-price.

The Bible sets up a vast dialectic about the idea of God, overcoming lower conceptions of God by higher ones, pathological ones by therapeutic ones. Yet this dialectic is not a completely unambiguous advance from lower to higher. The last book of the Bible is among its most violent, and the gospels themselves use too freely the language of dire threats and visions of torture. The dialectic continues in the interpretation of scripture across the centuries, as we learn to discern between the wholesome uses of the ancient text and its latent poisons. A canon within the canon emerges, and in practice the church proscribes the use of the more scandalous texts.

Today we can see scripture in historical and interreligious perspective with a clarity of vision that has no precedent. As we open ourselves to the challenge of scripture we need not be afraid to challenge it in return. 'Wrestling with difficult texts' is not a matter of apologetical acrobatics, but of frank pitting of our misgivings against what seems brutal in the old texts. The freedom with which Jewish exegesis tackles scripture, with the sense of equality that a son has before a Father, could be a model for a less constrained Christian relationship to the sacred texts.[15] Scripture often quarrels with itself. Jewish readers of scripture down the centuries have not hesitated to quarrel with God. The freedom of such a quarrelling hermeneutics can release in scripture the power to give illuminating ripostes to our questions. Reading the old violent texts today we think, 'That is how God spoke in those troubled times – how does he speak now?' The prophetic record becomes a stimulus to our own prophetic discernment as church.

The dialectical relationship thus opened up is full of paradoxes. The Bible was cited as a warrant for slavery, yet the Bible has been used as the greatest ideological weapon against slavery. Similarly the Bible has shored up patriarchy, yet if discerningly read it can become an effective weapon against patriarchy. The Bible has often been used to cement unjust relationships of power in society; to block progressive and democratic arrangements; to spread guilt and obscurantism about sexuality and

---

15. Declan Hurley points out, however, that 'Jewish interpretation allegorises and spiritualises the violent texts more than any other approach,' noting that 'much of Jewish exegesis of the Book of Job does its best to squirm out of any suggestion that the author intended to present a God who is capable of acting cruelly against one of his just servants.'

CHAPTER TEN

love; to foment suspicion and discrimination among peoples and faiths. Yet on all these fronts a discerning community can hear the Bible speak with another voice as well, and it is when the Bible is heard in this way that one recognises its power anew.

Christians judge the Bible not only from the standpoint of the modern conscience, but also under the impulsion of the Holy Spirit. The real, spiritual authority of scripture – its capacity to elicit faith and inspire hope – emerges when they wrestle with it in prayer and loving debate. They are moved to correct, in charity, Paul's occasional sexist, homophobic or anti-Semitic remarks, but they do so in order to free the core teachings of the apostle and make them audible today. They work on biblical traditions, cleansing them of their toxins, in order to retrieve them as living traditions for today.

The Christian Church has always enjoyed freedom over against scripture, seeing it as a book to be used. Revelation is not handed to one on a plate; it is an event that occurs when one reads scripture in community and in dialogue with the 'signs of the times', the phenomena of human joy and hope, war and reconciliation, need and promise, which were an essential point of reference in the theological thinking of the Hebrew prophets and which were again pointed to as an essential frame of reference by Vatican II. The theological claims about inspiration and inerrancy must be nuanced and modified in light of the actual dealings of the community with the hallowed text. These dealings have always been marked by selectivity; the community has trusted in its own instincts and in the leading of the Holy Spirit in deciding which texts in scripture spoke loudly and clearly and which others were best consigned to a decent obscurity.

For Christians the New Testament has been scripture in a more immediate sense than the old,[16] and its message has not been passed through the filter of allegorisation and other domesticating devices. Thus it is harder for Christians to attain a

---

16. As Joseph Ratzinger insists, in K. Rahner and J. Ratzinger, *Revelation and Tradition* (New York: Herder and Herder, 1966).

critical distance over against the New Testament. But gradually we are realising that no written words can be immediately identified with the Word of God. The words of scripture are exposed to all the vicissitudes of ancient historical writings, even at the level of textual transmission, and even such sublime writers as Paul and John were men of their time, using conceptual instruments that no longer fit contemporary mentalities. With Karl Barth we come to see scripture as attesting the Word of God, as a trace left by the long wrestling with the divine of the peoples of the old and new Covenants. We continue to develop that tradition, but critically, not taking any text of the past as a blueprint to be followed blindly. The same Spirit that confers on scripture its power is at work in the use and interpretation of scripture in the church today.

Fundamentalists in the Anglican Communion accuse alleged liberals of rejecting the sovereign authority of scripture over church. Yet the church has always lived in a perichoretic relationship to scripture. Scripture founds the church and embraces it; yet it is the church that established the canon of scripture and it is the present community of faithful who embrace scripture with their understanding and bring forth its sense for today. What in scripture becomes obtuse and unmeaningful cannot be cited as exemplifying that authority which scripture has over the church. There is no need to seek divine meaning in words that can perfectly well be explained by reference to the mores and mindsets of the ancient cultures in which they were formulated.

The Bible is a record of growth in the understanding of God from a primitive beginning, but the continuation of that growth depends on our own mature and responsible reading of the Bible. The Bible is a fictional machine for making God speak, by putting him on the stage in dialogue with human agents. Unless the dialogue continues today, the voice of God in scripture becomes a dead letter, or a crushing imposition.

Magical thinking stands in the way of this mature Christian use of sacred scripture. Such thinking embraces a literal understanding of scriptural sentences ripped from their contexts and thought to be transparently meaningful today. The sentences may be sheer absurdities – but that makes them all the more satisfying to one who brings the heuristic approach of magical thinking. A classic instance of magical literalism is Origen's alleged implementation of the gospel saying about becoming eunuchs for the sake of the kingdom.

To be sure, an element of magical thinking may be essential to religion: icons, relics, texts are merely what they are, but devoted love projects onto them numinous power, and they then indeed do become sites of healing and illumination. We must not banish such magic, but must translate it from the register of irrationality or superstition into that of a wise handling of 'skilful means'.

Some will resist the application in scriptural hermeneutics of wimpy contemporary notions of political correctness. They are happy that scripture is so full of blood, as it ensures the realism of the scriptural record. Mel Gibson's film, *The Passion of the Christ*, is praised on similar grounds, as bringing the terror of demonic violence, as unleashed against Christ, closer to modern consciousness. A sanitised Bible, pacifist and feminist and gay-friendly, would be as tasteless as the Pali Canon.

Yet the bloodlessness of Buddhist scriptures speaks a quiet word of reproach to us, urging us to advance to a new level of critical discernment in handling our own scriptures. Gloating over the defeat of enemies, even if they are God's enemies, and reveling in threats and fantasies of punishment, are attitudes that belong to a warlike culture. Scripture was born within such a culture, but ultimately tends to its overcoming, just as Buddhism overcomes the warlike culture of earlier Indian religion.[17]

---

17. Declan Hurley objects that the pacifism of Buddhist scriptures is facilitated in that they do not have the Old Testament concern with interpreting history through narrative. He adds: 'If the scriptures are a reflection on history, an attempt to see the guiding hand of God in the history of a people, the writer obviously has to deal with the issue of violence, because what people does not have its origin in violence? In that sense the Jewish scriptures are at least an honest acceptance of the

The lack at the origin

A Jewish psychoanalytical writer, born in Morocco, Daniel Sibony, has probed the dark side of monotheism. His work can be read in tandem with Karen Armstrong's work on Jewish, Christian and Islamic fundamentalism. Both writers help Christians to self-knowledge by showing them their own reflection in pathological aspects of Judaism and Islam.

All three religions live by a myth of the purity of their origins, a myth that breeds violence when it is threatened. Each religion offers a supremely satisfying identity, and the last word about the riddles of life and death. But supposing the identity is based on denial, on a papering over of cracks and flaws in its original construction? Some will attain intellectual and spiritual growth by opening up honestly to a recognition of these cracks and flaws. Others will see such honesty as apostasy and will bunker down in traditionalism and absolutism. The repressed insecurity of threatened identity will show itself in hostility to the rival who embodies the threat and becomes a scapegoat, as the Jews were for Christians throughout history. Throughout the centuries each of the three monotheisms proclaimed its own legitimacy in refuting that of the others. This fruitless apologetical debate is itself a fixational behaviour that indicates the true nature of the

---

violence inherent in Israel's history. The role of the exegete could therefore be one of helping contemporary communities to come to terms with their origin in bloodshed. Scripture then becomes a narrative of the tension between a people bathed in its own blood and that of its neighbours, and a God who continually calls that people to a different reality. There is something refreshingly honest and humble in both the Jewish and Christian approach to texts that are clearly obscene to modern consciousness. Just as the sacred writers who edited the sacred texts apparently never deleted anything but rather added to them and made corrective insertions, so today we leave what is there out of respect for it as a sacred text. Jesus replied to the question on divorce: 'It was because of your hardness of heart that Moses wrote this commandment' (Mk 10:5), and he then went to use scripture as its own critic. Applying this to a hermeneutic for interpreting the violent texts of the Jewish scriptures, one could say that in the Christian dispensation 'hardness of heart' can no longer justify the former injustices perpetrated out of fidelity to divine commandments.'

three religions. The splitting of human community into elect and reprobate, sheep and goats, is an intrinsically violent structure, pervasive in scripture. The teaching of Jesus, 'love your enemies', and his reaching across barriers to build inclusive community, go against this, but this is a virtuality that has to be drawn out of the texts by dint of careful spiritual and ethical discernment. In time of friction, this aspect of scripture is ignored; 'love your enemies' has hardly been the favoured slogan of the USA since 9/11. Instead the old dualism of good and evil comes into play.

The more relaxed vision of Vatican II marks a certain retreat of the question of identity, under the auspices of an inclusivism invoking the universality of grace and of divine self-revelation, in the spirit of the stories of Cornelius or of Paul's preaching at Athens in Acts and of the broad Logos-theology of the Apologists and the Alexandrian theologians of the second and third centuries. Unfortunately the spirit of sectarianism has revived as part of the general regression from the vision of Vatican II, tainting various Vatican documents such as *Dominus Iesus* (2000). The renewed worry about rival claims, which is causing ecumenism to flounder, perhaps indicates that ecumenical idealism about shared origins is bound to collapse back into the old game of 'my origin is better than yours'. Sibony proposes an alternative:

> Perhaps these three monotheistic currents will one day tolerate and pardon one another not because they derive from the same God and are 'brothers' (that kind of fraternity produces more wars than agreements, more rendings than ententes), but because they will find in themselves the same deficiency, the same type of infidelity to what founds them; because they will recognise themselves as children of the same original lack: each marked by a flaw at the origin, a flaw imputable to no one, in any case not to one's neighbour, a flaw intrinsic to the human and which other humans outside the religious field face as best they can.[18]

---

18. D. Sibony, *Les trois monothéismes: Juifs, Chrétiens, Musulmans entre leurs sources et leurs destins* (Paris: Seuil, 1997), 10.

A recognition of lack at the origin has surfaced occasionally in theology, only to meet with sharp repression, notably in the Modernist controversy. Some space must be made for what *Dominus Iesus* rejects, the sense that Christianity on its own is a broken and incomplete project, which needs to reach out humbly to other spiritual paths to find its proper role. Christ may be complete, but Christianity enjoys in practice only a very partial understanding of Christ and has to work on its legacy of deadly misunderstandings.

Recognition of the historical and unfinished nature of the Christian, Jewish and Islamic projects, and of the violent foreclosures that launched all three and that recur throughout their career, would certainly have a humbling effect on these traditions. Renouncing absolutism, they would think of themselves as modest and imperfect paths, and would refrain from brandishing the name of the God who unites and divides them as a warrant of legitimacy and superiority. Our construction of God is a powerful fiction, into which we have invested all sorts of delusive passions as well as the higher spiritual discernment that overcomes those passions. The voice of God in scripture is in the first place the voice of a dialectic going on within human consciousness, both individual and collective. The scandals of this discourse, even when canonised as infallible, bear witness to the divine in a negative mode : 'the ultimate is not here, seek it elsewhere', or perhaps, 'do not seek the ultimate at all, but live modestly in the conventional; do not seek certitude, but abide with questions'. This, of course, brings us into the vicinity of Buddhism, especially the Madhyamaka philosophy of conventional and ultimate reality and the Zen saying, 'If you meet the Buddha, slay the Buddha.'

It might be objected that if Christianity had begun by talking like this it would never have conquered the Roman Empire. It would have remained one of the spiritual talking shops of the ancient world, something like the Neoplatonists. No doubt we must discern in the rise of Christianity the powerful appeal of a liberating message on the one hand and abusive extrapolations on the other. In between them we can recognise necessary and legitimate moves, such as the formation of a strongly disciplined institutional church, which brought the danger of abuse. In the third century Origen honoured the critique of Christianity by Celsus, written eighty years earlier, with a long response in eight books. In the fourth century the critiques of Christianity by Porphyry and Julian, no doubt more informed and dangerous than Celsus, were unceremoniously burned. Repression replaced dialogue. The church was simply unprepared to meet the critical questions raised by these thinkers. Porphyry's demonstration of the inaccuracies in Daniel and the after-the-event status of its prophecies, for example, could have sparked an earlier birth of the historical-critical method in scriptural studies had the Fathers been able to face up to it honestly. But a battle for survival did not permit such disinterested investigations. Intra-Christian heretics received the same short shrift, their writings usually surviving only in quotations from orthodox opponents. The Vatican has apologised for certain excesses of certain Christians in their zeal for truth. But the violent repression of critical voices is coterminous with the exposition of Christian truth from Constantine to the nineteenth century. The insistence on the inerrancy of scripture is of a piece with this.

Psychoanalysis, like Buddhism, brings to awareness the passional projections that lay behind so much past certitudes and the coercion or violence to which they led. The history of the church and of Israel is largely – but not primarily – a record of these passions and delusions. To trace what is truly divine in it we must make a bonfire of our illusions, that is, not a casual or angry rejection of them but a penetrating analysis and dismantling, painfully, one by one.

For Sibony, religions are human constructions built in defence against feelings of peril, the anxiety of the unfounded, and the more religions become autonomous worlds (as the imaginative world of Israel and again that of the early church largely are) the more they give the measure of the fear they attempt to exorcise. Fortress religions seem unbeatable, the gates of hell cannot prevail against them, but the very necessity to build a fortress at all testifies to deep fear. Listening with the third ear to the questions, debates, solitary ruminations that religious themes arouse, one can detect in them a basic tone of anxiety. A sense of crisis, obscure guilt, a vision of the world as forgetting God or forgotten by God, rage against religious institutions, there are so many forms of religious maladjustment and alienation, and all of them have an intrinsic connection with the nature of religion itself. A false provision of origin cannot allay the anxiety of the lack of foundation. Detachment and trust are the religious response to the sickness of religion, a condition reached only by a working through of anxieties.

Defects at the basis of monotheistic constructions emerge in the course of their historical development. In Islam, a too great proximity of the divine voice, which speaks in the language of the people, prompts a too rigid adherence to the Qur'an that impedes modernisation and dialogue. The origin is too satisfying, too perfect, covering the original abyss with the veil of a fascinating language, that of the Qur'an; but this perfection 'encumbers it, prevents it from "moving" on the collective as well as on the individual plane, and seems to withdraw it from time and thus from history'.[19] The original imperfection engenders perpetual unease in the historical career of a religion. Denial can be sensed beneath the most firm affirmations, the secret suffering that they try to banish. Sibony sees the Jews as suffering secret guilt before the call of a God projected as demanding father, Muslims as suffering from the suffocating maternal fulness of their origin, Christianity as depending on the 'Christic *coup de force:* "an event of being" in which a man, Jesus, rises and fills or accomplishes the fault-lines of the Law'.[20] Sibony see the doctrine of forgiveness as another way of filling the existential fault indicated by the notion of God. Jesus merely 'gives them back God as the unforeseeable break that certainly is repaired and

---

19. Ibid., 19, 20.
20. D. Sibony, *Nom de Dieu: Par-delà les trois monothéismes* (Paris: Seuil, 2002), 19.

CHAPTER TEN

forgiven, but precisely they retain only the forgiveness'.[21] Religion is a play of anxious projections. God he sees as 'a figure of narcissism, individual or collective; narcissism of the origin, of identity, of becoming'.[22] 'If our reason does not reach "God", it is not because it is limited; it is that one cannot aim at a relation in which one is grasped and which operates exactly there where all our grasps fail; nor take for object a bond which serves us as subject or origin.'[23] In this situation, the distinction between belief and unbelief becomes secondary: 'The border passes between those who have a relation to that fault and those who do not'.[24]

Sibony may be in thrall to a Lacanian metaphysics of lack. The joy of the resurrection is a positive phenomenon, or rather a 'saturated phenomenon' (Jean-Luc Marion) that exceeds in reality the human categories we bring to bear on it. To reduce it to a violent coup does not do justice to the phenomenon. In general, humanity does not live from lack alone but from the givenness of the real on every level, a plenitude not a penury.

Buddhist vacuity accords with Sibony's God as lack. 'When that fault is filled in by a definitive call, this is named a "saviour". Today one thing is clear: the fault has triumphed over all the saviours, it traverses them.'[25] What if Jesus and the Buddha are saviours in virtue of their capacity to let themselves be traversed by the fault, by emptiness? Emptiness here does not triumph over salvation but is the key in which salvation is proclaimed.

'All that is is marked by a lack of being that makes of it a being in lack.'[26] We project onto God the same lack of being, in the passions he expresses in Genesis. The fullness of divine being bespeaks the sense of lack in those who project this vision of fullness. Buddhism takes its cue from that very sense of lack in order to open up to emptiness, rejecting characterisations of

---

21. Ibid., 61.
22. Ibid., 155.
23. Ibid., 234.
24. Ibid., 317.
25. Ibid., 318.
26. Ibid., 12.

the ultimate as fullness of being – these would be the heresy of substantialism or eternalism, which is considered just as poisonous as its opposite, annihilationism or nihilism. The texture of reality as we know it should be our guide to the nature of ultimate reality.

When scripture warns us not to aim at equality with God (Adam, the tower of Babel), could it not be read as warning us implicitly against the very projection of the kind of God that humans would wish to be – the projection of absolute power, immunity, self-sufficiency? From our very experience of lack and vulnerability can we not conceive of the divine otherwise, as some biblical texts begin to do? The inflated jargon of kenoticist theology, which has pressed the language of Buddhism into its service as well, misapprehends this need to rethink God as a kind of speculative gnosis. But the breakthrough required lies more in a dismantling of our false conceptions of God than in the erection of a new conception. Abiding patiently with the sense of lack, we trust in the graciousness of the ultimate.

In attempting to tackle the scandal of biblical violence, we find ourselves asking questions about the construction of monotheism itself and drawn into the project of rethinking the nature of the divine. This is not a vain exercise in speculation, but has a moral necessity, inspired not only by the modern conscience, but also, as I have tried to suggest, by the basic thrust of scripture itself. Scripture is not a dead letter but a text that comes alive whenever it is used as scripture, as a means for contemplating and sensing the presence of God. We know that it is not functioning properly when it produces rigid and violent mindsets. The overcoming of these, and of everything in the text that can breed them, is a necessary stage on the journey to a contemporary Spirit-filled understanding of the sacred text.

CHAPTER ELEVEN

A Response to Joseph O'Leary

Linda Hogan

I am grateful to Joseph O' Leary for his challenging and thought-provoking paper. There is no doubt that many aspects of his paper merit attention, and if this response afforded the opportunity to discuss the text thoroughly, one might explore further a number of points, including: how the absolutisation of individual life can become a form of idolatry rather than a form of respect; how the Christian tradition has made ill-fated and faltering exegetical and hermeneutical attempts to make sense of its 'texts of terror'; and how challenging for Christians is Sibony's comment that perhaps the three monotheistic currents will one day tolerate and pardon one another not because they derive from the same God and are 'brothers' but because they will find themselves with the same deficiency, the same type of infidelity to what founds them. Thus I expect that many listeners will have questions of this rich and complex paper to explore. In this short response, however, I wish to take up just one of the concerns that links this paper with one of the abiding themes in Enda McDonagh's theology, namely his concern with peace and his insistence that the eschatological dynamic within history requires that Christians be reconcilers, that they be peaceful justice-seekers.

It is a truism to acknowledge that the connections between religion and violence are complex and multifaceted. From the conflicts in Middle East and the Balkans to those in Southeast Asia and beyond, religion frames and legitimates political violence. Moreover, in international relations post-9/11 religious language and metaphors have acquired a new significance. In this context the emerging consensus appears to be not only that violence is intrinsic to religion, but also that religions incite, legitimate and intensify political violence. Indeed Professor O'Leary's reflection on scripturally sanctioned violence and the exegetical norms that the Christian tradition has generated gives a clear-sighted and compelling explanation of the dynamics involved with this strand of the tradition. However, as Professor O' Leary's paper also acknowledges, such an unambiguous indictment of religions is incomplete in that it fails both to appreciate the significant counter examples and to recognise the diversity that exists within religions on the issue of violence. Moreover, it ignores the religious roots of pacifism and the ethics of non-violence. Professor O' Leary's paper helps us to see how deeply rooted is this ambivalence about violence within the Christian tradition. But his paper also implicitly cautions us against limiting our discussion about violence to the religiously-sanctioned pathologies of holy war or just war. Indeed his paper also reminds us that if we focus on these pathologies exclusively then we deny the heart of the Christian tradition, its orientation towards the God of mercy and forgiveness.

A consistent feature of Professor McDonagh's work thus far has been his confidence that, notwithstanding the ambivalence that is present in the tradition, non-violence has a deeper claim on us than does violence. Jonathan Schell's recent work *Unconquerable World: Power, Nonviolence, and the Will of the People*,[1] makes a comparable claim, though his analysis is political and historical and he takes a wider view than one focusing solely on the Christian tradition. Schell does not deny that the twentieth century has been the bloodiest in history, nor does he believe that the move to non-violent action will come immediately, but what he does offer is an insight into a 'less-noticed, parallel history of nonviolent power'.[2] This is a story, as he says, of violence disrupted or in retreat – of great-power war immobilised by the nuclear stalemate, of brutal empires defeated by local peoples fighting for their self-determination, of revolutions

---

1. Jonathan Schell, *The Unconquerable World: Power, Nonviolence, and the Will of the People* (New York: Henry Holt and Company, 2003).
2. Ibid., 31.

CHAPTER ELEVEN

succeeding without violence, of democracy supplanting authoritarian or totalitarian repression, of national sovereignty yielding to systems of mixed and balanced powers.[3] It is the century of Mohandas Gandhi, Aung San Suu Kyi, Martin Luther King Jr., of Dorothy Day, Thomas Merton, the Berrigans, the Christian Peacemaker teams, the San Egidio and Mennonite peacemakers. In Ireland, though it has been a time in which political violence has recurred, it has also been a time in which Pax Christi, the Glencree Centre for Reconciliation, Encounter, the Irish Association and other organisations (with which Professor McDonagh has been centrally involved) have flourished. So Schell's book is in fact a chronicle of the good news of the twentieth century, and in the Irish context some of this good news too has been evident. Moreover, Schell notes the good news that, the violence of the last century notwithstanding, one can discern a slight, though significant, shift in the centre of gravity which, if nurtured, may provide a way of resisting the logic of violence which has captivated our political milieu.

Of course the purpose of Schell's book, mirroring the purpose of Professor McDonagh's work, is not merely to provide a chronicle, but rather to challenge us in our political analyses and action in the present. Schell argues in his book that the manner in which we narrate the past shapes the kind of future we can envision and enact. And so Schell's reading of our history is one which is dominated by conflict and violence, but one in which are discernible the seeds of reconciliation, peace and therefore hope.

Which leads me to an aspect of Professor McDonagh's current work that best embodies this preoccupation, namely, his joint appeal, with Stanley Hauerwas, 'to Christian Leaders and Theologians to Work for the Abolition of War'.[4] This beautifully

---

3. Schell, 305.
4. The text and comment are published in Hauerwas, 'Reflections on the "Appeal to Abolish War" or What Being a Friend of Enda's Got Me Into," in *Between Poetry and Politics: Essays in Honour of Enda McDonagh*, edited by Linda Hogan and Barbara Fitzgerald. (Dublin: Columba Press, 2003), 135-137

simple, yet audacious, proposal is that Christians should begin a discussion about war that would make war as morally problematic as slavery. Two hundred years ago, slavery not only existed but many people thought it was also morally unproblematic, and although slavery still exists, no one now thinks slavery can be morally justified. Thus the appeal is based on the claim that Christians have a moral imperative to work for the abolition of war. To this end it side-steps debates about whether the pacifist or just war traditions best reflect the tradition of the first centuries of Christian witness. Indeed, as Professor O' Leary's paper indicates, there is no simple way of resolving this debate.

Professor McDonagh's advocacy of a non-violent political ethic has become stronger and more persistent as his work has developed. He challenges us to consider why war has the grip it has on our moral imaginations, and why we so easily abandon politics and choose instead the unimaginative and destructive alternatives of violence. One could pursue this further to ask why the advocacy of non-violent solutions of conflict seem naïve or immoral, or finally how have we arrived at this place where our only vehicle for delivering populations from the complex synergy of poverty and violence is yet more violence. The 'appeal' and its subsequent development in a number of recent essays[5] challenges Christians to remember that they are gifted with and called to that flourishing in community in which to quote the psalmist 'justice and peace shall kiss'. Moreover, McDonagh claims that the 'eschatological character of this peace no more excludes its presence now as divine gift and its call to human beings to live it and further develop it any more than the eschatological character of justice excludes its urgent presence as gift and call.'[6]

There is no doubt that if we are to move beyond the logic of

---

5. See for example Stanley Hauerwas, Linda Hogan and Enda McDonagh, 'The Case for the Abolition of War in the Twenty-First Century', *Journal of the Society of Christian Ethics*, 25 (2005) 17-35 and 'From Shoa to Shalom' in McDonagh, *Vulnerable to the Holy*, (Dublin: Columba Press, 2004), 127-137.
6. Stanley Hauerwas, Linda Hogan and Enda McDonagh, 24

violence we need to find morally compelling and politically workable alternatives to war. But, as both Schell and McDonagh indicate, they do exist. The difficulty lies, not with our capacity to develop alternatives but in our failure to have a faith in and a commitment to the slow unglamorous work of non-violent political action. Yet, as Schell insists, 'the days when humanity can hope to save itself from force with force are over. None of the structures of violence – not the balance of power, not the balance of terror, not empire – can any longer rescue the world from the use of violence, now grown apocalyptic. Force can lead only to more force, not to peace. Only a turn to structures of cooperative power can offer hope.'[7] Through his theological and political work, Professor McDonagh pushes us endlessly to 'create peace in hope'. His prophetic and reconciling voice on this most contentious of topics was recognised recently when he was awarded the second Rosa Parks Peace Prize (Rosa Parks herself being the recipient of the inaugural prize). May he continue to disclose to us 'the arts of the possible'.

---

7. Schell, 345.

CHAPTER TWELVE

HIV/AIDS: The Expanding Ethical Challenge

James F. Keenan SJ

I broach anew the topic of HIV/AIDS with two central presuppositions. First, when Catholics hear the topic of Ethics and HIV/AIDS, they immediately think of 'condoms'; in order to get beyond condoms, so as to appreciate the complexity of the ethics challenge of HIV/AIDS, I shall offer no fewer than 10 topics for us to consider. Second, conversely, when others hear about the expanding ethical challenge of HIV/AIDS, they see the challenge as so vast, so foreboding, and so confounding that they throw up their hands and say, how can I do anything about this? For this reason I will direct the ten points to those who are in education, whether in theology, philosophy, nursing, secondary education, medical schools, university or graduate programming. I am speaking not as missionary, public health worker, physician, researcher, benefactor; I speak, rather, precisely as an educator to other educators, so as to confirm and to enlist my colleagues in the work of making HIV/AIDS an educational agenda item.

Let us begin then with the first topic: the urgency of the expanding ethical challenge as it impinges on us and our educational institutions.

I. THE EXCEPTIONALISM OF HIV/AIDS

On 8 February 2005, at the London School of Economics, Dr Peter Piot, Director of UNAIDS directly confronted the exceptionalism of HIV/AIDS. He asked, 'Is the AIDS pandemic so exceptional a threat that it is in a league altogether different to other infectious diseases or causes of ill health? Is the pandemic so exceptional a threat that its control should not be just one of many Millennium Development Goals but rather an overarching priority, a prerequisite to achieving the MDGs? Is the threat so exceptional that it demands a binding first call on the attention of political leaders as well as on finances? So exceptional that it demands that we undertake fundamental changes on many fronts if we are to succeed? Ladies and gentlemen: AIDS is exceptional. The response to AIDS needs to be equally exceptional.'

Piot offered four reasons for his claim regarding the exceptionalism of HIV/AIDS. First, he stated: 'an "epidemic equilibrium" or plateau is nowhere in sight – not globally, not at the level of epidemics in most countries, and not over the long term.'[1] The epidemic, then, is globalising rapidly; moreover, we can no longer locate it in certain hotspots either within a nation or region. It is diffuse. Consider this epidemiological information.

Although it was recognised only in 1981, by 1999 HIV/AIDS has become the 4th greatest cause of death in the world, accounting for 4.8% of all deaths worldwide and 3 million deaths per year (8,000 each day). In Sub-Saharan Africa AIDS is the leading cause of death, accounting for more than 1/5 of all deaths.[2] Today, with 42 million people living with HIV/AIDS and 25 million persons having died, 67 million persons have had their lives dramatically changed by this viral epidemic. Nearly 14,000 new infections occur every day, with the vast majority of these occurring in developing countries, through heterosexual transmission, by persons who are largely unaware of their HIV status. Half of new infections occur in women, and 2,000/day in persons younger than 15. The disease is not spreading evenly, however. Between 1999 and 2001, percentage increases of HIV-infected persons in various regions of the world ranged from a negligible increase in Australia and a 4% in North America, to an 89% increase in South/Southeast Asia and a 138% increase in Eastern Europe and Central Asia.[3]

---

1. Peter Piot, 'Why AIDS is exceptional' February 8, 2005 at http://www.aidsmatters.org/archives/100-Why-AIDS-is-Exceptional.html (March 20, 2005).
2. World Health Care Report, WHO, 2000.
3. UNAIDS.

AIDS has had a dramatic impact on duration of life, with adult life expectancy dropping by 15-33 years in some countries.[4] Although as recently as 2001 the UN had estimated that by mid-century the world's population would be reduced by at least 300 million because of the AIDS epidemic, that reduction has recently been revised to 480 million, with 47 million of the increased number of deaths expected to come from India and 40 million from China.[5] In short, not only has the epidemic not peaked in local areas, it has, instead, globalised: while in Botswana, Swaziland, and elsewhere in Southern Africa there is 40 per cent infection rate, we are seeing dramatic increases in Eastern Europe, India, China, and the Carribean. And now, India's 5.5 million people infected with the virus surpassed South Africa's 5.4 million.[6]

The second reason for insisting on the exceptionalism of HIV/AIDS is the exceptional nature of HIV's long gestation period that deceives us, so that the presence of the virus is not recognised until it is too late. This factor is very unusual because the HIV virus can remain undetected for up to six months after exposure. Moreover, without anti-retrovirals, it will develop into full blown AIDS, though maybe not for ten years.

Third, the impact on labour, economic and social infra-structures, and on children, is staggering. Consider this 'exceptional' data: by 2010, 1/10 children in sub-Saharan Africa will have lost one or both of their parents to AIDS (accounting for 29 million AIDS orphans). Countries such as the Central African Republic have closed more than 100 schools as a result of teacher deaths, and illness of parents often causes children (especially girls) to be pulled from school, both because of lack of school fees and because their efforts are needed to manage family farms.[7]

4. UN Department of Social and Economic Affairs, 2002, *World Population Prospects*, the 2000 Revision.
5. Naik, Gautam, 'HIV's Impact'.
6. 'India surpasses South Africa as Country with most HIV cases, Global Fund Director says,' Kaisernetwork.org, September 16, 2004 (available at http://www.kaisernetwork.org/daily_reports/print_report.cfm?DR_ID=25766&dr_cat=1)
7. UNAIDS, December 2001.

CHAPTER TWELVE

In response to growing numbers of unparented or poorly parented AIDS orphans living in large cities, in recognition of shrinking economies due to AIDS, and with HIV prevalence in some military populations as high as 60-90%,[8] the UN security council has met to discuss AIDS, not to consider its health ramifications, but because of the security implications of these numerous dramatic changes.[9]

Finally, HIV/Aids spreads predominantly through sexual activity and intravenous drug use. Inasmuch as there seems to be no soon-to-be-expected vaccine on the horizon, prevention becomes singularly important. But trying to persuade people to make behavioural changes in their lives, and being confronted simultaneously with a moral judgementalism from others, leaves the task of prevention with considerable handicaps.

These four factors – the absence of any epidemic equilibrium on the horizon, the deceptively long gestational period, the devastating impact on social and personal infrastructure, and the daunting behavioural challenges – make HIV/AIDS exceptional.

2. *The HIV/AIDS needs the help of Educators*

As the pandemic advances relentlessly we must examine ourselves critically, confronting the world, the church, and the academy by asking how, in 2007, after 26 years' experience, we are doing so poorly in the face of this epidemic? Those of us who work in educational institutes must especially ask: how well are we teaching?

This question was posed at a plenary session of the XVth International HIV/AIDS Conference held in Bangkok in July 2004 by Dr Mary Crewe of the Centre for the Study of AIDS at Pretoria University, South Africa. In light of such obvious failure, can we continue to educate as we do, or ought we to aim at a more transformative model of moral education?

In promoting the latter, Crewe reminds us that more than a third of all people living with HIV/AIDS are young people be-

---
8. Morin, Richard and Deane, Claudia, 'AIDS takes toll'.
9. Crossette, Barbara, 'Gore presides'.

tween the ages of 15 and 24, and almost two-thirds of these are girls. Crewe asks, 'Why is it left to young girls to bear the burden of the HIV/AIDS pandemic?' But as she poses this question in South Africa, those of us in the north are left with another question: How do we in the industrialised world teach 15-24 year olds at a time when their own generation in the developing world is so vulnerable? As we entertain this question, that is, as we seek to recast our educational institutions so as to transform our cultures and social structures, we must never lose sight of the primary concern that directly affects our students. To them, she says, we need to give a vision 'that they are valuable, rather than vulnerable.'[10]

I have noticed some developments, however. Last year, when I started teaching at Boston College, I offered a course for undergraduates entitled, 'HIV/AIDS and Ethics'. Fifty-seven students took it. What was particularly interesting is how much experience my students had. At least twenty students had already done immersion experiences in Africa, Latin America, or India. Others had done more local projects. But what they all lacked was academic studies that could complement their experience. They needed to read about the virus and its transmission, the narratives of the people infected and the people at risk; the issues related to prevention strategies and the need to develop more holistic and humane ones. They needed to know the power of stigmatisation and the role that cultures and churches have in promoting it. They need to understand the access programmes for people in the developing world, and the questions related to research and to patenting; and they needed to know where signs of hope are emerging. In short they needed an education.

This past year I offered the course again. I now have sixty-five students. Twenty-five of these have immersion experiences and many are going into such programmes next summer or next year. As undergraduates, these students have not yet begun

---

10. http://www.plusnews.org/AIDSReport.ASP?ReportID=3647 (May 12, 2005).

CHAPTER TWELVE

their professional degree programmes and so they can listen to their classmates wondering about how their areas of interest can be shaped by the pandemic. I have many students who say, I think I'm going into business, medicine, nursing, public health, communications, administration, journalism, philosophy, or theology, and I intend to see what I can do in that field for the people most immediately affected by the pandemic.

I have spoken at nearly two dozen universities of the need for course offerings in HIV/AIDS. At Boston College another faculty member, now in sociology, is offering an undergraduate course, and at each of the schools at which I speak and as I go around, one or two faculty tell me how they too are starting up courses on HIV/AIDS. So as to further this project, a student run network, entitled FACE/AIDS, will begin posting faculty syllabi of course offerings in HIV/AIDS for undergraduate students. We expect to become a catalyst for further, much needed courses.

3. Many Graduate Students in Theological Ethics Are Already Writing Theses and Dissertations on HIV/AIDS

James Olaitan Ajayi is a Nigerian diocesan priest whose dissertation at the Gregorian University was published; it focuses on the issues of economic justice and gender power dynamics as key concerns for addressing the pandemic.[11] Last year, Orbis Books published the dissertation of the Ursuline nun Maria Cimperman, in which she proposed a vision of the type of people we ought to become in a time of HIV/AIDS, and central to her claims is the call to be merciful.[12] Paterne-Auxence Mombe, a Jesuit from the Central African Republic, has just published his first book which details comprehensive care for persons living with HIV, *Rays of Hope: Managing HIV and AIDS in Africa*.[13] A

---

11. James Olaitan Ajayi, *The HIV/AIDS Epidemic in Nigeria: Some Considerations* 'Tesi Gregoriana, Serie Teologia, 93' (Rome: Gregorian University Press, 2003).
12. Maria Cimperman, *Fundamental Ethics in an Age of AIDS*, Ph.D. dissertation, Boston College, 2003.
13. Paterne-Auxence Mombe, *Rays of Hope: Managing HIV and AIDS in Africa* (Nairobi: Paulines Publications Africa, 2004).

French Assumptionist priest and AIDS physician is doing his dissertation on an ethics of vulnerability in a time of HIV/AIDS using the work of Enda McDonagh. Another French priest and physician, the Dominican Bertrand Lebouche, is finishing his dissertation on HIV/Aids and religion and has already published a book with Editions du Cerf, *Où es-tu quand j'ai mal?*[14] Ireland's Suzanne Mulligan finished her doctoral research at Maynooth on AIDS in South Africa, and is now teaching an HIV/AIDS and ethics courses at Milltown Park. The prolific writer turned doctoral student Gillian Paterson is finishing her doctorate on stigma and HIV/AIDS at Heythrop College. The Nigerian Jesuit, Agbonkhianmeghe E. Orobator, who did his dissertation in Leeds, has published with Paulines Publications, Africa, and now as the new rector of Hekima College in Nairobi teaches courses on HIV/AIDS and ethics at that school of theology. Incidentally, at the conference in Padova, the first International Crosscultural Conference for Catholic Theological Ethics, twelve of these new scholars were involved on panels on the specific topic of HIV/AIDS. Those papers prompted Mary-Jo Iozzio to invite thirty women moral theologians from across the globe to contribute to *Calling for Justice throughout the World: Catholic Women Theologians Considering the Moral Ramifications of the HIV/AIDS Pandemic*, published 2009 by Continuum.

Anyone looking to teach HIV/AIDS and ethics does not have to worry about a dearth of literature on the topic. New scholars worldwide are breaking important new ground in the field of HIV/AIDS.

4. *What These Works Reveal Is that People Most Affected by the Virus Live in Very Unstable Environments*

HIV/AIDS thrives where there is instability, a notion that is extremely important to appreciate. Those who are viewed as being 'marginalised' in any society are commonly described as those most at risk for acquiring HIV infection, but this characteris-

---

14. Bertrand Lebouché and Anne Lécu, *Où es-tu quand j'ai mal?* (Paris: Cerf, 2005).

ation, 'marginalisation,' doesn't quite get to the core of their vulnerability. HIV/AIDS breeds specifically where there is social instability, whether that means those who are affected by civil strife, military incursions or liberation armies in Uganda, Haiti, Sudan, or the Congo; those who are refugees in any part of the world; those in the prisons of Russia; those married to South African or Indian truck drivers who themselves live in very unstable worlds; those in debt-ridden nations on the verge of economic collapse; heads of families forced to migrate for employment, and those at home who await them; those who are drug addicts, whose own apprehension of themselves is itself unstable; those who are forced into sexual activity to support their children, their families, or their school fees; those who are overseas workers and fishermen; those who engage in clandestine homosexual activity in homophobic societies; or those girls and young women who are faithful to their marriages or to other stable sexual relationships, but whose husbands or partners put them at risk because of external sexual liaisons. In short, if we look for persons at risk for the virus or already infected by it, they are not simply marginalised people. They are people who are vulnerable precisely because their lives and their social settings lack the stability needed to live safely in a time of HIV/AIDS.

The economist Jeffrey Sachs emphasises the importance of this concept of instability when he writes, 'Since September 11 2001, the US launched a war on terrorism, but it has neglected the deeper causes of global instability. The nearly $500 billion that the US will spend this year on the military will never buy lasting peace if the US continues to spend only one-thirtieth of that – around $16 billion – to address the poorest of the poor, whose societies are destabilised by extreme poverty.'[15]

Sachs also notes that disease locks these unstable environments in with a barrier called infectious disease. He writes: 'Disease is not only a tragedy in human lives, disease is disaster for economic development ... the major reasons why many of

---

15. Jeffrey Sachs, 'The End of Poverty,' *Time*, March 6, 2005.

the poorest countries in the world, particularly but not exclusively in sub-Saharan Africa, are stuck in poverty is that the disease barrier is so great that it is blocking many different normal avenues of economic advance'.[16]

Buttressed against this barrier of disease within which instability thrives, more stable societies and institutions (including churches) create their own protective barriers. Again, Piot reminds us that 'the barriers to prompt and effective action are immeasurably magnified by taboo, denial and prejudice'.[17] This strategy is remarkable because in an almost perverse way these defensive barriers on the part of leaders in strong, stable cultures are antithetical to the attempts of ethicists, public health officials and clinicians to keep the most vulnerable persons uninfected. As opposed to supporting those public health preventive strategies (condoms, needle exchange, preventive education) which protect HIV-vulnerable individuals, some leaders and members of their societies perceive that the better and more important shields are those that keep risky individuals distanced from 'the general population,' or that are perceived as protecting social mores and orthodoxy from contamination.

5. *The Work of Shame, Stigmatisation and Moral Judgementalism Manages to Keep Those Most Affected by the Pandemic in Their Dangerously Unstable Worlds*

The strategy of keeping a distance is often backed by a deep moral judgementalism, whether explicitly stated or not. In his new book, *Breaking the Conspiracy of Silence: Christian Churches and the Global AIDS Crisis*, the Evangelical theologian Donald Messer examines compelling data from the HIV/AIDS pandemic and finds a church leadership that stands pathetically aloof, righteous, and judgemental. He appeals to several surveys, among them an informal one taken at a World Council of

---

16. Jeffrey Sachs, *Winning the Fight against Disease: A New Global Strategy*. Keynote Address to the 2003 Fulbright Scholar Conference, April 2, 2003, 1.
17. Ibid.

CHAPTER TWELVE

Churches gathering in Harare, Zimbabwe in 1998, in which 68 percent said they believed the pandemic to be a punishment from God. Only 48 per cent were willing as leaders to respond to church members with the virus, and only 25 percent would educate youth about related issues of sexuality and drug use.[18]

Moral judgementalism depends powerfully on the capacity to blame. This blame is deeply tied to the belief that those living in unstable situations cannot be trusted, and ought not to be admitted to the stable 'inner circle' of society. Moreover, since their condition is in many cases presumed to be their own fault, it does not merit the sympathetic, supportive, humanitarian response that other catastrophes prompt.

For example, the number of lives lost to the Indian Ocean Tsunami approached 300,000. This tragedy generated billions of dollars of supportive response worldwide immediately. Although HIV/AIDS causes the same number of deaths every 37 days, the will to commit concomitant resources to prevent such loss of life simply does not exist. Not only that, but if every 37 days another tsunami were to occur, we would witness a global effort of the highest priority creating a wall protecting all of humanity against the threat of such tsunamis. Faced with the fact that the HIV/AIDS pandemic does sustain the loss of ten tsunamis a year, we find no such interest in building a wall against the 'sea' of the virus. Desiring to protect ourselves from those at risk, we build a barrier against those living in unstable worlds. The biblical tradition of Job, whose narrative contradicts the deep-seated belief that we are the authors of our own troubles, apparently has no claim here.

6. A Central Task for Educators Today Is to Help Humanise the Face of HIV/AIDS

Eight years ago I invited Kevin Kelly and Enda McDonagh to join Jon Fuller, Lisa Cahill, Bob Vitillo and me in Boston to discuss a book project which later became *Catholic Ethicists on*

---

18. Donald Messer, Breaking the Conspiracy of Silence: Christian Churches and the Global AIDS Crisis, (Minneapolis: Fortress Press, 2004) 5-7.

HIV/AIDS Prevention. Today I use this book along with Donald Messer's in my course on HIV/AIDS. In our book, there are eight essays on such topics as how both the Catholic moral and Catholic bioethical tradition develops, on how casuistry works, on what are the issues of gender inequity and social justice, and Enda's fine essay on the kingdom of God; there are also twenty-seven other ones that describe cases from specific countries about the difficulties people face in unstable environs concerning local issues regarding prevention. My students love these cases.

I just finished sixty-five oral exams and when I asked the students what was the key learning experience for them in the first third of the course, it was not the data, but rather the narratives of these cases. For instance, they admire the character, described by Linda Hogan, of the Irish nun Sr Mary who, in trying to reach out to younger people in unstable families and settings, teaches them all the strategies involved in prevention and in doing that jeopardises her own relationship with the local church and even her religious community. Similarly they cite Peter Harvey's deeply troubling narrative about a woman who finally finds some stability in her life, only to have it robbed by the diagnosis of HIV/AIDS contracted precisely as she lived a life of turmoil. But the church, as Kevin Kelly notes in his essay, rather than acknowledging that the body of Christ has AIDS, distances itself from the woman's life by a profound moral barrier that alienates her from what was once her community of faith. The students are drawn in the same direction as they read the essays in Paul Farmer's landmark work, *Women, Poverty, and AIDS*.[19] There too they vividly report the encounters they had in the people they met in these essays.

In one narrative after another the students meet a never-before-seen person, and they enter into the narrative of her or his unstable life. One story was about the Ugandan Noreen

---

19. Paul Farmer, Margaret Connors, Janie Simmons, ed., *Women, Poverty and AIDS* (Monroe, Me: Common Courage Press, 1996.)

CHAPTER TWELVE

Kaleeba, whose family was devastated when her husband became infected, but Kaleeba found stability for her and her husband, and then built an international organisation to welcome others into her world. Two students were so moved by it that they contacted the author, Ugandan moralist John Mary Waliggo, and are going to stay with her for the summer. They literally are entering these narratives.

Students already having had immersion experiences fill out these portraits with their own accounts of their own encounters. In returning home, they are reporting what they have seen and what they have heard. I find these people are the new evangelisers, affirming our narratives, they are humanising the face of HIV/AIDS. As their generation comes under greater and greater siege throughout the world, they are introducing their classmates and their families and their professors to the people beyond the barriers.

7. Facing Prevention and Specifically the Condom
Because rates of infection are outdistancing rates of treatment, the issue of effective prevention strategies is even more urgent today than ever. Among these, the so-called ABC strategy is considered the most effective programme: A: Abstain; delay onset of intercourse until marriage. If you can't abstain, or are already in a sexual relationship, then B: Be faithful to that partner. If you choose (or do not have the freedom to say 'no' to) sexual relations, then C: use a Condom.

How reliable is the condom? We should acknowledge that condoms are not 100% reliable and that they can break, degrade under improper storage conditions or with inappropriate (petroleum-based) lubricants, and be poorly manufactured and incorrectly used. However, arguments that condoms provide no protection are refuted by studies involving their actual use. The largest analysis of published, peer-reviewed studies looking at the question of condom effectiveness was produced by the National Institute of Allergy and Infectious Diseases of the National Institutes of Health, USA, in July 2001. There it was noted that HIV is a very inefficiently transmitted infection when compared with other sexually transmitted diseases. For example, a single exposure to gonorrhea causes infection in 60%-80% of women. In contrast, after a single exposure to HIV, only 0.1% -0.2% of women become infected. The study found that use of condoms reduces the already low transmission rate of HIV by 85%. If one applied these data to 10,000 persons being exposed to HIV during sexual intercourse over a period of one year, in the absence of condoms 670 would become infected, but that number would be reduced to 90 if condoms were used consistently and correctly. The conclusion is clear: condoms are not perfect, but for those who choose (or are forced into) sexual contact, significant protection is afforded by this method.[20]

In view of such evidence of the effectiveness of condoms, Monsignor Georges Cottier, OP, then theologian of the papal household of Pope John Paul II and now Cardinal president of the International Theological Commission, was asked in an interview with Vatican Radio whether condom distribution might qualify as a 'lesser of two evils' approach. He responded: 'This is the question that moralists are asking themselves, and it is legitimate that they ask it.'[21] A few moral theologians, notably Kevin Kelly, have argued that any teaching on the condom inevitably must grapple with the teaching on contraception. Kelly argues that the teaching on birth control is itself the source of numerous dilemmas for Catholics, and that the issue of HIV prevention helps highlight the need to develop a more responsible birth control teaching.[22]

Others have argued differently, applying casuistic moral principles (lesser-evil, double effect, co-operation) to demon-

20. National Institute of Allergy and Infectious Diseases, National Institutes of Health, Department of Health and Human Services, 'Scientific evidence on condom effectiveness for sexually transmitted disease (STD) prevention', 20 July 2001 (available at http://www.niaid.nih.gov/dmid/stds/condomreport.pdf).
21. Catholic News Service, 'Papal theologian: AIDS-condoms issue legitimate to debate', 15 February 1996.
22. Kevin Kelly, *New Directions in Sexual Ethics: Moral Theology and the Challenge of AIDS* (London: Geoffrey Chapman, London, 1998.)

strate the compatibility of magisterial teaching on birth control with effective HIV/AIDS prevention methods.[23] These emphasise that in the case of HIV, the condom is not being used as a contraceptive device, but as a prophylactic against transmitting a deadly disease. They show how traditional principles acknowledge the legitimacy of such a distinction, and defend condoms for HIV/AIDS prevention while upholding – or at least not contesting – the validity of church teaching on contraception.[24] That distinction – between the therapeutic and the contraceptive – is found in *Humanae vitae*: 'The church does not consider at all illicit the use of those therapeutic means necessary to cure bodily diseases, even if a foreseeable impediment to procreation should result there from – provided such impediment is not directly intended for any motive whatsoever (paragraph 19)'.

These theologians have taken the casuistic position simply to acknowledge that bishops could support condom use without opposing *Humanae vitae*. Yet, twenty years later, moral theologians and many other Catholics are confounded by their hierarchy who persist in opposing condom usage by invoking the immutability of the birth control teaching. Catholics are astonished not simply because they are convinced of condom efficacy, but because their bishops seem to value their own teaching over the lives of those at risk: the present crisis is ultimately a threat to life itself, and not just a threat to sexual mores. The issue of protecting life, the heart of HIV/AIDS prevention strategies, does not appear to be at the forefront of their priorities. Thus, Melinda Gates echoed well the sentiments of many Catholics when she stated at the XVI International AIDS Conference: 'In the fight against AIDS, condoms save lives. If you oppose the

---

23. An application of each of the principles is made in Fuller and Keenan, 'Condoms, Catholics and HIV/AIDS Prevention,' *The Furrow* 52 (2001) 459-467.

24. For a review of these theologians' works, James F. Keenan, ed., assisted by Lisa Sowle Cahill, Jon Fuller, and Kevin Kelly, *Catholic Ethicists on HIV/AIDS Prevention* (New York: Continuum, 2000) 21-29 (Herein, Catholic Ethicists).

distribution of condoms, something is more important to you than saving lives.'[25]

Because of continued pressure from ethicists, public health officials, world leaders, and some of their own more enlightened brother bishops, these bishops will inevitably recognise the moral validity of the condom as part of a prevention strategy. As they do, they will need to decide whether to repudiate the birth control teaching entirely or to take the casuistic road and distance condoms as therapeutic from condoms as contraceptive. In any event, until they do, they undermine their own authority and leave many millions of lives at considerably more risk than they need to be.[26]

8. Concepts, Language and Advocacy Regarding Prevention and Access to Treatment

By this point, as educators we are realising how relevant concepts and language are for broaching the subject of HIV/AIDS. As the casuist Albert Jonsen notes, 'The public language ... of AIDS is as important as the science.'[27] In 1997, Jonathan Mann reflected on this claim and argued that the issue of casting a conceptual framework for ethically and politically analysing HIV/AIDS was urgent. To make his point, Mann put before public health officials a long recognised but rarely addressed insight: 'It is clear, throughout history and in all societies, that the rich live generally longer and healthier lives than the poor.'[28] In light

---

25. Melinda Gates, 'Address to the XVI International AIDS Conference, Toronto, August 13, 2006. http://64.233.161.104/search?q=cache: aXAhgbMiDxEJ:www.gatesfoundation.org/MediaCenter/Speeches/ MelindaSpeeches/MFGSpeech2006AIDS-060813.htm+Gates+%22oppose+the+distribution+of+condoms,+something+is+more%22&hl=en &gl=us&ct=clnk&cd=5 (visited 10/6/06)
26. Fuller and Keenan, 'Church Politics and HIV Prevention: Why is the Condom Question So Significant and So Neuralgic?' Linda Hogan and Barbara FitzGerald, eds, *Between Poetry and Politics, Essays in Honour of Enda McDonagh*, (Dublin, Columba Press, 2003) 158-181.
27. Albert Jonsen, 'Foreword,' E. Juengst and B. Koenig, eds, *The Meaning of AIDS*, (New York: Praeger Publishers, 1989).
28. Jonathan Mann, 'Medicine and Public Health, Ethics and Human Rights,' *The Hastings Center Report 27* (1997) 6-13.

CHAPTER TWELVE

of this one must ask, why then was the issue of poverty so rarely incorporated into the language of public health ethics? If poverty is so much a cause of the spread of disease, why wasn't poverty incorporated into the analyses and strategies of public health officials? Mann answered that 'Public health has lacked a conceptual framework for identifying and analysing the essential societal factors that represent the conditions in which people can be healthy.'

The language of bioethics until that point was based on principles like autonomy, beneficence, and non-maleficence; these principles gave the shape of a bioethics primarily concerned with the individual physician-patient relationship. But Mann was looking at the developing world, where many people do not have a physician let alone a relationship with one. Rather than using a language driven by individual relationships, he was looking for something that could analyse the social context in which people were both sick and poor. That is when Mann discovered in the language of human rights its integral comprehensiveness and moral urgency. Human rights language could link global campaigns for the right to access available medical treatments with equally effective and local strategic movements to obtain greater equality in political, economic and social forms of life.

Mann's work gave rise to two claims. First, Paul Farmer looked at the inequity of social institutions and how they embody 'virulent pathologies of power'. Reflecting on the deep connection between poor health and poverty, he saw the root causes of disease as being connected more to economics than to biology. He became particularly aware of the underlying social issues which made possible 'structural violence' against women and girls.[29] From a different perspective, Jeffrey Sachs studied

---

29. P. Farmer, M. Connors, and J. Simmons J, eds, *Women, Poverty and AIDS: Sex, Drugs and Structural Violence*, (Monroe, ME: Common Courage Press, 1996); P. Farmer, *Pathologies of Power: Health, Human Rights and New War on the Poor*, (Berkley: University of California Press, 1998); P. Farmer, *Infections and Inequalities: The Modern Plagues* (Berkley: University of California Press, 2002).

how disease affects social structures, that is, how disease makes people poor. While poverty certainly creates the conditions by which people become at risk for poor health, disease destroys their ability to escape from the very context that made them susceptible to ill health in the first place. 'Disease is not only a tragedy in human lives, disease is disaster for economic development.'[30] Coming from contrary perspectives, Farmer and Sachs did not contradict one another: rather, they keep us on track to see the deep and interlocking connections between poverty and disease.

Theological ethicists have paralleled these developments by bringing the language of the common good, social justice, solidarity and the option for the poor into their discourse. In many ways Lisa Sowle Cahill pioneered this shift, by engaging the traditional language of Catholic social justice so as to prompt us to be more attentive to issues of power and the distribution of resources.[31] Like public health officials, we ethicists realise that we cannot make the claims of what is fair unless we have the conceptual framework to understand and analyse why there are inequities and how they can be resolved. For this reason, ethicists have been able to examine many issues, for instance the issue of patenting and access to anti-retroviral medicines. What was once considered a simple issue of intellectual property is now confronted by the claims of the human right to basic urgent life-saving goods.[32]

---

30. Sachs J. 'Winning the Fight against Disease: A New Global Strategy' Keynote Address to the 2003 Fulbright Scholar Conference, April 2, 2003, 2 http://www.earth.columbia.edu/about/director/pubs/FulbrightSpeech0403.pdf#search=%22%22disease%20is%20disaster%20for%20economic%20development%22%22 (last visited, 10/6/06).
31. Lisa Sowle Cahill, *Theological Bioethics: Participation, Justice, Change* (Washington, DC: Georgetown University Press, 2005; Jon Fuller and James Keenan, 'The Language of Human Rights and Social Justice in the Face of HIV/AIDS,' *Budhi: A Journal of Ideas and Culture 8* (2004) 211-233.
32. Lisa Sowle Cahill, 'AIDS, Justice, and the Common Good,' *Catholic Ethicists* 282-293; Edwin Vasquez, *HIV/AIDS Epidemic, A Global Health Emergency: A Catholic Common-Good Approach to Patent Law Regarding AIDS Drugs*, STD dissertation, Weston Jesuit School of Theology, 2005.

This attentiveness to social justice and human rights also offers us analytical resources to address the underlying causes for on-going transmissions and therein lead us to more effective and comprehensive strategies for prevention. Here especially we can investigate better why women are so at risk today and why gender equity is such a needed component to HIV/AIDS prevention. The languages of human rights and social justice not only reveal to us that sexism and classism are causes of HIV/AIDS transmission, they also provide us a framework to investigate the proper ways of bringing such power inequities to an end.

9. Critically Considering the Care, Cultural Context, and Actual Delivery of Healthcare
As we become more familiar with the destabilising worlds where HIV/AIDS thrives, we are still going to need to respect the integrities of those environs. One of the most fundamental areas of investigation concerns the use of industrialised medicine and technology to respond locally to the crisis both to prevent transmission and to treat those already infected. While the initiatives are gravely needed, questions regarding the context of the local culture and the humaneness of the care being offered have been repeatedly raised by theological ethicists.

Occasionally, the attempt to respond to the HIV/AIDS crisis looks like an industrialised western military operation seeking to correct and remedy all that it perceives as wrong in a local setting. The language of 'targeting populations' and 'destroying the virus' capabilities' contribute to this perception. More problematic, however, are the way these operations often overrun existing infractures of local healthcare. These problems often arise from a failure to appreciate that healing and healthcare occur and are determined by local culture.

Four examples from *Catholic Ethicists on HIV/AIDS Prevention* help highlight how western technology has overlooked local context in HIV/AIDS treatment: Tanzania's Laurenti Magesa writes of the alienation of witch doctors and other African religion leaders from local prevention and treatment programmes in his native Tanzania; Mark Miller describes how the failures and successes in prevention strategies in western Canada depended on a direct engagement of first nation communities there; James Good recounts the unanticipated problems that faced those seeking to treat nomads in Kenya; and Paul Farmer and David Walton described the naïvete of condom distributors working in Haiti. There are many, many other instances.[33]

Inevitably, the turn to local culture raises a question regarding the quality and humanity of healthcare: does technology promote or reduce the humanity of healthcare delivery?[34] For instance, the hype that accompanies pharmacological capabilities often becomes more fascinating than the predicament in which HIV infected patients find themselves to be. The Ugandan theologian Emmanuel Katongole has raised a ringing critique of the inhumanity of certain policies that singularly rely on drugs and impoverish the overall tenor of healthcare in Africa.[35] (This is like focusing singularly on condoms without looking at the more comprehensive issues of sexuality, a point made brilliantly by CAFOD's Ann Smith in the London *Tablet*). These critical stances highlight how moral theologians must be alive to the possibility that the mode of delivery of much needed drugs could dangerously compromise local values and customs, as well as objectify and dehumanise the recipients of care and their care givers. In the light of the stigma still so deeply attached to HIV/AIDS, the question of the humanity and the context of healthcare is paramount.[36]

33. Laurenti Magesa, 'Recognizing the Reality of African Religion in Tanzania,' *Catholic Ethicists* 76-83; Mark Miller, 'Unmaking a Hidden Epidemic among First Nation Communities in Canada,' ibid., 84-91; James Good, 'HIV/AIDS among Desert Nomads in Kenya,' ibid., 91-96; Paul Farmer and David Walton, 'Condoms, Coups, and the Ideology of Prevention: Facing Failure in Rural Haiti,' ibid., 108-119.
34. Sharon R. Kaufman, *And a Time to Die: How American Hospitals Shape the End of Life* (New York: Scribner, 2005); Lebouché and Lécu, *Où es-tu quand j'ai mal?*
35. Emmanuel Katongole, 'AIDS, Africa, and the 'Age of Miraculous Medicine',' Padova.
36. On the issue of stigma see the essays by Linda Hogan, John Mary Waliggo, and NicholasPeter Harvey in *Catholic Ethicists*.

Theological ethicists need to be vigilant also about the research that more and more pharmaceutical companies are conducting in the developing world. In 1997 for instance, an extraordinary debate arose over experiments concerning drug programmes to inhibit transmission from mother to fetus.[37] That debate examined whether there were any grounds for compromising research protocols that normally hold universally. Do dire straits prompt us to suspend standards? If so, who bears the burdens when these standards are compromised? Our vigilance is imperative especially as microbicide investigations get underway.

10. Let Us Bridge the Gap and Become Sensitive Educators of HIV/AIDS
If bridging the gap between unstable and stable environs is what we must do, how do we do it? First, we must promote greater dialogue among advocates of these two very different strategies: those who are bridge-builders and those who are barrier builders. Through education and respectful conversation we must find appropriate means to build common ground, and especially to name and to raise up as models effective bridge-builders. Here I think of Kaleeba, Katongole, Cahill, McDonagh, Fuller and many others already mentioned. But I also think of the work of CAFOD (the Catholic Fund for Overseas Development of the Bishops of England and Wales) through its brave and well-argued attempts to confront the contemporary Catholic tendency to retrenchment and purity as opposed to the risks of mercy;[38] of Yale Divinity School's Margaret Farley, a Sister of Mercy, who established a circle of women in Africa to share in discourse about their experience of the pandemic and their role as care-givers in it;[39] and, finally, of Bishop Kevin Dowling's re-

---

37. Ronald Bayer, 'The debate over maternal-fetal HIV transmission prevention trials in Africa, Asia, and the Caribbean: Racist exploitation or exploitation of racism?,' *American Journal of Public Health* 88 (1998): 567-70.
38. http://www.cafod.org.uk/policy_and_analysis/commenteditorial/hiv_debate/tablet_article (March 20, 2005)
39. Margaret Farley, 'Partnership in Hope: Gender, Faith, and Responses to HIV/AIDS in Africa,' *The Mighty and the Almighty: Foreign Policy and God,* Yale Divinity School 2004, 16-20.

lentless efforts to move his brother bishops in South Africa to endorse effective prevention strategies and to promote a healthy and realistic discourse on sexuality.[40]

In his attempt to bridge the gaps, Donald Messer confronts the churches' need to advance AIDS prevention. He specifically challenges them to ask whether the messages of mercy, forgiveness and compassion have not been compromised by a barrier-driving agenda of purity, law, and judgement. Messer argues that not only is the welfare of those at risk for HIV infection being threatened by these approaches, but that the very integrity of the Christian character is also being jeopardised. Messer insists that AIDS is not a dirty word, and exhorts us to follow the example of Jesus. He outlines and examines seven stages toward a platform for a call to action: challenge the sexual practices of men; provide behavioural change education for men and women; reach out to the most impoverished women; reject patriarchal structures of church; champion human rights legislation and eradicate gender inequities; help women to protect themselves against HIV/AIDS and receive proper healthcare; protect the well-being of children.

Echoing both Mary Crewe and Enda McDonagh,[41] Kevin Kelly has proposed a new theology of AIDS and of sexuality that will reawaken us not only to the needs of those infected or at risk of becoming infected, but indeed to the very kenotic essence of the church.[42] Toward that end, we need then to draw our attention not only to those at risk, but also to those who create the barriers. We must remind them that for their own sakes they

---

40. Jon D. Fuller and James F. Keenan, 'Church Politics and HIV Prevention: Why is the Condom Question So Significant and So Neuralgic?,' Linda Hogan and Barbara FitzGerald, eds, *Between Poetry and Politics, Essays in Honour of Enda McDonagh* (Dublin, Columba Press, 2003)158-181.
41. Enda McDonagh, 'Theology in a Time of AIDS,' at http://www.cafod.org.uk/resources/worship/theological_articles/theology_in_a_time_of_aids (March 21, 2005); 'The Reign of God: Signposts for Catholic Moral Theology,' *Catholic Ethicists* 317-323.
42. Kevin T. Kelly, *New Directions in Sexual Ethics: Moral Theology and the Challenge of AIDS* (Geoffrey Chapman, London, 1998.)

must bridge this gap. This is what the gospels command, whether in the last judgement of Matthew 25 or in the Lucan Good Samaritan parable. In these and other instances, Christ's fundamental command is to be merciful. And as we see in the Good Samaritan story, the call to be merciful often requires us to sacrifice our desire to maintain purity.

What is mercy? I define it as 'the willingness to enter into the chaos of another.' I believe mercy embodies the heart of Catholic moral education.[43] On this note, then, I close by commenting on the church's merciful historical response in the face of another dangerous epidemic transmitted through sexual relations wherein instability and barriers played a very important role: the syphilis epidemic at the end of the fifteenth century.

In 1497, the *Compagnia del Divino Amore* (Confraternity of Divine Love) was founded in Genoa in 1497 by Chancellor of the Republic Ettore Vernazza as a group of laity and clergy committed to working for those suffering from shame: the poor, the prostitute and the syphilitic. Victims of syphilis, having been abandoned both by their families because of shame and by hospitals because of fear of contagion, found a welcome in the confraternity's *'gli ospedali degli incurabili'* (Hospitals for the Incurables). In 1499 they built the first hospital for the incurables in Genoa. In 1510 Saint Gaetano da Thiene built a hospital for the incurables in Rome at the church of Saint James on the Via Flaminia, so as to care for the piligrims who fell victim to syphilis on the pilgrimage to Rome! In 1517, the confraternity built 'the Hospital of Mercy' in Verona. Shortly thereafter Gaetano went to Vicenza to reorganise 'the Hospital of Mercy' there to serve the syphilitic. In 1521 the *Ospedale degli Incurabili* was opened in Brescia, and in 1522 Gaetano opened a hospital, still standing today, in Venice. In the same year a Confraternity chapter is founded in Padova, and within four years the mem-

---

43. Keenan, *The Works of Mercy: The Heart of Catholicism* (Lanham, Md: Sheed and Ward, 2005).

bers opened their hospital for syphilitics. In 1572 a hospital was opened in Bergamo and one in Crema in 1584.[44]

As did Christians in the early sixteenth century, we also find ourselves confronted with an 'incurable disease'. No one today remembers the narratives of those who excluded the victims of syphilis by establishing physical or social barriers of protection based on moral judgements of blame. Rather, history teaches us about the self-understanding of those who realised they were compelled by Christ's demand for mercy to identify with the burden of those at risk and to provide them with effective relief, comfort and companionship. They welcomed the incurables into their more stable world.

As educators in a time of HIV/AIDS, we are learning to appreciate the critical importance of attending to the concepts of justice, human rights, the common good, and the option for the poor. If we can be faithful to the need for a broadening and deepening of our approach, assuredly we will be able to develop a more competent and comprehensive strategy that encompasses bioethics, sexual ethics, public health policy and medical care. Similarly, by retrieving the lessons of mercy, we might be able to coax those who are afraid and entrenched in isolation into extending their hands and their resources from their firm centres of stability to those who live unstable lives in unstable settings. That movement, animated by mercy, is certainly what we need today, not only for those living in chaotic lands, but just as importantly for those living in the stable ones such as our own.

---

44. Alessandro Massobrio, *Ettore Vernazza. L'apostolo degli incurabili*, (Roma, Città Nuova, 2002). see, http://64.233.179.104/ search?q=cache:c5ecaoY-d4QJ:lettere2. unive.it/ deltorre/corso/materiali/Scuole.rtf+%22Compagnia+del+Divino+Amore%22+sifilide&hl=en (March 21, 2005)

CHAPTER THIRTEEN

Response to James Keenan

Raphael Gallagher CSsR

AIDS has outdistanced moral theologians in our response. Given James Keenan's statistics and illustrations it is a phenomenon likely to remain with us during our watch. There are some signs of hope among the emerging scholars: with their help, key questions can be identified, strategies outlined and cultural paradigms presented. In responding to Professor Keenan's paper, I acknowledge our debt for a splendid contribution and yet I want to probe other directions as to why AIDS has outdistanced us in theological research. The language of moral theology has enabled us to deal with some issues, like condoms, using the principles of the lesser evil and the double effect. These seem hardly adequate given the vastness, intricateness and interconnectedness of the moral issues raised by AIDS. The contribution of the language of human rights, the common good and social justice takes us closer to the core problems, as Professor Keenan indicates. But is this sufficient for a coherent and sustained theological response to AIDS?

The language of moral theology, in a time of AIDS, calls for a revision at three levels: the conceptual projection of God with which our discipline operates, the principles we use to analyse human reality, and the prudential choice involved in the application of the underlying God-concept and accompanying principles. Part of this revision will be a retrieval of neglected traditions; part will be a reformulation in the light of contemporary resources.

Moral theologians are excessively shy in exploring the conception of God at the heart of our reflection. Such questions are left to our systematic colleagues. This is a pity, and it means that moral theologians tend to assert certain ideas about God but leave them largely unanalysed. The normative language that pervades our discipline hinders us in the exploration of alternative concepts. Yet, others are available, such as the projection of a merciful God. 'A person who undertakes to praise God and yet will not exalt his mercy above all else had better keep silent'.[1] We cannot keep silent, so what would be the implications of this concept of a merciful God for moral theology in a time of AIDS?

The revelation of God's mercy is inseparable from the revelation of his transcendence and holiness. When, in the scriptures, Yahweh is revealed as 'the Holy' it is not only the remote holiness of omnipotence but holiness near to our humanity and communicated as a gift. The encounter of Yahweh with Moses outlined in Exodus is paradigmatic for this understanding.[2] Yahweh surely holds Moses at a distance but not so distant that he does not reveal himself as 'He who will bring his people out of Egypt'. The enduring memory of a transcendent yet essentially merciful God is an oft-repeated refrain in the Old Testament.[3] Some patristic analyses of the etymology of *misericordia* take this up by explaining mercy as compassion (that is, a passion in the human sense) for the evil endured by another person.[4] This concept of a God-like *misericordia* is not much present in recent Catholic moral theology. In the larger historical frame, this is traceable to the enduring influence of a stoical interpretation of mercy considered as a weakness, and therefore an evil. In the more immediate historical frame, it is a result of the moral theology of the manuals being constructed as dominantly normative: *misericordia* could be discussed only in the pastoral application of already established norms or within the ambit of spiritual direction.

---

1. *Taceat laudes tuas qui miserationes tuas non considerat quae tibi et medullis meis confitentur,* St Augustine, *Confessio,* Liber 6, Cap. 7, n. 12 (PL, 32, 725). Translation by A. Manson and L. C. Sheppard.
2. Exodus 33:18–34:10.
3. For example: Psalms 86:15, 103:8 and 145:8.
4. *Quis ignoret ex eo appellatam esse misericordiam, quod miserum cor faciat condolentis alieno malo?* St Augustine, *De moribus ecclesiae catholicae,* Cap. 27, 53, (PL 32, 1333). Translated by A. Manson and L. C. Sheppard.

CHAPTER THIRTEEN

The biblical concept of the transcendental merciful God (the God of *christostes* or *benignitas* in the Pauline sense[5]) suggests itself as the appropriate analogous way by which moral theology could consider an issue such as AIDS. When St Thomas discusses whether mercy is the greatest virtue he answers, characteristically, that it all depends.[6] In itself, it is the greatest virtue: existing in a particular subject, it is only the greatest virtue if it has no superior. Consequently, in God, mercy is the greatest virtue (or, more precisely, quality or attribute) because God has no superior. Therefore, when God reveals himself as God he does so in his mercy because there is no higher subject to whom one must appeal. It is important that moral theology invokes language about God analogously. Mercy, as a divine attribute exists only in God's will. But, crucially, that will is manifested in Jesus where it is precisely God's desire to be merciful that is revealed.[7]

Humanly, our capacity for mercy is limited by our knowledge and prejudices: theologically, by analogy with the will of God to be merciful, another perspective opens up. The will of God to be merciful is a response to the radical nature of human suffering, most especially the response to the human drama of sin. The Liturgy, in its invocation of God as *omnipotens et misericors Deus*, can give an indication of the appropriate language for moral theology.[8] There is not an anthropological reduction of God to human mercy, still less to the stoic presentation of mercy as weakness. The greatness of God is affirmed, most solemnly so in his will to mercy. Were this affirmation made more explicit as the theological conception of God operative in moral theology, our discipline would be energised to engage more honestly with

---

5. Confer Titus 3:4. 'But God revealed his eminent goodness and love for humankind and saved us, not because of good deeds we may have done, but for the sake of his own mercy.'
6. *Summa Theologiae*, 11a-11ae, q. 30, art. 4.
7. This is clear from the proclamation of the mission of Jesus in Luke 4:1-30: the parables of the Good Shepherd (John 10:1-9) and of the prodigal Son (Luke 15: 11-31) can be interpreted as confirmatory texts of this mission of mercy.
8. Confer the Collect of the Tenth Sunday after Pentecost in the Roman Missal.

the many dramas of AIDS which Professor Keenan has so vividly expounded.

Our ability to sustain this concept of God will be put to the test in our formulation of moral principles in situations of doubt, such as in the many conflictual experiences of AIDS. Moral theology does not operate solely with the alternates of moral certainty and moral relativism, though this is the contrast often portrayed. Theologically, for example, there are convincing arguments in favour of being a pacifist and convincing arguments in favour of a theory of the just war. Neither position is, as yet, absolutely convincing, and to espouse one in favour of the other does not make one a moral relativist. The terrain of moral reflection is coloured by provisional knowledge and atypical situations. Moral truth is not unattainable but its acquisition can be tortuously slow. Were we absolutely certain in the face of moral dilemmas such as AIDS, then we could formulate binding moral answers. But, as Keenan's paper amply illustrates, there are too many unclear aspects at the personal, social, economic and political levels. These uncertainties are not created by morality, as such, but by the multifaceted gradient of how AIDS spreads.

Moral theology needs to recover, or better, reformulate, a principled way of maintaining a coherent way of linking the theological concept of a transcendentally merciful God with the diversity of human character and the variety of moral situations.[9] The demise of the casuistry of the manuals need not be regretted: its general replacement by an intellectualist theory of the moral life (often invoking St Thomas) is not an adequate substitute.[10] What happened between St Thomas (died 1274) and

---

9. This is in line with the view of Gerson: 'The diversity of human character and mood is beyond belief: diversity not only among the mass of people, but in the same person: and in that person not only in different years or months or weeks, but also from day to day, from hour to hour and even moment to moment.' Jean Gerson, *De perfectione cordis* (ed. P. Glorieux, Oeuvres Complètes, Vol. 8, Paris, 1971, 129). Translation by M. Stone.

10. There are splendid books in this line, such as S. Pinckaers, *The Sources of Christian Ethics*, (T & T Clark, Edinburgh, 1996) translated Sr Mary Thomas Noble) and *The Pinckaers Reader*, (Catholic University of

CHAPTER THIRTEEN

the arrival of the post-tridentine moral manuals from the early 1600s may, curiously, have something important to contribute. This is generally regarded as a philosophically sterile period, but recent studies are indicating otherwise.[11]

The argument is not for a return to probabilism as a philosophical theory (its day is done) or to ask for a re-emergence of casuistry of the manual tradition. The question needing further study is: what were the philosophical debates behind both the emergence of probabilism and casuistry, as moral theology embraced them?[12] That is the interesting question. If we cannot possess knowledge of indeterminate things that impede other things, then we cannot in principle ascertain certain knowledge of future events. Hence, the uncertainty of our knowledge is a result of the indeterminacy of nature and not simply the result of limited human knowledge. For that reason, philosophers like Boethius of Dacia (d. c.1300) and others of the period developed the idea that we must content ourselves with knowledge that is concerned with events as they happen for the most part: *ut in pluribus, ut frequenter*. The evident indeterminacy of nature implies a level of probability as the stuff of moral analysis.

More interestingly, thinkers such as Henry of Ghent (d. 1293) John Duns Scotus (d. 1308) and John Buridan (d. c.1358) explored, along with the objective uncertainty of nature, the subjective doubts arising from the human *voluntas*. For these thinkers, practical decision making in cases of perplexity always takes place in a situation where there are several credible ends

---

America Press, Washington, 2005) edited by John Berkman & Craig Steven Titus, which offer a reconstruction of a way of moral reasoning by recovering neglected elements from St Thomas: in the case of Pinckaers, the notion of beatitude. I am less convinced by these approaches when confronted with the need to enter into the stuff of human tragedy at a practical level.
11. M. W. F. Stone, 'The Origins of Probablilism in Late Scholastic Thought. A Prologemenon to Further Study', in *Recherches de Théologie et Philosophie Médièvales*, 68 (2000) 1, 115-157.
12. J. Fleming, *Defending Probablilism. The Moral Theology of Juan Caramuel*, (Georgetown University Press, Washington, 2006) shows the need to rethink standard views about this period.

proposed by the human will. Good reasons will exist for a number of alternative choices, and given the plurality of alternatives a moral agent will be able to choose one of these over another. One can never be sure that what one chooses is in fact the 'best' thing to do. In the deliberative mess that moral judgements involve, uncertainty is an endemic feature of certain classes of moral decision. Intellectual prudence will not suffice because of the prominent role of the will in selecting human acts. The philosophers of this period thus developed a theory, generally but later called probabilism, to deal with objective intellectual uncertainty and subjective volitional uncertainty.

This may seem far removed from Professor Keenan's paper. But is it? What we are dealing with in AIDS is verifiable uncertainty about how it originated and spread, and subjective uncertainty about how a person can take decisions in particular cases. It is important that moral theology recover an awareness of the contingency of human action, and an appreciation that the accuracy of moral theology is of a different genre from that of the demonstrative sciences. Such an historical recovery will have advantages. It will illustrate that moral theology of this type is not moral licence or laxity but a method for ensuring responsibility in the absence of obvious moral certainties. In theological arguments, as in life, we work with provisional knowledge in arriving at judgements that are solid indicators of the road to fuller truth. This approach allows us to see moral theology as Christian discipleship (a concept central to Enda McDonagh's writings) but without reducing the argument hastily to the level of normative law. It is a practical theology that involves dialectical reasoning rather than a demonstrative theology deduced abstractly from principles. Such a moral theology seems particularly apt in a time of AIDS. Our conscience cannot be more certain than the premises, either intellectual or volitional, with which we operate. In uncertain times it may be useful to return, not to outdated probabilism or casuistry, but to the innovative thinking of the period between St Thomas and the Council of Trent as a source for a moral theology.

CHAPTER THIRTEEN

It is striking how James Keenan's analysis shows how boundaries cross in the moral analysis of AIDS: economic realities, sexual mores, political initiatives, biomedical advances. What is 'moral theology' is one issue, and not always clear. The confusion is confounded when a number of other disciplines cross lines with it: social morality, sexual ethics, and political theory. It is important to face AIDS in a multi-disciplined way but without the disintegration of the foundational approach to morality indicated in the previous points. This may be possible, if we make use of a theological approach implied in the stance of St Alphonsus Liguori. 'Some assert that it is sufficient to know the principles: they are altogether mistaken. The principles are few and known to all, even to those who have only an elementary moral knowledge. The greatest difficulty in the science of moral theology is the correct application of principles to particular cases, applying them in different ways according to different circumstances.'[13] 'Dear reader, my intention in writing this *Moral Theology*, which has a strictly practical goal, was not to present you with a thick scholastic treatment on "human actions". Rather, wanting to help with the salvation of souls, I have felt myself obliged to choose solely those questions which, in this area, we deem most necessary and useful to know for the conduct of life.'[14] The many faces of AIDS will present different moral dilemmas, and the circumstances of those dilemmas will indicate which principles are pertinent: the criterion of discerning the appropriate principles will be the salvation of souls, in the language of Alphonsus, which surely includes the good health of people, in our language.

Professor Keenan's exposition shows why he is recognised worldwide as an expert in the reality of AIDS. My comments are made in the spirit of supporting his approach, while suggesting

---

13. Alphonsus de Liguori, *Dissertatio pro usu moderato opinionis probabilis*, (Naples: Ex Typographia Benedicti Gessari, 1755), C. 4, n. 122. Translation S. O'Riordan.
14. Alphonsus de Liguori, *Theologia Moralis*, Vol. 2, Liber V (*De actibus humanis in genere*), *Tractatus Praeambulus*, (Rome, Ex Typographia Vaticana, 1907), ed. L. Gaudé. Translation P. Laverdure.

a different systematic approach to link the foundational concept of God, and the operative moral principles with a methodology for applying those principles in practice. If I have revisited the past history of moral theology it has not been with a desire to escape reality. It has been done in the hope that we can find insights there that will energise moral theology as we struggle with a drama that is surely, until now, outdistancing us.

CHAPTER FOURTEEN

Just Love:
Reordering the Moral Debate about Sexuality

Linda Hogan

It is a great pleasure to honour Professor Enda McDonagh and to celebrate his continuing contribution to the revitalisation of the life of the church. The theme on which I have been asked to speak is sexual ethics, and in so doing I intend to draw on strands in Enda McDonagh's work in order to suggest that, notwithstanding the progress that has been made in the last forty years, the church's teaching on sexuality continues to be in need of radical reform. It is evident that there is a yawning gap between what the church teaches on sexuality and what many Roman Catholics around the world believe. Over the past forty years this gap has increased and cannot simply be explained away by referring to trends like secularism, relativism and materialism. The reality is that many morally serious Roman Catholics do not find the church's conclusions about the morality of sex to be convincing and have formed different views about how the morality of sexuality is to be viewed. Nor is this simply a matter of people disagreeing about the morality of particular kinds of relationships or acts. The gap between what is taught by the hierarchical magisterium and what is believed and practised by many committed Catholics worldwide will not be bridged within the existing theological framework. Rather if the church is to move past this particular impasse then the debates about sexual ethics will need to be situated within a new framework. Hence my subtitle: 'Re-ordering the moral debate about sexuality'.

Theologians over the past four decades have identified elements within the theology and ethics of sexuality that are in need of reform. In the first place there is a recognition that the church needs to give due recognition to human experience in the moral discussion about sexuality and to see it as an important source of moral wisdom. In addition, theologies of sexuality need to be developed in ways that make space for those voices that have heretofore been absent from theological reflection. In particular, theological reflection needs to include the critical voices of women worldwide, who have not only been silent, but who have often been silenced in this regard. Moreover, the church needs to be open to the recognition that change in the theological premises and in the methodologies employed is likely to lead to different conclusions about critical issues. It is notable however, that even where there have been changes in the church's theology of sexuality, these have not been accompanied by comparable changes in the conclusions reached about the morality of particular processes, acts or relationships. Thus in some cases the theology has changed, the methodologies have been modified, but the conclusions have stayed the same.

Enda McDonagh has written extensively about the ethical issues associated with sexuality. Over the years he has courageously raised difficult questions about the church's teaching on contraception, mixed marriages, divorce and second unions, on homosexuality and same-sex unions. Moreover, his writing on sexual ethics has consistently reflected his confidence that the lives of ordinary men and women are significant sources of moral insight. Indeed the most striking dimension of his writing on sexuality is that it is written with an overwhelming sense that at the centre of all of these protracted debates are individual men and women struggling to live just and loving lives. Whether he is writing about HIV/AIDS or same-sex relationships his theology begins and ends with the lives of persons-in-relationship. This is no abstract discussion; the objective is never simply to conform to a pre-determined position. Rather, the animating core of his reflection on human sexuality is the person. His theology is embedded in the fabric of real life and respects the wisdom that lies therein. In this brief comment, I will draw on some dimensions of Enda McDonagh's theology in order to suggest ways in which the moral debate about sexuality needs to be re-ordered. Reflecting on the implications of his theology, I wish to highlight three dimensions: in the first place the language of love needs to be supplemented by the language of justice; secondly, the focus on sexual acts needs to be replaced by a focus on sexual relations; thirdly, in its contribution to the public debate about sexuality, the church's own language needs to convey a respect for human dignity and ensure that no person is damaged by the manner or tone in which discussions about sexuality are conducted.

Reordering the Debate: Love and Justice
It would be wrong to claim that Enda McDonagh has developed a definite framework for sexual ethics. Rather it is more accurate to say that the emerging insight from his work is that the critical question to be asked and answered in all these contexts is: 'What does it mean to love justly?' This is explored explicitly in an essay initially written to mark the 60th birthday of Martin Pendergast, former Director of Catholic Aids Link, entitled 'Love and Justice: In God and Church, in Sexuality and Society' and republished in his recent collection *Immersed in Mystery: Enroute to Theology*.[1] This essay proposes that in Catholic theologising about sex the discourses of love and justice need to be brought together. Indeed he sees the re-positioning of these two discourses to be essential if there is to be any prospect of resolving the increasingly entrenched differences within contemporary Catholicism on the ethics of sex.

It is important to acknowledge that, in the past sixty years, we have witnessed a profound change in the manner in which the Catholic moral tradition has thought about sex. The first critical development, in the 40s and 50s, related to a move from the idiom of law, to the idiom of love. Theologians like Bernard Häring and Gerard Gilleman were significant, but none was more important than Herbert Doms. In his *The Meaning of*

---

1. Enda McDonagh, *Immersed in Mystery: Enroute to Theology*, (Dublin, Veritas, 2007), pp 165-175.

Marriage published in 1939 he argued that the theology of marriage should regard the experience of married people as a theological resource and that the tradition should begin to construe sexuality's meaning in terms of a range of values, especially intersubjective ones, and particularly the value of love. From the vantage point of today it may seem strange to be noting how radical this transition to the language of love in moral theology has been. However, the move away from the language of law has been one of the most important developments in moral theology for centuries. The subsequent fifty years have seen many Christian theologies of sexuality develop in this direction, and there is no doubt that the theology of John Paul II has been influential in reinforcing this theological approach to human sexuality. The more recent development, and one with which Enda McDonagh has been strongly associated, has been an approach that brings the language of justice (as well as the language of love) into considerations of the morality of sex. In particular in his writings about HIV/AIDS he insists that issues of sexuality can never be analysed exclusively in personal terms but rather that issues of inequality and disempowerment also have a bearing on how an adequate ethic of sexuality can be developed. Thus in the work of Enda McDonagh, as well as that of Kevin Kelly and Margaret Farley and others, it becomes ever more clear that, rather than being fixated on the morality of specific acts, Catholic sexual ethics would be better served by attempting to give a nuanced answer to the question of what it means to love justly. There will inevitably be many different answers to this question in circulation within the Catholic tradition. However, what is crucial, to quote Enda again, is that we recognise that 'the relation between justice and love is critical to any authentic theology of Christian living', and especially to any authentic Christian theology of sexuality.

There is no doubt that a Christian sexual ethic that is structured around the norms of love and justice would deal differently with the many contentious issues with which we are grappling today. Indeed in framing the moral questions about sex within

CHAPTER FOURTEEN

the dialectic of love and justice an entirely new way of seeing becomes possible. In particular with the dual focus on love and justice the significance of the moral quality of sexual relationships, rather than of sexual acts, comes more clearly into view. Moreover, when we focus our attention on the relational dimensions of sexuality, the moral questions to be asked are different. In the next section I wish to explore what it might mean to reorder the debate by focusing on relationships, not acts, in the specific context of same-sex relationships.

Reordering the Debate: Relationships not Acts
Within the Catholic tradition we seem to have no framework within which to talk about the morality of homosexual relationships, and thus no coherent way of contributing to the debate about legal recognition for same-sex couples. Rarely, if ever, do the texts that issue from the teaching offices of the church speak about homosexual relationships or construe the question in relational terms. Instead, typically in the Catholic tradition the moral concerns are discussed in terms either of the orientation of persons, of homosexual acts or of homosexual activity. This reluctance to accept a relational rather than a mechanistic definition of homosexuality means that the tradition has no way of conceptualising, and therefore no way of evaluating, homosexual desire in the context of relationships. Moreover, it is for this reason that the issue of legal recognition for same-sex relationships has been so difficult; this is the first time that the church has really had to face the reality that the moral questions pertaining to homosexuality involve us in a discussion about committed, mutual, faithful relationships.

If, however, it is the dynamic between love and justice that frames the moral discussion about same-sex relationships, then an entirely different set of questions become important. No longer is the question of sexual orientation the central one, but rather the critical questions are those that pertain to the moral quality of the sexual relationship. Assessing the moral quality of sexual relationships is a complex and nuanced affair. However, the kinds of questions that will help us understand the moral quality of sexual relationships are likely to be questions such as: whether a relationship enhances the dignity of each of the individuals involved; whether the relationship is a mutual one; whether it is a committed and faithful one; whether it is a truthful one; whether it is generative (either in a biological or a social sense); and whether it aspires to embody the values of justice and care. Moreover, when we consider the social context we will need to ask whether the common good will be enhanced or diminished if legal protection is afforded to particular forms of relationships, such as same-sex relationships. Again there will be good reasons why people are likely to disagree on this matter. Although it is not possible here to develop these arguments, I would suggest that legal recognition of same-sex relationships would be likely to support rather than to threaten the common good and that a moral framework constructed around the dynamic of justice and love helps one to see this clearly. Thus for example one might suggest that the common good might be enhanced if there is: legal recognition of faithful, mutual committed relationships; social protection for the different models of family life that exist in the state; respect for the equality of citizens; mutual respect based on an understanding of and a valuing of diversity; and political stability arising from the equal treatment of all citizens. In each case one might say that these are components of the common good that are protected with the legal recognition of same-sex relationships.

Reordering the Moral Debate: Respecting Human Dignity in Public Discourse

That the Catholic Church, along with other faith-based groups, has the right to participate in public debate on matters of social significance, including sexuality, is accepted. Moreover, it is important that faith-based groups have the space to engage in public debate using the kind of language that best reflects each group's deepest held convictions. In this way it is hoped that the public debate will enable a society to come to a consensus about

CHAPTER FOURTEEN

how particular values can best be protected and promoted. However, in communicating the teaching of the hierarchical magisterium on sexuality, and especially on homosexuality, the Catholic Church faces a number of challenges, not least of which is how this teaching can be communicated without demeaning those whose sexual lives do not conform with official church teaching. There is no doubt that the language of condemnation through which many discussions about sexuality is conducted is experienced as unjust, discriminatory and deeply uncharitable. Moreover, it may even be the case that some of the official church documents could be regarded as homophobic, and therefore illegal in some jurisdictions. One hopes that in time the official position on same-sex relationships will change and that eventually such relationships will be regarded as having value and meaning in ways analogous to heterosexual relationships. However, while the negative evaluation persists one hopes that the church will seek to ameliorate the damaging effects of its language of condemnation.

Of course honesty in public debate is also important and here again the church faces a challenge, namely, to communicate the diverse views that exist within the church on many sexual issues and to remind its various audiences that over the centuries the church's teaching has changed, sometimes radically. The church's moral tradition is discursive. It is shaped and transformed through its engagement with other traditions and disciplines, and in response to the *sensus fidelium*. Yet, this discursive character of the moral tradition is rarely highlighted by the church in its public utterances. Thus many people, including many Catholics, are not aware of the changing and changeful character of the church's moral tradition and therefore fail to understand that what is currently taught can and often is transformed as our understanding of particular issues grows and develops. Too often the impression is given that what is taught can never be amended. Yet the moral tradition of the church is replete with examples of issues on which the teaching has changed including slavery, human rights, usury, marriage and abortion, to name but a few.

The tradition is enhanced, not undermined, when its discursive character is acknowledged. Such an acknowledgment is essential if we are to have an honest debate about sexuality, a debate that is characterised by the norms of justice and love.

Over the past forty years our knowledge and understanding of sexuality has grown significantly, as has our appreciation of the nature of the moral issues that are at stake. Throughout his career Enda McDonagh has made a significant contribution to the debate, particularly with his insistence that together the norms of love and justice provide the cornerstones for a framework within which a Christian ethic of sex can be elaborated. This paper seeks to pay tribute to Enda's contribution by considering the implications of adopting this framework in relation to the pressing issue of same-sex relationships. There is no doubt that the terms of our debate about sexuality will change radically when the central question is whether a relationship is characterised by justice and love, by what Margaret Farley calls just love.[2] One looks forward in hope to the time when such a theology will shape both the church's own reflections on sexuality and its contributions to the public debate on the matter.

---

2. Margaret Farley, *Just Love: A Framework for Christian Sexual Ethics* (New York, Continuum, 2006.)

CHAPTER FIFTEEN

Conflicts and Human Rights: A Global Perspective

Noel Dorr

Introduction
I believe that in Japan the state honours very distinguished persons by designating them 'Living National Treasures'. If we had such a system here in Ireland I think most of us here would want to nominate Enda McDonagh for that exalted status.

All of us who know Enda know that he is multifaceted. Each of us has experienced the glint and sparkle of some of those facets. But we have also come to know – indirectly perhaps and by reflection – that there are many other friends, in a wide circle, who look from other angles and see other aspects of the man which emit an equally luminous gleam.

I have been asked to speak on 'Conflict and Human Rights: A Global Perspective'. This is a topic which, even if the coincidence is not exact, seems to me to bear very directly on peace and justice – two areas of deep concern to Enda. A concern for justice permeates much, if not all, of his work; and he has pursued his concern for peace most recently in an impassioned 'Appeal to Abolish War' which he and his friend Stanley Hauerwas launched in 2002, with the help of Linda Hogan of the Irish School of Ecumenics at TCD.

Conflict and Human Rights: aspiration and reality
That conflict, injustice and abuses of human rights are still part of the human condition in this opening decade of the 21st century is all too evident. We inherit from the 20th century a structure for the maintenance of international peace and security which is now worldwide – that is the United Nations and its Security Council; and quite a dense network of international human rights agreements, conventions and commitments developed

over the second half of that century. It is clear that both of these systems are fragile and inadequate.

The aspiration and the rhetoric were high when the UN Charter was drafted in 1945. It begins with a Preamble in which 'We the peoples of the United Nations' express a determination:

> 'to save succeeding generations from the scourge of war …', and 'to reaffirm faith in fundamental human rights, in the dignity and worth of the human person, in the equal rights of men and women and of nations large and small …'

But the reality, more than sixty years on, still falls far short of the aim. When we read about what is happening today in Burma, Darfur and Zimbabwe, for example, or consider the dreadful but little-known conflicts in Eastern Congo, or the hopeless mess in Iraq, it is hard not to feel a righteous and justifiable anger at what seems to be a chronic failure by the UN to live up to these aims. We do not always realise that the blame lies elsewhere – with the member states who fail to live up to the commitments they made in accepting the charter.

I readily acknowledge, however, that both the UN as a structure for the maintenance of international peace and security, and the network of human rights commitments which we have evolved over the second half of the 20th century, are fragile and far from adequate. Too often they prove ineffectual in curbing human folly and callousness. But even though they are inadequate, they still go a long step beyond anything which humankind was able to achieve in earlier times. I do not wish to dampen the indignation we rightly feel at their inadequacies. But I would argue strongly that the world would be much worse without them; and that such hope as we have of achieving a better, more just, and more peaceful world order in the 21st century depends in large measure on our ability to maintain and develop them.

In putting that argument to you this morning, I will look briefly first at our present international system and how it evolved. I want at the outset to show you just how novel these structures are in comparison with anything that humanity was able to achieve in earlier times.

CHAPTER FIFTEEN

The international system today

I start by drawing your attention to an obvious fact. Our world today is organised into about 200 sovereign, independent states each of which, in principle at least, accepts the sovereignty of every other.

It was not always like this. At the start of the 20th century a large part of the globe was ruled or dominated by a small number of countries of the developed world. One historian estimated recently that in 1913, just before the First World War, some 65% of the world's land and more than 80% of the world's population were under some kind of imperial or colonial rule. This changed radically during the course of the 20th century as the principle of self-determination was put into effect – slowly after the First World War, and much more widely and rapidly after World War II. Today there are no more empires or colonies, no more unexplored or unclaimed territories. In our time, humanity, by its own choice, has organised itself into a world of sovereign, independent states.

Erosion of Sovereignty

Of course this is not a full description of our world today. States may be sovereign in principle but their economic sovereignty has been eroded greatly through the pressures of globalisation. This is especially true in poorer and weaker countries. States have also limited their sovereignty voluntarily by their adherence to various agreements and conventions. EU member states have gone further – they have agreed to pool part of their sovereignty and exercise it in common through supranational institutions.

State frontiers are increasingly porous. People everywhere are linked in new ways, through rapid developments in communications and transport, trade, commerce and financial exchanges, travel, migration and cultural exchanges of all kinds. Nor are states the only significant 'actors' in the international system. Multinational corporations are wealthy and powerful. Non-Governmental Organisations, too, can exert considerable influence across national frontiers. In recent times, too, some states have been attacked by faith-based groups who believe that they have a divinely-ordained mandate to replace the institutions of the modern secular state by structures which give full and exclusive effect to their particular religious values and beliefs.

Nevertheless, for most of the world's peoples, including ourselves here in Ireland, the sovereignty of each individual state is still the fundamental organising concept. The sovereign territorially-based state is certainly the only humanly-established social or political structure in the modern secular world which makes an absolute claim on those who belong to it; it is the only such structure able to mobilise its members to go to war; and the only such structure which demands a loyalty which requires them to be ready, if necessary, to die in its defence.

Why the international system today is distinctive
There have been states of one kind or another in various parts of the world since antiquity. But there are several features which make our present international states system distinctive:
- it is now global in its reach – it has become so in my lifetime, if not in yours. For the first time in human history, there is a single, worldwide international system;
- its basis is the sovereign, independent, territorial state. Each such state claims a right to maintain an army to defend itself;
- the states within it may differ greatly in size, in wealth, in importance, and in their systems of government, but each accepts, in principle at least, the sovereignty of every other;
- the states which make it up co-operate through common institutions but, being sovereign, they recognise no over-riding authority superior to themselves.

State sovereignty
Political scientists trace the origins of this present international system back to early modern Europe when stronger and more unified states began to emerge. A new sense of the sovereignty of individual states developed – particularly after the great split

CHAPTER FIFTEEN

in 'Christendom' at the Reformation and the so-called 'Wars of Religion' which followed. This emerging international system was new and distinctive by comparison with the multi-layered levels of feudal authority which had prevailed in medieval Europe. It was not only that the states in the system were now asserting themselves as sovereign and independent units. It was also that, notwithstanding obvious differences in power and status between them, each state, in principle at least, had come to accept the independence and sovereignty of every other. The religious issues which had torn Europe apart since the Reformation, were accommodated now through the principle *cujus regio, ejus religio*, which asserted that the internal affairs of a state, in matters of religion in particular, were a matter for the ruler of that state to determine. Another, broader maxim of the time which further emphasised the sovereignty of individual states, was *rex imperator est in regno suo* – the king is emperor, which is to say supreme ruler, in his own kingdom.

This emerging international system was limited to Europe at first. It evolved there further over time, and in later centuries, as Europe came to dominate the world, it spread more widely. In the 18th and 19th centuries, new states on the European model emerged to independence in the Americas. In the 20th century, as the principle of self-determination worked itself through, the system extended to the world as a whole.

Notwithstanding the pressures of globalisation, the organising principle of international life in our time is still that of the independence and sovereignty of states and this is likely to remain the case for the foreseeable future. I am not commending this – I am simply pointing to the fact that most of humanity still seems to hold with great stubbornness to this concept, to the extent of fighting and dying to establish and maintain it. Some of our own parents and grandparents did so in the first half of the century and we still cling to Ireland's sovereignty today. Even within recent decades, new states have emerged to independent sovereignty, peacefully or through conflict – in such places as former Yugoslavia and East Timor.

At the international level, too, the principle seems to be solidly entrenched. The UN Charter states quite explicitly that 'The Organization is based on the principle of the sovereign equality of all its Members' and that 'Nothing contained in the present Charter shall authorize the United Nations to intervene in matters which are essentially within the domestic jurisdiction of any state ...' And as late as March 2005 in a report on UN reform the former Secretary General, Kofi Annan, emphasised that: 'Sovereign states are the basic and indispensable building blocks of the international system.'

Conflict between States
What can be done to avert conflict and advance human rights in such a world? If humanity has organised itself, as it has, into separate sovereign states; if each such state makes an absolute claim on the allegiance of its citizens; if each maintains armed forces to defend its sovereignty; and if there is no superior, overall authority capable of imposing peace, order and justice, then the task is clearly a difficult one.

Certainly in Europe in recent centuries, war was frequent. It was not seen as contrary to international law – indeed it was accepted as a normal part of international life even up to the First World War. Von Clausewitz in the early 19th century characterised it as 'the continuation of political intercourse by other means'; and the distinguished British scholar, Sir Michael Howard, quoting a Victorian predecessor, goes so far as to say that 'war appears to be as old as mankind but peace is a modern invention.'

At first these wars were limited in scope and largely involved professional armies. As the technology of weaponry improved, however, and massed armies drawn from whole populations on the model established by Napoleon became the norm, war became ever more destructive and the need to develop systems for averting international conflict became correspondingly more acute.

CHAPTER FIFTEEN

Structures for conflict-prevention
I want to touch briefly on three significant efforts to do this which have been made over the past two centuries and which led up to the United Nations of today. Each followed a general war between the major powers.

1. The Congress of Vienna 1815
The first such effort at a large-scale peace settlement which would re-order the international system was at the Congress of Vienna in 1815 where the victorious allies sought to re-create on a more stable basis the European system of independent sovereign states which Napoleon had overturned. Their main concern was how to maintain a 'balance' between the Great Powers since they believed that that would be the best way to maintain the peace and stability of the system for the future. In addition they agreed to consult between themselves at times of crises through a loose arrangement described as 'the Concert of Europe'. We might think of this today as a first outline sketch for the UN Security Council. The 'Concert' was limited in scope, however, and no standing body or organisation was created. It did work to some extent, however, particularly during the first half of the 19th century and it helped to avert some crises which could have led to another general war.

Nevertheless, war was still accepted as an inevitable part of international life right through that century. There were occasional wars in Europe – including the Crimean War and the Franco-Prussian War; wars of liberation as well as wars between states in Latin America; a dreadful Civil War in the United States; and of course continuing wars with native peoples along colonial frontiers as European powers in the so-called 'civilised world' sought to secure or extend the territories of the 'uncivilised world' over which they ruled. Still, there was some progress: at least there was no continent-wide or general war after the Congress of Vienna for another hundred years.

BEAUTY, TRUTH AND LOVE

The Hague Peace Conferences
Although it was not one of the three efforts at a general international settlement, I should also, in passing, mention a worthy peace-promotion initiative taken by the Czar of Russia at the very end of that century. He seems to have had a premonition of coming disaster. He invited other governments to attend a peace conference at The Hague directed to 'the maintenance of the general peace and a possible reduction of the excessive armaments which weigh upon all nations'. Some 25 States, including the US and four others from outside Europe, attended a first Conference in 1899; and 44 states attended a second conference in 1907. Some things were achieved – a Permanent Court of Arbitration helped to prepare the way for today's International Court of Justice; there was some codification of the rules of war and the rights of neutral states; and some improvement in humanitarian law including the rules on prisoners of war.

Most poignant to read today, however, in view of what was to follow in the 20th century, were two Declarations adopted at the first Peace Conference of 1899: the first prohibited 'the launching of projectiles and explosives from balloons'; the second, the use of projectiles, the object of which is the diffusion of asphyxiating gases.'

2. The Versailles Peace Conference 1919
The cataclysm which the Czar feared did come in 1914 with the outbreak of the First World War. This was a truly global war: we are still living out some of its consequences. After the war, came the second of the three efforts to create a system to avert conflict between states to which I referred. The 19th century idea of peace maintained through a balance of power was now discredited. Instead, at the Versailles Peace Conference in 1919, US President Woodrow Wilson persuaded the other Allies to create a 'League of Nations' based on the new concept of 'collective security'. His aim was to create 'a community of power', and give it effect through standing international institutions established under a covenant accepted by all member states and binding on

CHAPTER FIFTEEN

all. The League duly came into being but sadly Wilson failed to persuade his own country, the US, to join.

The League had some successes in the 1920s but in the 1930s it proved weak and ultimately ineffectual when faced with Japanese militarism and the rise of aggressive totalitarianism in Germany and Italy. It virtually collapsed at the end of that decade and the world slid again into war.

The Kellogg-Briand Pact
In those years between the two World Wars, there was one other worthy – and noteworthy – initiative which I think I should mention here in passing. This was nothing less than an international pact against war.

The aim of the League Covenant had been to put in place procedures to moderate and delay the resort to war by states in dispute and oblige them first to seek alternative means of resolving their quarrel. It did not prohibit war entirely. In the late 1920s, however, a great majority of the world's states signed a new Treaty which did just that – an early model, one might say, for the McDonagh-Hauerwas 'Appeal' in our day. This was the so-called Kellogg-Briand Pact – an international treaty remarkable for its brevity no less than for its ambition. In two short substantive articles, the signatory states renounced war as an instrument of policy and agreed that they would never seek to settle disputes or conflicts by other than pacific means. William T. Cosgrave signed in 1928 on behalf of the Irish Free State. By 1933 some 65 States in all had signed the document though some important states such as the US, the UK and France added important qualifications to their acceptance of the treaty. Still, the new treaty seemed to be a major step towards abolishing war between nations. Sad to say, however, in 1939, barely six years later, the world collapsed again into an even greater and more disastrous war.

3. *The United Nations*
In 1944-45, towards the end of that war, the main Allied Powers

began the third major effort in the past two hundred years to create a system to avert conflict between states. That was the essential aim and purpose of the United Nations as conceived by the wartime leaders – Roosevelt, Churchill and Stalin. It is worth remembering that the UN was not created by idealists – these were tough, realist, wartime leaders engaged at the time in an all-out conflict with no parallel in previous history. Since they took time to plan the new organisation while that war was still in progress, we must assume that they took it seriously as a system for conflict prevention.

The UN as they conceived it in 1944 and 1945 could be described as a continuation of their wartime alliance into the post-war world. It was over-optimistic to suppose that the alliance of convenience against a common enemy between the US and other Western powers on the one hand and the Soviet Union on the other would continue indefinitely: the UN Security Council was soon split apart by the Cold War.

Over more than sixty years since then, however, the UN has grown into something quite different – something which its founders may never have intended. It has become the first universal organisation of states in history. Its charter has become a kind of fundamental constitution for international society; and around it has grown a large family of organisations and agencies which structure and order many aspects of international life. This makes the UN of today an organisation of great importance – even if the record of its central organ, the Security Council, in maintaining international peace and security is a very poor one by comparison with the ambitious aims set by the preamble to the charter which I quoted at the outset.

There is a great deal more which I would like to say about the UN but there are space constraints. So I want to conclude by talking about the second of the two issues I have been asked to cover, that is human rights. This is a most important issue and one on which, I will argue, the UN has achieved some considerable success even though there is much more to be done.

CHAPTER FIFTEEN

HUMAN RIGHTS

International concern – a recent development

Until the mid-20th century there was no internationally accepted charter of human rights. Nor indeed were most states prepared to accept that the abuse of individual human rights within a state could be a matter of legitimate concern to the international community as a whole. Very much to the contrary; as I have explained, the system of international law which had developed in Europe from the 17th to the 19th century regarded it as a matter for each government to interpret its obligations in relation to its own citizens or to others present within its territory. Other states had no standing to complain except in cases where there was some very specific agreement affording protection to aliens.

Post World War I

The carnage of the 1914-18 war gave rise to radical new thinking about international relations. US President Woodrow Wilson in particular was imbued with moral purpose, and he pressed at the Versailles Peace Conference in 1919 for the creation of a more principled international system which would be given effect through the League of Nations. He spoke frequently of morality, and argued in public speeches that 'in the Covenant of the League the moral forces of the world are mobilised and international law is revolutionised by putting morality into it.'

The League, as I explained earlier, was essentially a 'collective security' organisation. But the new moral tone which Wilson injected into international relations is reflected in several articles of the Covenant as well as in provisions in the peace treaties about the treatment of minorities in certain European countries. The Covenant, for example, required member states of the League to 'endeavour to secure … fair and humane conditions of labour for men, women and children, both in their own countries and in all the countries to which their commercial and industrial relations extend.' They also undertook 'to secure just treatment of the native inhabitants of territories under their control'. Furthermore, the League's 'mandates' system, which was a kind of guardianship by particular member states over former German colonies, described 'the well-being and development of … peoples' in these territories as 'a sacred trust of civilisation'.

The inclusion of these provisions in the Covenant of the League and in the peace treaties can be seen as a significant first step in a new direction. Older international law principles had stressed the sovereignty of states. Now, however, some issues bearing on the rights of individuals were beginning to be accepted as matters of legitimate concern to the international community as a whole. But there was still no concept of a full-scale international codification of human rights as such – still less of internationally accepted mechanisms and structures to promote their implementation.

World War II concentration camps
The decisive event which changed the thinking of states was the Second World War – in particular the opening of the Nazi concentration camps at the end of the war. It became clear that millions of human beings had been systematically exterminated; and, furthermore, that in the camps there had been a detailed, methodical brutalisation and dehumanisation of each individual; a careful collection not just of the valuables but of the clothing, human hair and dental fillings of those who went to the gas ovens. The final sick irony was the inscription which still stands over the gateway at Auschwitz '*Arbeit macht frei*' – work makes us free.

The effect was to reduce human beings methodically to the status of objects to be used and discarded – the precise opposite of the great German philosopher Kant's injunction that every person ought to be treated as an end in themselves and not simply as a means to some other end. And these were policies which had come, not out of barbarism or ignorance, but from the heartland of western civilisation. The horror of all of this gave a new and decisive impetus to two important ideas: human rights, as such, must in future be a matter of legitimate international concern; and the international community must not, ever again, remain passive when genocide occurs.

CHAPTER FIFTEEN

Human Rights in the UN Charter

The major Allied Powers in preparing the first draft of the UN Charter in 1944 were, however, still extremely reluctant to accept any weakening of national sovereignty. So they included only one brief reference to the promotion of 'respect for human rights and fundamental freedoms'. In 1945, however, before the Charter was adopted, the smaller and middle-sized states at the San Francisco Conference succeeded in inserting somewhat clearer and more explicit human rights provisions.

The 'Purposes' of the UN are listed in Article 1 of the Charter. The first of these is 'the maintenance of international peace and security'. But another 'Purpose' listed in that very same Article is

> '[to achieve international cooperation] ... in promoting and encouraging respect for human rights and for fundamental freedoms for all without distinction as to race, sex, language, or religion ...'

This was an advanced formulation for the time. Even more so was its inclusion in the document – an international treaty – accepted by fifty sovereign states and open in principle for signature by all 'other peace-loving states'. This was something quite new in international life. The sovereignty of each state was still an established principle but from now on there was a new and potentially subversive principle to set alongside it as part of the new world order which was emerging from the chaos of war: the 'dignity and worth' of each human person was to be respected; and furthermore this was henceforth to be a matter of legitimate concern to the *community* of states.

It is true that the Charter speaks of 'promoting' and 'encouraging' respect for human rights. It stops short of using words like 'safeguard,' 'guarantee' or 'enforce' which some states would have preferred. The major powers of the day were simply not willing to go that far at that time. Furthermore, in setting out the 'purposes' of the UN that first Charter Article makes a distinction between the way in which each of the two 'purposes' I have mentioned is to be achieved. International peace and security is to be maintained by 'effective collective measures' – that is by the UN itself through the Security Council. Human rights, however, are to be a matter for 'international co-operation' between its member states.

The result, as I see it, is that in this and in many later articles there is a kind of tension built into the Charter. The founders in 1945 clearly intended the United Nations to be an organisation of sovereign states dealing primarily with inter-state conflict. So they inserted a specific provision in the Charter which precludes the organisation from intervening in 'matters which are essentially within the domestic jurisdiction of any state'. But many other provisions envisage that the organisation is to develop an active role on human rights matters. It has done so over the past half century; and, in doing so, I would argue, has gone much farther than the founders may ever have intended.

Negotiation of Human Rights instruments
To start with in the late 1940s two most important documents were negotiated under the auspices of the UN.

One was the *Genocide Convention* which places a binding obligation on all states which are parties to it to act forcefully to stop genocide and requires them to act to punish the perpetrators as individuals, notwithstanding that they may plead sovereign immunity. This was an important breach in the established principle of 'non-intervention' in the internal affairs of states.

The other was the epoch-making *Universal Declaration of Human Rights* of 1948. Formally speaking this is not a legally binding document. But it would be hard to exaggerate its importance. In adopting it, the community of nations, for the first time, committed itself to a solemn declaration enumerating a wide range of fundamental rights and freedoms. The Declaration has had a significant influence on national constitutions, on domestic law and on court decisions in a number of countries.

It has also set an agenda for all that followed. Over the next half century, through detailed and patient work the UN has developed a network of human rights covenants and conventions. These are binding international treaties and agreements which elaborate on, and give effect to, many of the general provisions of the declaration. In themselves of course they certainly do not ensure an end to human rights abuses. But, taken together, they form an increasingly dense and ordered web of human rights obligations which constrain the vast majority of states who have agreed to be bound by them, much as the ship-wrecked Gulliver on the beach was bound by the threads of the Lilliputians.

I have spoken of a tension in the UN Charter between 'non-intervention' and human rights provisions. Although that tension is still there, the balance tipped somewhat after the influx into the UN from 1960 onwards of something over one hundred newly independent states. The effect was to bring together the two worlds of the 19th century – the so-called 'civilised' world of developed countries and the so-called 'uncivilised' world which the colonial powers had seen as open for appropriation. Now there was a single, unified, international system based on sovereign independent states and an organisation – the United Nations – in which all of those states were represented and, formally at least, entitled to be equal members. The newly independent states, mainly from the developing world, were now a majority in the General Assembly and they were strongly opposed to colonialism and apartheid. They refused to accept that the Charter provision barring intervention in matters of 'domestic jurisdiction' could apply to either of these two issues. This helped to erode the stricter construction of that provision which had prevailed when 'western' countries were the majority.

But there is a limit to how far this has gone: the sovereignty of each individual state is still a fundamental principle; and the new member states, which have recently gained or regained their independence, are particularly sensitive about anything which might infringe on their own national sovereignty. In some of these states there are autocratic leaders and oppressive regimes which are unwilling to concede to the international community any right to monitor or judge their record on human rights. Other states with less to hide nevertheless retain vivid memories of phrases such as 'civilising mission', and 'concern for the well-being of the native peoples' which states of the developed world used in earlier times as a cover for colonisation. This makes them suspicious, even today, of any further weakening of the Charter article on 'domestic jurisdiction' such as they think would be inevitable if the international community were to develop a stronger, and more intrusive role on human rights matters.

Evaluation

My argument here is that what has been done on human rights over the past half century, through the UN and otherwise, is significant and important. But there is a much darker side which must be faced. Gross abuses of human rights continue in many parts of the world; and it is hard not to feel a righteous and justifiable anger about what seems to be the chronic inability of an organisation based on a charter which speaks of 'the dignity and worth of the human person' to curb and punish man's inhumanity to man.

This view is put most trenchantly in a recent book by the distinguished human rights lawyer Geoffrey Robertson QC:

> Diplomacy is the antithesis of justice: it brokers trade-offs which always allow oppressors to escape punishment. Global enforcement of human rights standards cannot confidently be entrusted to the United Nations, with its lamentable record of doing so little to staunch gross abuses by countries of any significance (or even by insignificant countries, if they are protected by powerful alignments).

His indignation is understandable. But his complete rejection of diplomacy and of the United Nations goes too far.

It is true that the UN is not able to enforce human rights standards but is there any other body or organisation which can? A great deal has been achieved by the United Nations over the past sixty years through the slow, patient and imperfect processes of

CHAPTER FIFTEEN

diplomacy to weave a fabric of internationally accepted human rights law and obligation in a world where states still insist on their sovereign independence and are ready to fight to maintain it. The covenants and conventions which have been negotiated under UN auspices over that period cover many different aspects of human rights; they have been signed and ratified by large numbers of states; and many provide for regular reporting back and monitoring of implementation.

To those of us who are rightly angry when we hear about injustice, diplomacy may indeed, as Robertson suggests, seem to be the antithesis of justice imposed righteously and by forceful means. But peace too is a value – though it is often in tension with the whole-hearted pursuit of justice. Force, even if righteously used, still means conflict; and the blood that is shed, even where the conflict is undertaken righteously and for worthy motives, is still real blood. Too often, it is the blood of innocents.

That said, however, there is room for much greater, more concerted, and more effective, pressure by the international community on states which commit or allow gross abuses of human rights.

The UN Charter, as drafted in 1944-45 envisages the role of the Security Council as that of maintaining 'international peace and security'. The founding states wanted to limit its authority to international conflict, that is conflicts between states. Today, we need a much broader understanding of 'peace and security': it ought to mean, not just the absence of war between states but peace and security for their peoples. Or, as the former UN Secretary General Kofi Annan put it some years ago, there is a linkage between various aspects of human living:

> We will not enjoy development without security, we will not enjoy security without development and we will not enjoy either without respect for human rights.

In recent years there has been growing support for the idea that the UN Security Council should be able to authorise direct and forceful intervention on humanitarian grounds to stop gross abuses of human rights, verging on genocide, within a state. In 2005 a high level panel on UN Reform argued for this. They accepted that each government is responsible in the first instance for promoting the welfare of its own citizens. But if a government fails completely in that responsibility and is guilty of gross oppression of its own people, then, in the view of the panel, the Security Council should step in to exercise an overriding 'responsibility to protect' on behalf of the international community as a whole. They argued indeed that this is already 'an emerging norm' in international law and practice. Their view was supported by Kofi Annan who had set up the panel.

At a Summit meeting held at the UN later that year, Heads of State and Government from around the world went some way towards endorsing this approach. In the document which they adopted at that meeting they said

> ... we are prepared to take collective action, in a timely and decisive manner, through the Security Council, in accordance with the Charter, including Chapter VII [which allows the Council to use forceful means to enforce its decisions], on a case by case basis and in co-operation with relevant regional organisations as appropriate, should peaceful means be inadequate and national authorities manifestly fail to protect their populations from genocide, war crimes, ethnic cleansing and crimes against humanity.

This is a carefully qualified expression of support for what is still a new and controversial concept in international law and practice.

Many countries of the developing world, however, are particularly dubious about whole-hearted acceptance of the idea of legitimating outside intervention, even for the best of motives, in the internal affairs of sovereign states. That still seems to them to be close to the 'civilising mission' which some European powers claimed to be exercising in the 19th century and which, in practice they used as an excuse for the extension of colonial rule. Developing countries are also dubious about the failure so far to

CHAPTER FIFTEEN

broaden and reform the UN Security Council where the five major powers from the Second World War still exercise vetoes as Permanent Members. For these reasons, I think, it will be some considerable time before the concept of an international 'responsibility to protect' is widely accepted and implemented in practice.

Conclusion
That said, however, I will still argue that in a world like ours where each state clings stubbornly to its sovereign independence, diplomacy and negotiation are not to be despised. They may often be the necessary and honourable way of averting the greater injustices of war. And they can be a means of working, slowly, patiently and imperfectly, over time, towards that always distant ideal of justice for all in a world at peace which would, I think, be Enda McDonagh's most fervent prayer.

CHAPTER SIXTEEN

Listening to the Voices from the Margins

Stanislaus Kennedy

It is a great privilege for me to be invited to pay tribute to Professor Enda McDonagh. Enda has been a source of inspiration to me for the past forty years. His commitment to the dignity of every human person was always to the fore, especially those at the margins, always to the poor. Really, I'm delighted to speak today on behalf of people on the margins.

> *Some People*[1]
> Some people know what it is like
> To be called names in front of their children
> To be short for the rent
> To be short for the light
> To be short for the school books
> To wait in Community Welfare rooms full of smoke
> To wait two years to have a tooth looked at
> To wait another two years to have a tooth out (the same tooth)
> To be out of work
> To be out money
> To be out of fashion
> To be out of friends
> To be in for the Vincent de Paul man
> To be in space for the milk man
> To be in hospital unconscious or the rent man (St Jude's ward, 4th floor)
> To be second hand
> To be second class
> To be no class

---

1. Poem with permission from Rita Ann Higgins

CHAPTER SIXTEEN

> To be looked down on
> To be walked on
> To be spat on
> Some people do know what it is like
> and other people don't
> Some people's children know what it is like
> And other people's don't.

Not being marginalised myself, I feel deferential about speaking for the people who do live on the margins, the people that Rita Ann Higgins talks about in her poem. But part of being a marginalised person is that you don't have a voice, or at least not a voice that is listened to, and because society does not usually listen to the voices of marginalised people, I venture, in all humility, to speak on their behalf.

Consistent and relative poverty

The most marginalised people in our society live in 'consistent poverty'. The government recognises that a person is living in 'consistent poverty' if they haven't sufficient resources to be able to keep their home adequately warm or cannot afford two good pairs of shoes a year or to buy Christmas or birthday presents for their family. Between 7% and 8% of our people in the Republic of Ireland live in consistent poverty. They are older people or people who have long-term illnesses, physical or mental, or they are lone parents or people who are caring for a disabled child or other relative. Homeless people fall into this category, and the long-term unemployed, but also some people who work in poorly paid and insecure jobs.

As well as all these very poor people, we also have 22% of our population living a little above that limit, in what is called 'relative income poverty'. People in relative poverty are those who have to live on less than 60% of the median income. At the moment, the income level that defines relative income poverty for a single person is €209.87 a week or, in the case of a family of four, the figure is €486.90, which averages out at less than €122 a week each, to cover rent, food, heat, power, clothes and shoes, schoolbooks, household items and small luxuries like sweets or DVDs or cigarettes. You wouldn't have much left over after all that to save for a holiday or for Christmas presents and it is very easy for an emergency, such as someone in the family going into hospital or a washing machine breaking down, to spiral quickly into financial disaster.

And yet, there is no official recognition of relative income poverty. Officially, people on this level of income are recognised as being 'at risk' of poverty, but this level of very real financial stress is not even acknowledged as a form of poverty in its own right. It is as if the government is saying to people living at this obviously inadequate income level that they are living only in some sort of virtual poverty; that they are somehow not really poor. But it is very real poverty to try to manage on that kind of money. And not only is that poverty real for the individuals trying to cope with it, but the numbers living in this kind of poverty are growing.

Poverty is always hard and always nasty but poverty is much harder to bear in the midst of plenty. It is bad enough to be poor, but to be poor in our consumer society is to be excluded from what is valued by society – from education beyond the basic level, from jobs other than the most badly paid, and from the Irish success story. In this newly successful society, those who don't succeed financially, socially and politically are seen as failures, losers, non-productive, useless. It is not good to live your life feeling you are despised by the majority and considered a burden on the state. It does not nurture the kind of self-esteem a person needs in order to function well as a member of a family, a community, a workforce and a society. Poor people in a rich society learn to internalise this view of themselves as useless, unproductive and burdensome; this compounds their sense of powerlessness and makes it even more difficult for them to move out of poverty. It is not poor people's unworthiness that keeps them poor; but their *sense* of unworthiness, inculcated through years of being ground down and despised.

We have put in place a system to measure consistent poverty

CHAPTER SIXTEEN

and relative poverty in this country on a regular basis, but we have no system that routinely measures poverty in terms of access to healthcare, to housing, to education, to social support and to transport. But even without having the statistical information we should have, it is obvious that it is the poorest people who are most affected by difficulties of access to services like these, and the situation of people who are poor is made immeasurably worse because the public services and the social supports that they need are inadequate and inaccessible and in many cases not available at all.

From the margins of the health service
Poor people suffer because the gap between those who can pay for services and those who cannot pay has widened. Those who can pay get what they need; those who can't don't. This is especially true than in the health service. In spite of our recent affluence, Ireland has never recovered from the health cuts of the 1980s, and our provision of healthcare compares poorly with that of other countries. The proportion of GDP spent on public healthcare by the Irish government is 5.5%, compared with 6.6% in the USA, 8.6% in Germany, 7.8% in Sweden, 7.4% in France and 7.3% in Denmark.

Sick people who live on the margins of our society have to wait for treatment, and the waiting lists are often very long. In December 2006, for example, there were 15,096 adults and 2300 children waiting for surgical procedures; there were 4425 adults and 402 children waiting for medical admission; and around 30% of both adults and children had been waiting for longer than a year.

While some people are queuing up for hours on end, sometimes even days, on trolleys or even plastic chairs in A&E, more and more people are buying their way in the health service, taking out health insurance, which makes the gap between the public and the private wider and deeper. And the inequity reaches beyond the waiting lists and the A&E bottlenecks. It permeates the system. Private patients have their medical care delivered by consultants; public patients receive 'consultant-led' treatment with their care provided mainly by doctors who are still in training, whose working hours are unacceptably long and who may be inexperienced and inadequately supervised. In recent times there has been increasing reliance on the private sector to provide additional services in the health sector. This practice is being promoted as a quicker means to achieve progress. But this trend reinforces unfairness in an already inequitable system. A national healthcare system must have fairness at its core, and it must be based on the recognition that healthcare is an essential service, not a commercial product. It is more than 30 years since Irish society found it possible to eliminate the distinction in the way public and private patients access GP care; it is high time to start a process towards achieving the same goal in the delivery of hospital care.

From the margins of the education system
The slippery slope into social exclusion really gets under way in school. During our affluent years, thousands of young people have come flocking in to second and third level education, and yet there is a minority for whom the education system, far from being a release of potential, has in fact been a frustration of their potential. These are the 18% of young people in this country who leave school without attaining any qualification at all. They are almost all children from economically and socially deprived communities, and they face the risk of being unemployed or of finding only a poorly paid job in adulthood. In this sense educational disadvantage is an important reason why children who are poor become poor adults. The unemployment rate among early school leavers in the 18-24 age group was 19% in 2006, compared to 8.2% for all persons within that age category. Put in another way, an extremely high proportion (43%) of young people who leave school early are either unemployed or economically inactive, and they find it hard to make up later in life for that lack of education in childhood.

These are mostly children who didn't get on well at school, and who certainly didn't enjoy school. Such children have prob-

CHAPTER SIXTEEN

lems at school mainly because they grow up in poor homes, where there is very little space, very little money, very little self-esteem and very low expectations and, consequently, not much motivation to do well at school. It is hardly surprising that children from such homes do not feel very connected to school. They may not have the proper uniform; they many not have a warm coat, or the money for books or the extra things that other children have. Such children start at a disadvantage, especially if they haven't learned, before starting school, through play and encouragement, the key skills of taking turns, sharing and resolving conflicts peacefully. If they come from very poor homes, they probably have not learned the curiosity and confidence that form the basis of being ready to learn. And so instead of being a place of wonder, fun, encouragement, motivation, school quickly becomes a place of broken hopes, broken dreams, broken spirits.

Many children from poorer homes have difficulty with the discipline required to sit still and to concentrate for long periods. Many never learn to read or at least not sufficiently well to be able to follow what is going on. Not being able to read properly and being at school is like spending your day with people who speak a language that you don't understand. The humiliation of feeling that you are seen as weak or stupid or less confident than everyone else, who can read, is difficult to handle. And children who are alienated from school, who can't concentrate, who haven't learnt to read well, get bored. They get into fights, they cause aggravation to hard-pressed teachers, they cause trouble, maybe they get into a spot of bullying, and gradually the teachers get fed up and see their behaviour, which is really a natural reaction to feeling excluded, as lack of interest or a threat or even wilful provocation or a form of badness.

And so the alienated child begins to miss classes, miss half days, miss many days. Initially the school tries to get him back on track, but the effort is half-hearted because there is a secret relief that one more thorn in the side has been removed. When a child believes that he is no good at school, he distances himself from the school, and then he comes to be perceived as somebody who cannot avail himself of what the school has to offer. The problem is located in the child rather than in the school or the education system, and the child finds himself in a cycle of poor self-esteem that affects everything he thinks about himself and everything he does, maybe for the rest of his life.

Today 9.4% of our children under 14 years of age – that is 79,000 children – live in consistent poverty, and 175,000 children under 14, that is 21.2% of our children, are living in relative income poverty. These children cannot avail properly of our education system; they are quite simply too poor to function at school, too poor to learn to read, too poor to integrate into the life of the school and do well and go on to second or third level. There is so much going on in their lives, so many problems and difficulties, that it is just too hard, too alienating, too depressing to cope also with the demands of school.

And so, for all the excellence of our education system in so many ways, we have 22.6% of the Irish population who are identified as functionally illiterate. These figures represent a failure of the education system, but they also represent what it means to be poor in Ireland today.

From the margins of the housing system
The waiting list for social housing is now significantly longer than it was in 1996. Today there are 43,684 households waiting for housing. That is 70% higher than it was 10 years ago. And while they are on this waiting list, families and individuals are depending on the private sector to rent them flats or houses. That sector is very insecure and tenants are vulnerable. The flats that are rented to people on the housing list are at the bottom end of the market, where accommodation often lacks basic necessities and essential facilities, and some places are not even suitable for human habitation. Here individuals and families who are trapped in poverty have to live in terrible conditions. They may not be actually on the streets and they may not be physically roofless but they are homeless nevertheless, because they lack the very basic constituents of a home.

CHAPTER SIXTEEN

In addition to those nominally housed, but effectively homeless people, there are 5,000 people in Ireland who are actually and literally homeless. In other words, they are wandering around and living by going from hostel to hostel or even sleeping on the streets.

We have made some efforts to combat homelessness in this country. Additional hostel places have been made available recently and some of the hostels have been modernised. But despite these improvements, some homeless people still have to sleep rough at night because all the emergency accommodation is full. Some hostels provide inappropriate accommodation in dormitories, where drug-free young people have to sleep next to drug-users and where vulnerable homeless people have to share facilities with career criminals. In such places, homeless people sleep with their runners under their pillow for fear they will be stolen during the night. There are still emergency services for homeless people that infringe their dignity, fuel their frustration and anger and make them wonder why Ireland's prosperity has passed them by.

Private rented accommodation has traditionally been a route out of homelessness. However, as the cost of housing escalated over the past 10 years, so also has the cost of rented accommodation. Homeless people are entitled to a rent supplement from the state towards the cost of renting private accommodation, but there is a limit to the amount the state is willing to contribute. The standard is 130 a week in Dublin for a single person, less in other parts of the country, but this amount barely covers the cost of a small bedsit in Dublin which may be in very poor condition. To make matters worse, the state will not always agree to pay the deposit (equivalent to four weeks' rent) that is always required in advance, and in any case it can be extremely difficult to find landlords who are willing to accept tenants reliant on welfare payments. For all these reasons, the escape route of private rented accommodation is very limited. Some homeless people who have the patience – and the bus fares – to persevere for weeks and months may manage to acquire settled accommodation, but it is increasingly difficult.

A better route out of homelessness is social housing, but the waiting lists for local authority accommodation are growing – with over 43,000 households on the waiting list, the wait can be anything up to five years – and this means that homeless people find it more and more difficult to get access to social housing. Single homeless people, particularly men, are constantly being pushed to the very bottom of the waiting list, since priority is given to families with children, and single men may simply never get local authority accommodation.

From the margins of immigration
Immigrants make a huge contribution to Irish society through taking up jobs where there are labour shortages and, once they are established in our system, they contribute like everyone else by paying their taxes. They also have an important contribution to make to the social and cultural life of the country. We in Ireland are relatively new players on the immigration scene and we are slow to recognise that when we look for workers it is human beings who come.

We have to learn that the human person who comes to this country to fill a job vacancy is not just a work unit but a person who has needs – not just economic needs but social, political, spiritual and psychological needs. Migrant workers are welcomed to Ireland to fill the labour shortage, but there is not much protection of their rights as workers, they have virtually no right to be reunited with their families, and they have no right either to long-term residency status. This makes migrant workers feel very insecure.

For asylum-seekers it is worse again. While their cases are being processed – which can go on sometimes for many years – asylum-seekers have to live under the 'direct provision' system, which means that they are supplied with accommodation, food and basic necessities and a very small amount of spending money, but they are not allowed to work. For people who have provided for themselves and their families all their lives, this is very demeaning and frustrating, and it can go on for a very long

CHAPTER SIXTEEN

time. Ireland is one of only a few EU countries that refuse to allow asylum seekers to take up employment.

It's important for a country like Ireland that is receiving immigrants to remember that immigrants are not only individuals. They are members of a family and belong to various social networks. They are rooted in a culture and a tradition. They are people with ties to home and homeland.

We need a coherent and cohesive long-term strategy for immigrants. We need a rights-based approach to immigration: we need to recognise immigrants' right to family reunification and their right to long-term residency. We need also to recognise their right to integrate into our society. We need to allow people to cherish their own culture while also learning to respect Irish culture; in other words, we need to develop integration policies that are based on shared values.

From the margins of the justice system
During the last recent general election campaign, political parties were competing with one another to prove to the voters that they were going to be toughest on crime. Yet in truth there is little reason to believe that any of the parties claiming to be tough on crime is serious. None of them seems to have the kind of policies that evidence-based research tells us would actually reduce the incidence of crime. Instead, the political parties have put forward proposals that are framed to appear tough on crime, but in reality they are only tough on criminals. Being tough on crime is an entirely different matter: in fact, being tough on criminals can often mean being soft on crime.

Most strategies to control crime favoured by politicians seeking votes are actually ineffective or counter-productive, because they do not seek to understand and eliminate the causes of the offenders' behaviour. Despite a huge amount of evidence that shows how limited prison is as a method of addressing crime, our deeply rooted bias in favour of imprisonment continues, even in the face of the colossal annual cost (€90,000) of keeping a person in custody. Between 1996 and 2006 our prison population increased by 1,000; if imprisonment is supposed to suppress crime, it can't be working, because crime has not decreased at the same rate that imprisonment has increased.

There is certainly a role for imprisonment as part of a society's response to crime, but prison needs to be firmly located amongst an array of responses, all of which should have the objective of moving offenders away from crime. These responses need to be focused on assisting the offender to address the issues underlying his or her offending behaviour, issues such as addiction, effects of trauma, poor education, mental illness and lack of suitable accommodation.

Instead of speaking of alternatives to imprisonment, we might think instead of prison itself as an alternative form of punishment, which would be used for the most serious crimes; and in the case of less serious crimes, only after all the other options have failed.

From the margins of drug use
Our statistics on illegal drug use are very outdated. In 2000-2001 we had 14,500 heroin users, of whom 12,500 were in Dublin. In 2003 a survey found that 3% of the population were using cocaine at some time in their lives. In 2004 a survey found that 40% of 15-year-olds had tried cannabis. But even without up-to-date statistics, we know from what is happening around us that the use of illegal drugs is a serious and growing problem. Cocaine use is spreading rapidly among all social groups and to every city and town in Ireland.

Polydrug use (the use of several drugs simultaneously) is increasingly the norm among drug users and addicts, and this makes dealing with their drug problem a much more difficult task. Drug misuse is at the root of a great deal of crime perpetrated in Ireland, including not just drug-related offences themselves but the thefts and burglaries that constitute 80% of all offences committed.

With just one year left to run, the National Drug Strategy has failed in many respects. Waiting lists for methadone treatment

CHAPTER SIXTEEN

vary from location to location, but a two-year wait is normal for some categories of heroin users, including homeless people. Less than 30 detox beds are available. Given the scale of known drug use this is lamentably inadequate. Even though the Midterm Review emphasised the importance of aftercare, no accommodation for this purpose is available apart from two small houses in Dublin, which were already up and running before the review. Neither have any rehabilitation services come on stream.

There clearly needs to be increased provision in all four categories of drug services: detox, treatment, rehabilitation and aftercare. Common sense, not to mention common humanity, would demand that services should be sufficient to allow any user who wants to obtain treatment for their drug problem to do so without undue delay.

There is an urgent need to ensure co-ordination and cohesion among the services. Too often, gaps can occur so that a person who has completed one stage in the process of recovery is unable to access the service at the next stage, with the result that he or she relapses and the progress achieved is undone.

Since drug misuse is no longer confined to major cities, the full range of services needs to be accessible to people in all parts of the country. In addition to services to deal with misuse there is a need for further development of prevention services and a wide education programme. Early intervention programmes are completely under developed in Ireland.

People addicted to heroin and families affected by addiction are among the most marginalised in society. The majority of heroin users come from a background of marked socio-economic deprivation and educational disadvantage. It is clear that problematic drug use is related to poverty and social exclusion and is highly concentrated in residual local authority areas which have been written off and have become dumping grounds for vulnerable households.

There is a disproportionate concentration of families who are on the fringes of the labour market, whose children underachieve at school and who experience poor health, in the most deprived areas. Clearly there is a need to address the causes of heroin addiction, which is so disproportionately concentrated in these disaffected communities. This requires large-scale investment to regenerate those areas if we are serious about attacking the drug problem.

There is also a need for an honest debate on drugs. Much of the public debate takes place in either a moral context, where people involved in the debate are eager to be seen to condemn drugs (because 'drugs are bad') or in an emotional context of fear. A debate based solely on moral or emotional arguments won't do anything to deal with the problem. We need to address the drug issue not by demonising illegal drugs and drug users or by scaremongering but by examining the outcomes of evidence-based research from around the world on what policies and treatments work in prevention and rehabilitation, what policies can actually reduce the harm done to individuals and families and society by illegal drug use.

Bringing the margins into the centre
For decades we were told that we had to create wealth before we could distribute it. When we did create enormous wealth there were no proposals to redistribute it. There were no such plans on the part of any of the parties during the last election. There are no plans to engage in any comprehensive redistribution that would improve the social protection we provide and that would take everybody out of consistent poverty and reduce to close to zero those in relative poverty. Unless there is a radical change in our policies and priorities, the situation of people living in poverty will continue, with the poor becoming more marginalised. The reason for this is that poverty is not just a by-product of poor economic performance. Poverty is structured into the way our society operates. I am not just talking about consistent and relative poverty. I am also talking about housing poverty, health poverty and education poverty. If poverty is to be eradicated we must have a change of attitude in policies and priorities. As long as society operates on the principle of individualism

CHAPTER SIXTEEN

and personal achievement, so long will we have poverty. What we need is a strong social policy and an agenda that will ensure that we have equitable distribution of our resources.

The challenge for our policy-makers is to ensure that the benefits of our economic growth are distributed across health, housing, welfare, education and transport in a way that will benefit all and ensure all our citizens are served with equal respect and according to their needs. This is not how we operate at the moment. We have become a class-conscious society. We are wealth-conscious, and we are afraid of losing any of our newly acquired comforts. During the election, we heard a lot about putting more money into people's pockets through tax cuts and holding this out as a prospect for improving living standards. But standards of living in developed countries cannot be equated only with levels of disposable income. If we are to enjoy good standards of living, everyone has to be able to access good-quality services as the need arises. The problem with focusing on just making sure that people have a higher disposable income is that this simply supports inequality: the more income people have to spend, the more likely they are to buy their way past poor-quality public services. Paying for services in the private sector solves the immediate problem for the people concerned, but it also creates inequality, because for people who live on the margins of society, this is not an option and never will be an option.

If we want to bring the people who are on the margins in to the centre, we need to come up with new ideas about how we organise society economically, socially and politically. To nurture such new ideas, we need to encourage debate, and encouraging debate on new ideas about society means that we need to overcome the profound anti-intellectualism of our political structures and culture.

This is our responsibility as citizens. It is not just the government's responsibility. It is up to all of us to press for these changes. It is vitally important that we take ownership of our responsibility as citizens. The gap between individualism and community-mindedness will only be filled by having a sense of ownership.

BEAUTY, TRUTH AND LOVE

It is our time, our place, right here now in this village, in this neighbourhood, in this town, in this city. What happens here and now is our responsibility; what happens tomorrow is our legacy. We are all responsible for the time we live in. We hold that responsibility jointly and we hold it now.

CHAPTER SEVENTEEN

Theology and Poetry:
'Loose-leafed through the Cosmos'

Patrick O'Brien

Sometimes the title comes first: for a poem, an essay, a talk, a painting. On other occasions it occurs afterwards when the completed work suggests it, even supplies it with a sudden phrase. The title given to this contribution is both beginning and end. It is also maybe the very structure of the talk, or perhaps more accurately its lack of structure; 'loose-leafed' thoughts drifting from the mighty forests that are theology and poetry. The title is also suggestive of the event we are celebrating. 'Loose-leafed' hinting the many leaves of the many books that Dr Enda McDonagh is gifting to Galway-Mayo Institute of Technology, 'through the cosmos' pointing to the universality of his interests and influence. A mind alert and alive to so many fields of thought and feeling.

Therefore the provenance of the title is appropriate. It is a phrase from Seamus Heaney's translation of Canto XXXIII of Dante Alighieri's *Paradiso* section of *The Divine Comedy*. There, finally, Dante is face to face with God, under divine light. There the union of the Triune God is creating a union of all things. Heaney's translation of the complete verse is as follows:

> In the depths of it I beheld infolded
> bound by love into a single volume
> what is loose-leafed through the cosmos, far and wide[1]

It is the love of God which makes one of all things. Everything is, until that final reconciliation, a dim reflection of

---

1. Quoted in Linda Hogan and Barbara Fitzgerald, eds, *Between Politics and Poetry*, (Dublin: Columba Press, 2003), p 13

that light, that creative force which holds all things in being, in *The Divine Comedy's* final line *'l'amor che move il sole e l'altre stelle'* ('by the love which moves the sun and the other stars' – Seamus Heaney). The dim reflection includes the poem itself. Despite the necessary admission of his inadequacy before God, his inability to describe 'what no eye has seen no ear heard', Dante's *Divine Comedy* is the supreme expression of an age when people could imagine a unity of all things. Politics, poetry, theology, science could conspire together in joy. *The Divine Comedy*, in its pilgrimage from hell to heaven creates a visionary universe, a cosmic force-field of meaning. With Dante the vernacular Italian language is enabled to fuse together the theology of Thomas Aquinas, the politics of Florence, the regime of Christendom, the science of astronomy, the early stirrings of love in a young man. All is grist to the mill of Dante's imagination.

It is a world, a cosmos, which is breaking up even as it is articulated. Christendom will disappear. Schism and Reformation will tear the veil of the church to shreds. Empires, all claiming the cross as a standard bearer, will be involved in genocidal conquests around new worlds discovered. Science will go its own way, so that even the deep theological and poetic truths of Genesis are lost in the seas off the Galapagos Islands. Absolutes will bend low before Einstein. Infernos become this-worldly in concentration camps, gulags, in Hiroshima and Nagasaki. It will not be possible again to have a poet, or a poem, which will dare to know all, to include all. Dante stands at the peak of a mountain we can no longer climb.

However, he still stands guard over poetry. Twentieth century verse can be read in many ways as a homage to Dante. Eliot and Pound bow before him. Irish poetry today is pupil of the Florentine master. Most obviously in Seamus Heaney, but W. B. Yeats, Thomas Kinsella, John F. Deane, Ciaran Carson have been in his class. I suppose it is no small surprise that the attraction has, by and large, been to the *Inferno*. Not now because, as with Milton, the devil has the best lines, but after the trenches of the First World War, the horrors of Hitler and Stalin we have looked

CHAPTER SEVENTEEN

into our own human eyes and seen evil look back at us with the grimace of death. 'Inferno', 'hell', 'the rough beast' of Yeats, has residence on earth.

Even the very possibility of poetry is called into question. Adorno's questioning of poetry's right to exist in the vicinity of Auschwitz for all its power is answered in the poetry which confronts the evil. To name the 'rough beast' is to begin its taming. So when Paul Celan seeks to redeem the German language after its subservience to Nazi infiltration, it becomes an affirmation of life over death, barely. Somehow the music of the fugue rises in the ashy air. His poetry avails, uses, subverts imagery from the psalms, from the history of Israel, to find a stuttering hope. True words begin to redeem the times. Another example of this can be found in the poets confronted by the nihilistic materialism of Stalin's Russia. One could give many examples from the great generation of poets who wrote in that dark age – Mandelstam, Pasternak, Akhmatova and Tsvetayeva into the following period of Brodsky in Russia and poets of the stature of Milosz and Herbert in Poland – but two examples must suffice here to make my point. These texts at once define the slavery and overcome it. Pasternak's *Doctor Zhivago* is a novel in which theology and poetry ate together in confronting the forces of death. In it the final victory of life is declared in the book's final chapter which is a collection of the poems written by Yuri Zhivago. The novel's theology is, in the words of Thomas Merton, 'a Christianity reduced to its barest and most elementary essentials'.[2] It is a novel set in the time between the crucifixion and the resurrection, when the forces of death seem to have conquered life, love, hope. But victory is declared by the existence of the poems in the easter garden of the last chapter. There, where the seasons of the year, the cycle of the liturgical calendar , events in the lives of the Zhivago and Lara and the life of Jesus Christ in the gospels work together to create both judgement and reward. A novel which

---

2. *The Literary Essays of Thomas Merton*, (New Directions Press, 1981), p 43.

opens with the death of a beloved mother, ends in a poem of resurrection, concludes with this verse:

> And on the third day I shall rise again,
> Like rafts down a river, like a convoy of barges,
> The centuries will float to me out of the darkness.
> And I will judge them.[3]

Like Dante's Beatrice, Lara has been Pasternak's living, loving, loved woman but also Mary of Nazareth, Mary Magdalene, and also the very feminine Spirit of God.

If Pasternak's *Doctor Zhivago* is set between Good Friday and Easter Sunday, the defining poem of Russia's twentieth century, Anna Akhmatova's *Requiem*, is firmly placed on Good Friday. The incident that inspired the poem is told in what Akhmatova names 'Instead of a Forward':

> In the fearful years of the Yezhov terror I spent seventeen months in prison queues in Leningrad. One day somebody 'identified' me. Beside me, in the queue, there was a woman with blue lips. She had, of course, never heard of me; but suddenly came out of that trance so common to us all and whispered in my ear (everyone spoke in whispers there): 'Can you describe this?' And I said 'Yes, I can.' And then something like the shadow of a smile crossed what had once been her face.[4]

Anna Akhmatova's promise to that woman, to Russia herself, is the poem *Requiem* and the central section of that poem is named 'Crucifixion'. There you find these words:

> Magdalia beat her breast and wept, while
> The loved disciple seemed hammered out of stone.
> But, for the Mother, where she stood in silence, –
> No one as much as dared to look that way.[5]

---

3. Boris Pasternak, *Doctor Zhivago* (Everyman Library, 1991), p 507
4. 'Requiem' by Anna Akhmatova, *Selected Poems*, translated by D. M. Thomas, (Penguin Classics, 2006), p 87.
5. Ibid, p 94.

CHAPTER SEVENTEEN

Central to that poem (and indeed to the cross itself) is the moment when Jesus prays the anguished poem, Psalm 22. In both *Doctor Zhivago* and *Requiem* theology and poetry are one. In both we are led to Jesus, and the Jesus praying poetry on the cross is himself a poet.

Any Christology which fails to understand this, which does not imagine the image-maker, Jesus, is less than satisfactory. Everything in the life of Jesus reveals him as a man of the Book, who in turn is adding to the Book by his stories, parables, the poetry of the Beatitudes. The Books of the Jewish Testament which echo in his words, which resound in his own own discovery of himself are books of poetry: the hymns of the Suffering Servant in Isaiah; the disconcerting imagery of Jonah in the belly of the Leviathan; the innocent suffering of Job. So many of the images of himself are poetic, out from the depths of the psalms, especially the Good Shepherd of Psalm 23. The faith of Judaism is in poetry: they are people of the Book and, at its most glorious and most profound moments of understanding, it is poetry. The outstanding example of this is the Book of Job. In terms of the prose narrative it is to be no more than another narrative of the duel between good and evil. But the pressure of the events described turns the carbon of prose to the ice cold diamond of a poetry which challenges conventional religion, wisdom itself, to something new.

As nowhere else the poetry holds God under intense examination. Suffering, innocent suffering, demands a poetry which in turn demands a new theology of God. The deepest, darkest and profoundest theology of scripture is the poetry of Job. Poetry goes where theology fears to tremble.

All the darkest questions of the Old Testament are the ones faced by Jesus: Job, Jonah and Qoheleth sit by the shadow of the cross, with Mary, Mary Magdalene, with John the Divine, with Anna Akhmatova, Yuri Zhivago. The Jesus on the cross is a poet who imagined new worlds in young poems and also bare Beckett lines on a tree which has no leaves and then only one. And if Jesus is a theologian he is a theologian of stories, parables honed by a poet's eye for detail. Jesus seeks to tell of God with stories that never mention God. Instead we have prodigal sons and prodigal fathers, we have shepherds, vineyard owners, Samaritan travellers. It is in the stories that God lives, but between the lines, somewhere in their rhythm, in their syntax of freedom. I am reminded of something Thomas Merton said in his introduction to *The Wisdom of the Desert*, his anthology of the sayings of the desert fathers and mothers: 'They were humble, quiet, sensible people, with a deep knowledge of human nature and enough understanding of the things of God to realise they knew very little about him. Hence they were not much disposed to make long speeches about the divine essence, or even to declaim on the mystical meaning of scripture. If these men say little about God, it is because they know that when one has been somewhere close to his dwelling, silence makes more sense than a lot of words.'[6]

When the stories of Jesus and the story of Jesus become theology rather than story they can lose their impact and revolutionary freedom. They lose their life-blood. Perhaps the best example of this is the Eucharist. It is the meal of a poet. We must presume that Jesus took a long time in choosing his memorial gift. Other possibilities must have tempted him. Lighted candles, lilies of the field, roasted lamb. Indeed the list is endless, for everything that lives and moves is a sacrament of the creator God and the Spirit at play in the universe. But out of scripture, out of memory, out of a poet's eye for a black skillet pot on the crane in an open fire, the wine drenched wedding feast and the slaking of thirst after harvest, he chose bread and wine. Our varied, divided understanding of their nature has come I feel because we think of Jesus as a philosopher walking in the disputed streets of Athens rather than a poet hungry for life, and urgent about those who hunger. A poet, musician, artist is one whose words, notes, marks are real. They create in the doing. The real presence of Jesus in the bread and wine is the reality of the poet

---

6. *The Wisdom of the Desert*, Thomas Merton, (Sheldon Press, 1961), p 14.

CHAPTER SEVENTEEN

Jesus, Son of the Father who created out of the words spoken over the void, over the wasteland of Job, Eliot, Ecclesiastes, Becket. Not just are theology and poetry one at their best, but the subjects of theology, the Triune God, are the poetry of creation.

Thus theology must be a study of creation, and of creators. One of the abiding contributions of Enda McDonagh to theology has been his work on creators like Gerard Manley Hopkins, Tony O'Malley, John F. Deane. In his introduction to the catalogue of Tony O'Malley's 'Good Friday and Easter Paintings' Enda McDonagh makes the central link between creativity and redemption. Where in the darkness of O'Malley's colours, indeed out of their darkness, an Easter light is creating itself. The Risen Christ is the poet Jesus revealing the word of a creative God dancing in light, among the flowers of a spring garden.

In a way we are back where we started. Dante's *Divine Comedy* begins ina Good Friday descent into hell and ends in the fullness of Easter light. As do *Doctor Zhivago*, 'Requiem', Hopkins' dark sonnets, John F. Deane's 'Man Handling the Deity', Tony O'Malley's paintings. Poetry insists on the final victory of its judging word. Even when the words, the paint, the notes are inadequate. Like Beckett characters under the single leafed tree one must go on 'staining the silence'. Even when the parable teller Jesus, the poet of Beatitude Hill, is nailed to seven bare sentences of love, forgiveness, trust, despair, thirst and hope the creative act continues. Finding new ways of failing better theology are words seeking the poetry of God. All poetry, all creative work, are expressions of a plenitude God on genesis morning and a God nailed to minimum notes on a dying Friday afternoon. 'Loose-leafed in the cosmos far and wide' all are pulsed with the rhythm and blood of a God of love. God's love for all – victims of war and violence, aids, strugglers for peace and justice, creators of works of beauty and truth, Mayo farmers and teachers and footballers – has been the central motif of all Enda McDonagh's writing and teaching. Let me finish with the final stanza of Seamus Heaney's translation of Canto XXXIII of 'Paradiso'. It speaks it own praise:

So I was lost in study of that sight:
I yearned to see how the Image had inscaped
The circle and is co-extensive with it.

But my own wings were not equal to the flight
Except that my mind was struck by a bright bolt
And in a flash was granted all it sought.

Here power upholding high imagining failed,
But as a balanced wheel revolves and whirrs
My will and my desire were now revolved

By the love which moves the sun and the other stars.[7]

---

7. Quoted in Between Politics and Poetry, p 15.

CHAPTER EIGHTEEN

Art: A Gateway to the Transcendent

Anne Harkin-Petersen

The Tate Modern has one room set aside for nine paintings by twentieth-century painter Mark Rothko. The first impressions on entering are that this room bears no resemblance to any other in the gallery. Little by little, it becomes clear what is different. In the first instance, the lighting is understated. There is no harsh illumination of the paintings on the walls. There is no stark demand by the lighting to draw attention to the work. Like the steady advance of a chromatic scale the body adjusts to the containment of the space. Initial apprehension is replaced with tranquillity. Gradually, and gently, an awareness of the paintings intrudes upon the perceptive senses. Slowly it enters the psyche how huge these paintings are. The size alone momentarily halts the comprehensive process and the paintings demand respect.

The size of each painting is considerable and while three have the same measurements, with the vertical side being the longest, two others are identical, but with greater length in the horizontal direction; another two are equal in vertical length to the first three mentioned, but the horizontal lengths do not conform to one another. The remaining two paintings have different measurements. All in all, it must be understood that only some element of conformity can be found as regards size. The subtlety of each painting is unique.

To demonstrate the content of these paintings it may be helpful to examine one in detail. Simply titled, *Black on Maroon*, this painting measures 266.7 x 457.2 cm, a rectangular oil painting on canvas. The colours, as the title suggests, are of maroon and black. They merge in and out of one another in unequal measure along the borders of the painting. Where one colour begins and the other ends, is not clearly defined. What could only be described as two cloudy maroon panels, pillars, or figures of unequal width but corresponding depth, appear to hover above, or present themselves as somehow external to the black background, which itself seems to float out of a bed of maroon. The brushstrokes imply a haphazard approach that might result in confusion but no such effect is felt. Dynamism coexists with an induction to calm. The effect is enigmatic.

The room is not empty, so the viewer is alerted to the fact that there is something intriguing about this space. What enters the viewer's mind is an awareness of the inclination to stay, to find out what it is about these paintings that others find so fascinating. What is it about these particular works that places them in such a prestigious setting and, what is it about them that attracts and holds such attention? Can a link be made with some other occurrence where an awareness of shared experience invites participation? What does this say about the intention of a work of art? Has the role of art a wider value than either its monetary or sensory value? The viewer is alerted to a sense of communal intrigue that these paintings obviously radiate.

With no intrusive change of rhythm, contradictions begin to challenge the understanding. Despite their large size the impact is non-threatening. The palette for all nine paintings is limited to black, maroon and red. But these colours exude a pulsation that is spellbinding, rather like the persistent rhythm of a Bach prelude. The invitation to become involved is proffered and accepted. By now, accustomed to the dim atmosphere, the viewer becomes aware that these canvasses contain little or no overt representation or recognisable symbol. They are simplicity itself, it seems. Bands of oil colour of various depths and widths, in maroon and black and red, sometimes horizontal, sometimes vertical. Yet their affect is anything but simple. The challenges continue.

The occurrence is one where the viewer may become lost in reverie; from deep within excitement stirs and fires the imagination. The oppositions remain. The experience is overwhelming, and unforgettable, soothing and exhilarating. The seductive in-

CHAPTER EIGHTEEN

vitation to linger, and participate, grows stronger while, all the while the viewer is being drawn step by step, into an enthralled trance. The ritual, between the viewer and the paintings, rises and falls like the rhythm of a dance, a dance that reaches to a crescendo of joy and excitement, then falls to the depths of contemplation and trance. The incorporation of the viewer is complete.

Considering the range of emotions and thought processes inspired by such an experience as described above, surely the most pressing question that now arises is how do Rothko's paintings stand in relation to what is popularly considered the most desirable in works of art? How relevant is such an experience in a climate where it appears that the current yardstick for measuring works of art seems to depend solely on acquisitive and monetary values?

The dilemma that faces all of us at the present time revolves around what might be considered a work of art. In fact more than ever our individual judgement is put to the test. For instance the expectation and emphasis in contemporary times seems to have set aside the more noble facets of artistic endeavour and concentrated quite simply on the viability aspect. Only recently it has been reported extensively in the media about the prices being obtained for what could be considered gimmicky artefacts. It seems incredible that what is being encouraged by a fickle art market is the more outrageous and novel. It might be fair to say that a reasonable perception of the contemporary art world, judging by the publicity surrounding the sale and purchase of certain purported works of art, e.g. the auction of work by British artist Damien Hirst, may be that it has set aside or apparently forgotten about aesthetic values. Hal Foster in *Art in Theory* makes the point that the role of the artist in the contemporary world and the role of the viewer have expanded, the artist 'becomes a manipulator of signs more than a producer of art objects and the viewer an active reader of messages rather than a passive contemplator of the aesthetic or consumer of the spectacular'.[1]

---

1. Charles Harrison and Paul Wood, eds. *Art in Theory 1900-2000: An Anthology in Changing Ideas* (Malden: Blackwell, 2003) p 1038.

If a universal value is applied to a work of art surely there is no compulsion upon the individual viewer to examine the content in any great depth. Therefore the aesthetic experience may be deemed unnecessary. If the only criterion by which a work of art is valued is its material value then the work of art is robbed of a more esoteric possibility and, consequently, so is the individual. Therefore, one would have to question how is it possible for such an object to encapsulate a demand for perceptual sensitivity, to open up a portal into mystery and foster deep contemplation on holistic values. As James Elkins remarks regarding contemporary attitudes, 'We are on a strict diet of ironic detachment; we permit ourselves slim rations of pleasure, but genuine transport is strictly forbidden.'[2]

Since the earliest recorded history of the human race, the visual image is recognised to be a primary source of communication. Therefore it is important that the visual image convey an exemplary idea or predominant message, the purpose for which the work of art is made. This is partly what distinguishes a work of art from just any visual image. For instance, the Egyptians created images for the tombs of the dead. These images were made with geometric regularity and keen observation of nature. The main purpose, or the exemplary idea, behind the images was to help and guide the soul on its journey into the afterlife. In later times, when St Augustine introduced the theory of God as light, Christian artists used the principle of light as one of the main metaphors to explore metaphysical and redemptive properties. In the Middle Ages visual art was one of the main vehicles for instruction, particularly in the values of the Old Testament. In earlier times symbolic reference kept the focus within certain parameters partly because a consensus on symbolic meaning was possible: particular symbols implied certain meanings, for instance at the time of the Renaissance, an image of a dog in a painting implied faithfulness. With the advance of time, education and scholarship, the exemplary idea has become more open to individual interpretation.

---

2. James Elkins, *Pictures and Tears*, (New York: Routledge, 2001) p 129.

CHAPTER EIGHTEEN

Part of the confusion that abounds today is because the symbol itself has no basis in any reality and symbol is a conglomerate of any number of phenomena. Nature is being sidelined in favour of simulation. An added problem is that several experts can explicate the meaning of any given symbol. Universal opinions are handed down and take the form of dogma. Answers to questions must fit into either the yes or no category. One consequence is that the question and answer test syndrome is perceived to be the most reliable evaluation system. Any opinion that cannot fit the criteria of technological expertise and the rapid fire question and answer syndrome would appear to have no value, or might be viewed with suspicion. One result appears to be that the individual's own integrity is relegated by expert opinions and, therefore, the value of individual integrity is placed at risk in the rush for a sterile judgement of value.

Reason demands that an explanation for all phenomena ought to be possible. But a problem that arises when confronted with works of art such as the Rothko's defies logic. Where can an explanation be found? Is there any connection to be made between this and any other known experience? In order to analyse the above experience a careful examination of what exactly has occurred here is necessary.

Hugh St Victor (1096-1141), a medieval French theologian and mystical writer, describes contemplation as 'an easy and clear-sighted penetration of the soul into what is seen'.[3] G. W. F. Hegel (1770-1831), a German philosopher of the Enlightenment period, also affirms the involvement of visual art with the soul and spirit and maintains that a work of art 'should disclose an inner life, feeling, soul, a content and spirit'.[4] It is not unreasonable therefore to consider that an inducement to reverie is a primary and essential component of the effect Rothko's paintings activate in the viewer. Secondly, the paintings act as a catalyst

---

3. Umberto Eco, *Art and Beauty in the Middle Ages*, (New Haven: Yale University Press, 1986), p 10.
4. G. W. F. Hegel, 'Lectures on Aesthetics', in Richard Kearney and Rasmusson eds, *Continental Aesthetics*, (Malden, MA: Blackwell Press, 2001), p 102.

that encourages an experience, which may be analogous with the experience of mystery. Thirdly, the experience draws attention to the notion that traditionally a reverential experience is induced by a deeply ritualistic or spiritual moment. Finally, the link with the long tradition of aesthetics as the source of possible enlightenment is suggested.

There is much recorded evidence throughout the history of art that will confirm the relationship between contemplation, soul, transcendence and art. If contemplation is defined as an act that demands intense lengthy thought especially on a spiritual dimension, then the concept of mystery is not far behind. A concept of mystery is perceived to be present when we have a sense of the sacred, the numinous or the more than ordinary. Considering the description of the event of the Rothko paintings as referred to here it is reasonable to state therefore that the experience of the Rothko paintings evokes a sense of mystery.

To assist a better understanding of how to approach works of art a brief examination of historical validation of what constitutes the aesthetic is called for. It is suggested that such validation may help redress the balance in favour of a more holistic development of the human being rather than emphasise the more acquisitive attitude that appears to be what is being promoted in the present time.

As already remarked there is no ambiguity in stating that the primary purpose of art is its role as communicator. What is firmly established from a study of the history of art is that art has many roles, that of teacher, social analyst, spiritual and moral guide. Several writers support the idea that the aesthetic experience must benefit the individual and elevate the consciousness of society at large. Books, such as, Monroe Beardsley's *Aesthetics from the Ancient Greece to the Present*, Umberto Eco's *Art and Beauty in the Middle Ages*, E. H. Gombrich's *Symbolic Images*, or *An Anthology of Continental Aesthetics* edited by Richard Kearney and David Rasmusson are just some publications that throw light on the subject.

Consider for a moment what is meant by aesthetics, the

CHAPTER EIGHTEEN

philosophical branch of art history – 'The study of what is immediately pleasing to our visual or auditory perception, or to our imagination; the study of the nature of beauty; also, the theory of taste and criticism in the creative and performing arts'[5] – and its relevance to the experience of an art work.

Within the history of art, a record of similarly described experiences validates their authenticity. However, from art historical evidence that is available there is no standard agreement on the criteria that can induce an aesthetic experience. All that can be stated is that at different times, subjective considerations are in the ascendancy and objectivity is relegated and vice versa. The history of aesthetics makes it clear that there is no continuous conduit that leads from the Ancient Greeks until now. In fact the history of aesthetics might be compared to a maze that shows many different routes leading to various points at which the traveller must pause, and reassess what has been learnt along the way. Nor is there conclusive evidence in the history of art to define how the constituent parts of any works of art produce the complete aesthetic experience.

What is clear is that detailed arguments to support the value of art and the aesthetic experience can be verified by history. Plotinus (205-70BC), St Augustine (354-430), St Thomas Aquinas (c.1225-1274), Marcilio Ficino (1433-1499), Albrecht Durer (1471-1528), Immanuel Kant (1724-1804), Edmund Burke (1729-1797), G. W. F. Hegel (1770-1831) and more recently, Søren Kirkegaard (1813-1855), Martin Heidegger (1889-1976), Theodor Adorno (1903-1969) and Edward Said (1935-2003) are just some of the many scholars who attest to the interactive relationship, between the artist, the viewer and a work of art that encompasses the aesthetic experience and the consequent holistic effect upon the human being.

Initially, the contents of a work of art can be judged at two levels, the objective and the subjective. As far back as Plato and Aristotle there is evidence of the tension between such apparently obvious oppositions. What becomes clear, in the history of

---

5. Thomas Mautner, *Dictionary of Philosophy*, (London: Penguin, 2000), p 8.

aesthetics, however, is that the relationship between what is objective and subjective is mirrored in the oppositions between the empirical and the transcendental, the universal and the individual, the reasonable and the sensual, the realistic and the imaginative. Some works of art reflect the logical, reasonable, empirical proposals to understand what is perceived to be reality. Other works of art, at different periods of history, are more concerned with the imaginative, intuitive, emotive, sensual, metaphysical, interpretations of reality. Neither opposition, however, actually reflects the complete picture. A third dimension is needed to explain what happens when confronted by a work of art.

Ideally there must be a dialectical possibility between the artist and the work of art that must in turn synthesise with the viewer, in order to create the climate for the aesthetic experience. In other words, a tripartite relationship is formed between the artist, the work of art and the spectator to validate a truly aesthetic experience. A synthesis such as this indicates the presence of a ground from which to propose a new thesis. The importance of the aesthetic experience is then guaranteed and so is the possibility of a continuum.

Whether the aesthetic experience may mirror, or form a link to any other known life experience, gradually impinges upon the mind. To concentrate for a moment on the links between the aesthetic experience and other known experiences may help to establish a more equitable and a less singular valuation system than what appears to be in vogue presently when considering works of art. For instance, many insightful references to the relationship between art and spirituality, the soul, and metaphysics can be found throughout the history of art and aesthetics. Two of the most prominent proponents of spirituality in art must be Immanuel Kant and G. W. F. Hegel. Kant gives the requisites for fine art as imagination, understanding, soul and taste. Hegel remarks that, 'The universal need for art is man's rational need to lift the inner and outer world into his spiritual consciousness as an object in which he recognises his own self.'[6]

---

6. Hegel 'Lectures on Aesthetics', p 107.

CHAPTER EIGHTEEN

Spiritual consciousness is a natural conduit to metaphysical considerations. Metaphysics conjures up the concept of mystery. The word mystery has several connotations such as apprehension, anticipation, excitement, dread, curiosity, and endlessness. However, the most valid seems to be related to an out-of-world experience, in other words, a transcendent experience. Therefore, it does not require a major leap of faith to the analogous identification of the aesthetic experience with the religious or spiritual one, particularly if the notion of reverie is taken into the equation. The journey through the history of aesthetics itself takes on all the attributes of mystery as it leads from one idea to another. Once again to refer to the experience of the Rothko works of art it is reasonable to say that an air of mystery surrounds both the paintings and the experience of them.

Religion is traditionally related to metaphysics. In a Western Christian tradition mystery is easily associated with the notion of the religious ritual. In the same tradition an aesthetic experience is most easily linked to a notion of sacrament. In the words of James Elkins, 'The glow of a Rothko painting might be a sign of God or even a sign from God; but it also could just be a reminder of God'.[7]

The first important element in a religious ritual is a sense of the sacred. Secondly, a natural evolution is the judicial stage, followed by coherence and finally appreciation. Really this coincides with Kant and his *Critique of Pure Judgement*. From reading Kant it becomes clear that what is necessary in a work of art is sufficient association of ideas that will bring the viewer to a state of thought or contemplation that will focus the mind on an ideal worth pursuing. Hegel's studies and insights substantiate and augment Kantian theory. Hegelian emphasis is on the work of art as a spiritual activity and it 'should disclose an inner life, feeling, soul, a content and spirit'.[8]

If in Western Christian tradition the simple definition of sacrament is a sign and symbol of the sacred, then it is not so

---

7. James Elkins, *Pictures and Tears*, p 175.
8. Hegel, 'Lectures on Aesthetics', p 102.

difficult to imagine that a true aesthetic experience is most easily linked to a notion of sacrament. Sacrament is a sign and symbol that arises out of the experience of our lives. In other words, a short explanation of the role of sacrament in Christian tradition shows that it is linked to the most important events in the life of any human being. Therefore the purpose of sacrament is to call to mind certain important events and link them with the idea of mystery and transcendence and, as Joseph Martos explains, sacrament can only be effective so long as it is relevant to life. He says, 'Sacraments are not for the unconscious, the asleep or the dead. They are for the awake and aware, the living the growing'.[9]

Birth, communion, initiation to adulthood, relationships, reconciliation, dedication and death are what form the basis of Christian sacraments. There can be no argument that such events are essential, they are individual yet impinge on the community, and so there is an obvious connection to the exemplary idea. As Michael A. Cowan remarks: '[I]n sacred moments our depths resonate with the web of life; we touch on ultimate meanings and mysteries'.[10] Art is also a communication through sign and symbol of the exemplary idea. What is required to appreciate sacrament is similar to what one needs to appreciate visual art. An open mind, multiple or complex referents, universality, the positive and fundamental interest in promoting human values that can produce an uplifting, thoughtful, contemplative reaction in whoever participates in either. This recalls the experience as described by the writer when confronted with the work of Mark Rothko in the Tate Modern in London.

To summarise, the initial reaction to the experience of the Rothko paintings are feelings of reverence and awe coupled with a sense of mystery. The overwhelming desire is to hold this remarkable event within the safety of the individual mind, how-

---
9. Joseph Martos, *The Catholic Sacraments*, (Delaware: Ml Glazier, 1983), p 17.
10. Michael A. Cowan, 'Sacramental Moments: Appreciative Awareness in the Iron Cage' in Regis A. Duffy OFM, ed, *Alternative Futures for Worship*, (Collegeville: Liturgical Press, 1987), p 35.

CHAPTER EIGHTEEN

ever, consequent to the mysteriousness of the happening, the impulse to share the experience with others becomes necessary. The reactions evoked bring a sense of wonder and transport the viewer to an inner contemplation that can easily be equated with reverence and transcendence. What is suggested here is the very authentic and important role that art plays in the overall holistic evolution of human beings. The mystery is that the Rothko paintings bring this about and it is impossible to say why. However, what is essential is an open mind and a willingness to be transformed by the experience. The aesthetic experience not only facilitates a concept of mystery, it embodies mystery.

Subsequently, another question that arises must centre on the validity of the aesthetic experience, as it can be related to the cultural climate of today; in other words the relevance of the aesthetic experience in the contemporary world. Given the strong emphasis on shock value, material value, and the promotion of works which do not engender such a deep resonance within the human heart, it becomes more imperative that the individual exercise her or his particular judgement on what is being put forward by the art market as works of art. It could be construed that the contemporary message being delivered by works of art is one of complete materialism. This is too cynical an attitude to adopt. Art cannot be relegated to a cul de sac. Whether the message it conveys is derisory or cynical, or positive and affirming, art always commands a response. What should be remembered is that throughout history there has been a core element of thought that has never completely forgotten or ruled out the transcendental tradition first attributed to the Classical period of ancient Greece. So, on the other hand, evidence to support the importance of the aesthetic experience can still be recognised in the work of many thinkers and many artists.

Through the whole journey of the history of art what dominates is the intrepid enquiry of so many philosophers, theologians, critical theorists, and critics, into the enigmatic experience that is provoked by a work of art. The journey is all about enigma, mystery, illusion and ephemera. The aesthetic experience cannot be quantified and qualified except in so much as it is construed to be impossible to contain within any logical explanation. The aesthetic experience can be partially understood but is never completely understandable. The closest interpretation may be how it relates to the mysterious.

An aesthetic experience is inexplicable, wondrous and enigmatic. A work of art is an affirmation of the individual, not alone as the individual *per se* but the individual as a member of a community. A work of art is made for the community; otherwise it would have no function. A work can have many different agendas: it can be for enjoyment, as an anarchic political statement, or as a conscious reminder of some important truth. Ideally, it is a synthesis of the sensuous and the reasonable to produce an ephemeral third dimension, the aesthetic experience. This is what makes a work of art essential, haunting, magical, spiritual, and inspiring. Art as a medium of such an experience can therefore be a gateway to the transcendent.

CHAPTER NINETEEN

Reclaiming Beauty

Mary Gordon

There is an American children's game called 'Telephone,' called, I believe, across the pond, 'Chinese Whispers'. One person whispers a phrase or sentence to the next person, who whispers it to the next, who whispers it the next, and so on down the line. The point of the exercise is the malleability of language. So if child 1 whispers into the ear of child 2 'Uncle Henry's beard is long,' by the time the message is passed to child 12, she will have heard, 'Punch a wren and hear a song.'

Something like that happened with the title of this paper. I thought I had conveyed it as, 'Giving Beauty Back,' making a gerund of the words of Hopkins' found in the poem, 'The Leaden Echo and the Golden Echo': 'Give beauty back, beauty, beauty, beauty, back to God, beauty's self and beauty's giver.' But somewhere along the line, I learned that my title had somehow been transformed into 'Reclaiming Beauty'. When I heard it, it seemed to me a much better thing, a change that pleased me very much indeed, leading me, as I am neither Presbyterian nor Greek, to name the transformation neither predestination nor fate, but grace.

In my original, pre-graced way, I thought of invoking Hopkins' words because they were given to me by Enda once in a particularly Enda-like way. I was spending a few days with him in Mayo, and it was a time in which I was particularly discouraged about writing, my own writing, and the enterprise of writing in general. It seemed to me a vain and a foolish endeavour. Better, as Yeats would say, to 'break stones in all kinds of weather,' or as my Irish grandmother would say, to get down on my knees and scrub a floor, which might do someone some good and get my mind off things. Torturing me especially was the question: why in a world so full of suffering and injustice should I devote my time and energies to stitching words together in a way that might create a well made cloak, with the improbable dream of a radiant one – a cloak that might be visible to no one but myself, or only a very few. And even at the best, even if the pleasure rendered by the creation was vouchsafed to many, for how long would the pleasure last, and what lasting effect might it have on any life? Even as I use the word vouchsafe, I become conscious of the effect of an early liturgical life on the mind or ear of the writer. Would anyone not brought up in the pre-Vatican II Catholic church have access to the word 'vouchsafe?'

But I digress. To get back to my point: I was suffering from the malaise connected to writing that my husband describes as 'I'm going to give it all up and become a physical therapist' mode.' I may have asked Enda if he thought I should enroll in a physical therapy course … I don't know, it might have happened …it was rather late, and we'd been drinking red wine. I don't think he responded to that particular question. Rather, he reminded me of the Hopkins poem, which speaks of a way of overcoming the despair, not only the despair born of the folly of making, but the Proustian despair at the passage of time. Enda gave me the lines, 'Give beauty back … to God's self, beauty's self and beauty's giver'. From these lines I felt that the making of beautiful things was a duty rather than a luxury. Not that Enda would invoke the word 'duty'. I don't think I've ever heard the word 'duty' pass his lips. Rather, Enda heartened me: he gave me back my heart. In his characteristically gentle way, Enda has a facility for creating change in the human heart without the changed person realising that a finger has been laid upon him or her. Rather, one feels a warm breath. A sense of accompaniment I can only imagine (you will forgive me for courting blasphemy) might have been what the disciples felt when they met Jesus on the road to Emmaus. I am always pleased at the incarnational detail in Luke's gospel: the provision of a menu: Jesus and the

CHAPTER NINETEEN

disciples eat broiled fish. I believe Enda is quite fond of broiled fish.

So, when I agreed to be part of today's celebration, I had pledged myself to say something about beauty. And as I am very well known for being a woman of my word, I must finally get down to it. I will begin by a definition of beauty. In doing this, I will invoke the great American writer, James Thurber. He begins an essay, 'How To Tell Love From Passion' in the following way. 'To start with, we must determine how to tell love from passion. By love we mean that pleasant feeling which we all know exists. But when I say passion, I mean passion.' And so I will bypass the work of centuries of aestheticians and say simply, we know something is beautiful by the lifting of our hearts caused by an experience whose roots are in the senses.

Having solved that problem I am now free to move to my main subject. If I don't quite know what my main subject is, I know, at least what it is something like. I want to say something about what I think of as Enda's vision, and how that vision is something I would love to incorporate into my own work as an artist. It is a vision of faith, and hope, and love. A vision at once tender and searing, forgiving and prophetic. A vision which is hopeful, not optimistic – hope against hope, not pie in the sky. A vision that takes in the possibility of human evil, but does not rest there, because it is moved by the human story: its inventions, its surprising moments of heroism, its unpredictable potential for doing better than it ought to, better than it had planned. I hear Enda's voice in my memory when I am in the midst of a bout of particularly vicious self flagellation for one of my many lapses of attention, compassion, justice. When I think that there is no hope for me and I ought to simply stay in bed and cover my head with my pillow and then my blanket, I hear Enda's voice saying, 'You're all right, you know.' And I often think of Enda when I read Georges Bernanos' *Diary of a Country Priest*. The last words of the dying young priest are, 'What does it matter, grace is everywhere.' Or in an alternate translation, 'What does it matter: all is grace.'

Enda's vision is profoundly and ineluctably religious. But there have been others speaking here, others with far more authority and expertise than I, who have spoken about him as a theologian. His vision is also profoundly political, and others have more right to speak of that aspect of his life and work. But an aspect of his vocation that is less well known is his appreciation of the arts and his importance to artists, and it is this aspect of his vision, the part that connects to the work of contemporary artists, that I would like to focus on today.

How can a contemporary artist, one who finds her or himself living in a time known as post-modernism, incorporate a religious vision into her or his work, one that is neither nostalgic nor repressive? I think there is a connection between this problem for the artist, and the problem of identity for a contemporary priest. One of the central problems for a contemporary, whether or not we wish to enroll ourselves in the ranks of the post modernists, is how to create a proper relationship to the past. A certain strain of post-modernist thinkers see the past largely as sham and entrapment, and their mission is to show up the contradictions and obfuscations that have resulted in repressions which are sometimes murderous. After such a project, there is little residue of love or appreciation; the relationship to the past seems to be reduced to a combination of aggression and defensiveness. The artist who wishes to have a relationship with the great works of the past, a relationship which is neither blind to historical realities and accidents, nor slavish in its appreciation, is, it seems to me, in a similar situation to that of a contemporary priest. There is of course, one major difference. A priest is surrounded by a cohort of believers; an artist must understand that to be a believer places her or him in the realm of the suspect.

The late great John McGahern, in an article written shortly before his death, explored his path from belief to unbelief – the more common one for the contemporary artist. It is no accident, I suppose, that the only time I met John McGahern was in Enda's company; the meeting was set up by him, and we shared a lovely lunch, Enda, McGahern and his wife Jacqueline and I, in a

CHAPTER NINETEEN

restaurant by a river in county Longford, the county that my grandmother had left for good in 1896. Here are McGahern's words:

> I grew up in what was a theocracy in all but name. Hell and heaven and purgatory were places real and certain we would go to after death, dependent on the judgement. Churches in my part of Ireland were so crowded that children and old people who were fasting to receive Communion would regularly pass out in the bad air and have to be carried outside. Not to attend Sunday Mass was to court social ostracism, to be seen as mad or consorting with the devil, or at best to be seriously eccentric. Work stopped each day in shop and office and street and field when the bell for the Angelus rang out, as in the Millet painting. The Rosary celebrating the mysteries, closed each day. The story of Christ and how he redeemed us ran through our year as a parallel world to the solid world of our daily lives; the feasts of saints, Lent and Advent, the great festivals of Christmas and Easter, all the week of Whit, when it was dangerous to go out on water; on all Souls' night the dead rose and walked as shadows among the living.
>
> Gradually, belief in these sacred stories and mysteries fell away without my noticing, until one day I awoke, like a character in a Gaelic poem, and realised I was no longer dreaming ...
>
> Before the printed word, churches have been described as the Bibles of the poor, and the church was my first book. In an impoverished time, it was my introduction to ceremony, to grace and sacrament, to symbol and ritual, even to luxury. I remember vividly the plain flat brown cardboard boxes in which tulips for the altar, red and white and yellow, came on the bus in winter when there were no flowers anywhere.
>
> In 1903, Proust wrote to his friend George de Lauris: 'I can tell you at Illiers, the small community where two

days ago my father presided to the awarding of the school prizes, the curé is no longer invited to the distribution of the prizes since the passage of the Ferry laws (on secular education). The pupils are trained to consider the people who associate with him as socially undesirable, and in their way, quite as much as the other, they are working to split France in two. And when I remember this little village so subject to the miserly earth, itself the foster-mother of miserliness; when I remember the curé who taught me Latin and the names of the flowers in his garden; when, above all, I know the mentality of my father's brother-in-law – town magistrate down there and anticlerical; when I think of all this, it doesn't seem to me right that the old curé should no longer be invited to the distribution of the prizes, as representative of something in the village more difficult than the social function symbolised by the pharmacist, the retired tobacco-inspector, and the optician, but something which is, nevertheless, not unworthy of respect, were it only for the perception of the meaning of the spiritualised beauty of the church spire – pointing upward into the sunset where it loses itself so lovingly in the rose-coloured clouds; and which, all the same, at first sight, to a stranger alighting in the village, looks somehow better, nobler, more dignified, with more meaning behind it, and with, what we all need, more love than the other buildings, however sanctioned they may be under the latest laws.

When a long abuse of power is corrected, it is generally replaced by an opposite violence. In the new dispensations, all that was good in what went before is taxed indiscriminately with the bad ...'

The most dramatic change in my lifetime has been the collapse of the church's absolute power. This has brought freedom and sanity in certain areas of human behaviour after a long suppression – as well as a new intolerance. The religious instinct is so ingrained in human nature that it is never likely to disappear, even when it is derided or

CHAPTER NINETEEN

suppressed. In *The Greeks and the Irrational*, E. R. Dodds proposes this lucid definition and distinction: 'Religion grows out of man's relationship to his total environment, morals out of his relations to his fellow man' ... If the true religious instinct – our relationship to our total environment – will not go away, neither will its popular equivalent seeking signs and manifestations and help in an uncertain and terrifying world.

McGahern's life was lived far away from participation in anything having to do with the official church, and certainly, it would be hard to imagine someone who had more right for feelings of resentful alienation: his career was blighted by the censorship that was a product of the Irish theocracy whose main prop was the hierarchy of the church. His movement, though, from belief to a wafting memory of aesthetic attachment is not unusual among artists and intellectuals. What is unusual, and typical of the man, is a quiet consideration of the value of those habits that he himself felt incapable of adopting, or unwilling to adopt. His evocation of Proust – or Proust's evocation of life in an early twentieth century Norman town – sails dangerously near nostalgia but, as is so often the case with a craft in the hands of a great writer, complications render mere nostalgia impossible. Unlike McGahern – and probably because he hadn't been hurt by his early brushes with the church – Proust doesn't refer to the abuses that the anti-clericals devoted themselves to extirpating. He recalls only the kindly, abstracted and scholarly curé (who will later make his way into *Á La Recerche du Temps Perdu*) and the spiritualised beauty of the spire which (and this is where genius enters) 'loses itself so lovingly in the rose coloured clouds' and which partakes, unlike other architectural feelings, of meaning and needed love.

McGahern and Proust have much more nuanced responses to the subject of religion than some of the writers at a literary conference I have just recently attended in New York. It was organised by the international writers' organisation, PEN. The subject of the conference was faith and reason.

The convenor of one particular panel urged his audience to acknowledge that all the progress in human history that had taken place in the last two hundred and fifty years had taken place in spite of religion, not because of it. That all the freedoms that we point to as the most precious possessions of the West were the work of people who had set themselves against the church and the machinery of belief. He insisted that religion has done nothing but harm in the recent history of consciousness. Salman Rushdie, the President of American PEN, declared that we had to admit that the source of most of the world's greatest contemporary problems could be laid at the doorstep of religion. Some of the speakers at this conference felt compelled to gesture with the tips of their chins towards Bach and Bellini, to acknowledge the importance of Gothic Architecture or Gregorian chant. But, they insisted, that was then and this is now. And now, as we live now, the speakers at this conference insisted, it is important to return to the glory days of post-Enlightenment atheism, source of all progress, toleration, justice, preservation of rights.

I felt alienated listening to these speakers; I felt foolish, cowardly, unmasked. Then, a Pakistani novelist spoke of the necessity to remember that either faith or reason followed to excess could bring about horrors. Then an Italian invoked Dante, insisting on the importance of the invisible. Toni Morrison read from her novel *Paradise*: two sermons on two different ministers with opposing understandings of the love of God.

In thinking of these speakers, and pondering the words of John McGahern and Proust, I have approached some light marks that might suggest the shape of the position of the contemporary postmodern artist who tries to make sense of a life devoted to art, a life that is also, however irregularly, however incompletely, saturated by faith.

If we call ourselves post modernists, that is because we can't think of any other way of defining ourselves that acknowledges the enormous influence of modernism. The poet Robert Pinsky has suggested that perhaps some of us might be more satisfied with the term, 'neo-modernists,' suggesting a less embattled re-

CHAPTER NINETEEN

lationship with our forbears. Whatever we call ourselves, we know that we are the heirs of some of the important characteristics of modernism, including a new examination of the relationship of the present to the past, and an attentiveness to form that takes into account contemporary technological and scientific reality, an insistence on the primacy of sense experience, and a belief that as purveyors of vision, the artist has taken over the role of the priest. Absent from the understanding of most modernists is the conviction that moral positions and questions of justice are the business of art. 'Poetry makes nothing happen,' W. H. Auden said. Joyce had no time for Irish politics; Proust made a brief foray into the public world by witnessing the iniquities of the Dreyfus affair, but quickly withdrew into his cork lined room. Virginia Woolf was a feminist and a socialist, but as is the case with Jane Austen, of whom it has been said that, reading her books, no one would know the Napoleonic Wars had taken place, Woolf's novels concern themselves primarily with the interior world. And sometimes when the great modernists entered the political arena, as is the case with Ezra Pound, who was imprisoned for supporting Mussolini, one wishes they had stayed out. Even Yeats and Eliot confused political ideas with a nostalgic and elitist longing for a past that never existed: their leanings were importantly un- or anti-democratic, and in Eliot's case, anti-Semitic.

The modernist ideal of the artist takes the Romantic ideal of the poet in the ivory tower and ratchets it up a few important notches. For the high modernist, the great artist places her or himself above the crowd, and has no real interest in reaching the crowd, or even helping the crowd to catch up. The post modernist, in rejecting the priestly robes donned by the Modernist, and in his or her insistence on there being no fixed points, no universally reliable truths, in his or her rejection of the unquestioned supremacy of an Enlightenment enlightenment, has most typically found him or herself unwilling to engage in the search for wisdom, finding even the category delusional or risible, or at best naïve. So the typical post modernist position is ironic, making the best of a bad business by offering a few good jokes. Or creating a dazzling surface. Or else it acknowledges the modern gluttony for violence and oversimplification by offering violence and a bright, cartoonish menu for the overstuffed.

In this climate, where would the place for a vision such as Enda's, a vision that tries in the words quoted by McGahern, to create a 'relationship with our total environment,' a vision at once hopeful and tragic, insisting that life is meaningful, looking to politics and the natural world – and, importantly to art, as the manifold places where this religious meaning is to be found. How would an artist living in our time create moments of vision that would reflect the spirit Enda embodies in his priesthood, a spirit of faith and hope and love. A faith, hope, and love lived against long odds. And witness: for Enda is one of those who hungers and thirsts after justice, and cries out in a prophetic voice when he sees its violation.

Having set out the lineaments of such a vision, I am going to provide some examples of its inclusion. I will not offer samples of the work of two of Enda's favourite poets, Eavan Boland and Seamus Heaney, on the grounds that for an American to bring them into a room such as this would seem like a species of carrying coals to Newcastle. By way of Pittsburgh. And so I hope not to be practising what might seem like a too common American fault: the offering of a native product as a proof of superiority. Rather, I hope to share with you the work of writers, two of whom, both American women, are not as well known in Ireland: Flannery O'Connor and Elizabeth Bishop. The third, Czeslaw Milosz, is American through the gift of the tyrannous twentieth century: a native of Lithuania, he spent the last half of his life in Berkeley, California.

The first poem is by Elizabeth Bishop, and it is called 'Filling Station'

> Oh, but it is dirty!
> – this little filling station
> oil soaked, oil permeated

to a disturbing, over-all
black translucency.
Be careful with that match!

Father wears a dirty,
oil-soaked monkey suit
that cuts him under the arms,
and several quick and saucy
and greasy sons assist him
(it's a family filling station),
all quite thoroughly dirty.

Do they live in the station?
It has a cement porch
behind the pumps, and on it
a set of crushed and grease-
impregnated wickerwork;
on a wicker sofa
a dirty dog, quite comfy.

Some comic books provide
the only note of colour—
of certain colour. They lie
upon a big dim doily
draping a taboret
(part of a set), beside
a big hirsute begonia.

Why the extraneous plant?
Why the taboret?
Why, oh why, the doily?
(Embroidered in daisy stitch
with marguerites, I think,
and heavy with gray crochet.

> Somebody embroidered the doily.
> Somebody waters the plant,
> or oils it, maybe. Somebody
> arranges the rows of cans
> so that they softly say:
> Esso-so-so-so
> to high strung automobiles.
> Somebody loves us all.

The second poem I offer is by Czeslaw Milosz. It is about the painter Corot; the fifth in a series called 'At Yale.' Its proper title is Yale University Art Gallery – Jean Baptiste Corot (1796-1875) 'Port in La Rochelle' ca. 1851

> His name is luminosity. Whatever he saw
> Would bring to him, would humbly offer
> Its interior without waves, its silence, its calm.
> Like a river in the haze of an early morning,
> Like a mother of pearl in a black shell.
> So, too, this port, in an afternoon hour
> With its slumbering sails, its heat.
> Where we wandered perhaps, heavy with wine,
> Unbuttoning our waistcoats, for him was airy.
> It revealed radiance in the disguise of a moment.
> These small figures are real till today:
> Here are three women, another is riding
> A donkey, a man is rolling a barrel,
> Horses in their collars, patient. He, holding his palette,
> Called out to them, summoned them, led them away
> From the poor earth of toil and bitterness
> Into this velvety province of goodness.

This passage from Flannery O'Connor's story 'Revelation' occurs at the very end. Mrs Turpin, the main character, a smug, self-satisfied, self-made woman, is shocked when a young woman who sits across from her in a doctor's office, infuriated by her racist and classist ramblings, calls her an 'old wart hog from hell'. Home with her literal pigs, she has her mystical vision.

CHAPTER NINETEEN

Like a monumental statue coming to life, she bent her head slowly and gazed, as if through the very heart of mystery, down into the pig parlour at the hogs. They had settled all in one corner around the old sow who was grunting softly. A red glow suffused them. They appeared to pant with a secret life.

Until the sun slipped finally behind the tree line, Mrs Turpin remained there with her gaze bent to them as if she were absorbing some abysmal life-giving knowledge. At last she lifted her head. There was only a purple streak in the sky, cutting through a field of crimson and leading like an extension of the highway, into the descending dusk. She raised her hands from the side of the pen in a gesture hieratic and profound. A visionary light settled in her eyes. She saw the streak as a vast swinging bridge extending upward from the earth through a field of living fire. Upon it a vast horde of souls were rumbling toward heaven. There were whole companies of white trash, clean for the first time in their lives, and bands of black niggers in white robes, and battalions of freaks and lunatics shouting and clapping and leaping like frogs. And bringing up the end of the procession was a tribe of people whom she recognised at once as those who ... had always had a little of everything and the God-given wit to use it right. She leaned forward to observe them closer. They were marching behind the others with great dignity, accountable as they had always been for good order and common sense and respectable behaviour. They alone were on key. Yet she could see by their shocked and altered faces that even their virtues were being burned away. She lowered her hands and gripped the rail of the hog pen, her eyes small but fixed unblinkingly on what lay ahead. In a moment the vision faded but she remained where she was, immobile.

At length she got down and turned off the faucet and made her slow way on the darkening path to the house. In the woods around her, the invisible cricket choruses had struck up, but what she heard were the voices of the souls climbing upward into the starry field and shouting Hallelujia.

Why have I chosen these words to exemplify what I believe is Enda McDonagh's spirit? First, because they are beautiful, and they honour the highest standards of language and imagery, and in the process of giving beauty back one must labour to return only the first fruits. These writers have done the backbreaking labour of creation, as Enda has done the backbreaking work of thought, study, writing, and ministry. Second, because they are images of grace, grace which is by its very nature unearned and surprising. And each suggests a part of Enda's greatness: the Milosz poem, in its celebration of luminosity and goodness, speaks to the brilliance of Enda's mind and the consolatory power of his presence; the Bishop, in its comic acceptance of our flawed human nature, culminating in a vision of unconditional love; the O'Connor, in its witnessing to something more final than human injustice, while acknowledging it, and pointing out the limits and futility of dreams of middle-class order.

If there were a theology under whose roof each of these three works could find a home, it would be a theology of incarnation. A theology which insists that the mixed is our lot, that privileges neither the corporeal nor the invisible, but insists on a both/and. And in the poignancy of the incarnation, the hybridity which is central to Christian understanding, a crucible is created in which the major product must be mercy, compassion. A refusal of the death dealing appetite for purity and perfection which my friends at the PEN literary conference assume is the only language a person of faith can speak.

I am far from a professional theologian, but I can offer the suggestion that what marks Enda McDonagh as a theologian is that he is a theologian of incarnation. His is a theology that insists that the divine word never divorces itself from the realities and demands and failures and triumphs of human flesh. And incarnation, too, is the business of artists. We are ambassadors

CHAPTER NINETEEN

between the seen and the unseen. For a writer in particular, working as we do with language, our toolbox packed with sounds and images, we traffic across realms: smuggling, importing, manufacturing, marketing what we find in the warehouse of our minds.

The priest and the artist are engaged in impossible works, impossible tasks. Why do we do it? Why work at this task which is doomed not to succeed? Beckett had a sign tacked above his desk: 'Fail. Fail again. Fail better.'

Another kind of priest than Enda is, in another age, might have answered this why question with the words : 'For the glory of God.' Enda might answer more simply, 'It's what I do, you know.' And today we honour him in all his doings, we praise our friend, our admired companion on the road, who provides for so many of us that, light, transforming breath of life – which is, after all, another word for inspiration.

List of Contributors

NUALA BURKE lives in Castlebar, Co Mayo, and has studied theology at TCD and All Hallows College, Dublin.

CHARLES CURRAN, a priest of the diocese of Rochester, New York, is Elizabeth Scurlock Professor of Human Values at Southern Methodist University, Dallas.

JOHN F. DEANE has published several collections of poetry and some fiction. He founded Poetry Ireland and *Poetry Ireland Review* and is a member of Aos Dána.

NOEL DORR has served in the Department of Foreign Affairs, most recently as Secretary General (1987-1995). He is Chairman of the Governing Body of NUI Galway.

EUGENE DUFFY is Lecturer in Theology and Religious Studies at Mary Immaculate College of Education, University of Limerick.

SEÁN FREYNE was Professor of Theology at Trinity College, Dublin and is currently Director of the Joint Programme for Mediterranean and Near Eastern Studies at TCD.

RAPHAEL GALLAGHER CSSR is Professor of Systematic Moral theology at Accademia Alfonsiana, Rome.

MARY GORDON is a novelist, short-story writer and literary critic, and is McIntosh Professor of English at Barnard College, New York.

PATRICK HANNON is emeritus Professor of Moral Theology at Maynooth College.

ANNE HARKIN-PETERSEN is a visual artist with an interest in philosophy.

STANLEY HAUERWAS is Gilbert T Rowe Professor of Theological Ethics at the Divinity School, Duke University, Durham, North Carolina.

BRENDAN HOBAN is Parish Priest of Ballina, Co Mayo, and a writer and broadcaster.

LINDA HOGAN is Professor of Ecumenics and Head of School at The Irish School of Ecumenics, Trinity College, Dublin.

JAMES KEENAN SJ holds the Founder's Chair in Theology at Boston College.

STANISLAUS KENNEDY is a Religious Sister of Charity and the founder of Focus Ireland.

VINCENT MACNAMARA is a member of St Patrick's Missionary Society and has taught moral theology at Maynooth, Milltown and the Gregorian University, Rome.

+ MICHAEL NEARY is Archbishop of Tuam, formerly Professor of Sacred Scripture at Maynooth.

PATRICK O'BRIEN is Parish Priest of Caherlistrane, Co Galway, and a poet and broadcaster.

JOSEPH O'LEARY is a priest of the diocese of Cork and Professor of English Literature at Sophia University, Tokyo.

NOLLAIG Ó MURAÍLE is senior lecturer in Irish at the National University of Ireland, Galway.